Cheating the ferryman

Cheating the ferryman

The revolutionary science of
life after death

Anthony Peake

This edition published in 2022 by Arcturus Publishing Limited
26/27 Bickels Yard, 151–153 Bermondsey Street,
London SE1 3HA

AD008733UK

Printed in the UK

CONTENTS

CONTENTS

PART 4 – THE PROOF

PROOF FROM QUANTUM PHYSICS

PROOF FROM COSMOLOGY

PROOF FROM NEUROLOGY

PROOF FROM EXPERIENCE

PART 5 – THE INSTANTIATION ARGUMENT

'Were it offered to my choice, I should have no objection to a repetition of the same life from its beginning, only asking the advantage authors have in a second edition to correct some faults of the first. So would I if I might, besides correcting the faults, change some sinister accidents and events of it for others more favorable.'

Benjamin Franklin

PROLOGUE

What happens when we die?

This is the ultimate question and one that has probably exercised human beings from the moment they became self-aware. Throughout the ages, various ideas and beliefs have engaged people. Although these have been numerous, they effectively come down to three options. These are:

1. You cease to exist.

This means that everything about you, all your hopes, dreams, loves, hates, are for nothing. You will never meet your loved ones ever again.

For billions of years, you did not exist, and for billions of years, you will not exist. In effect, something existed for a vanishingly small amount of time when considering the age of the universe. This something perceived something and then disappeared as if it never existed at all. It spent this small amount of time believing it had some form of inner existence, but, if modern science is believed, these 'perceptions' were simply an accidental outcome of blind evolution, an 'epiphenomenon' of brain processes.

There was no point to this life other than its short existence.

Morality and humanity have no meaning in this scenario. This life could have been lived in an orgy of brutality and nastiness or in a caring, loving way. The universe is totally indifferent to this. Indeed, in such a scenario, the only rational approach to this short life is a life of hedonism and self-gratification and/or suicide, which is the only way that such a creature can take any control in a deterministic and indifferent universe rapidly moving to a state of total heat-death.

Nothing matters and life is pointless. Then you die, and that is it.

2. You die and go to Heaven or Hell.

Heaven seems to consist of an eternity of worshipping God surrounded by other 'elect' – that is, those who through their actions on Earth have been rewarded with an eternity in Heaven, whose only motivation is to bask in the glory of this God.

Hell consists of eternal torments. Whether you end up in either place is decided by what you do with the vanishingly small amount of time you are allocated in the one and only life you ever have.

This life can be a hundred years or a hundred seconds; it matters not one jot how long you are given. That is it. There is no appeal and no chance to realize that you made mistakes in your life or any second chance to put things right. You had one chance, and you either got it right or wrong. Of course, 'right' and 'wrong' are at the whim of a deity who uncannily reflects the values of whichever society embraces that deity.

There used to be the concept of Purgatory whereby you could spend time regretting and atoning for the 'wrongs' you did in your life. But there is still no chance to correct these mistakes or put into practice what you have learned from this one life. But you will live for all eternity in spirit form.

Eternity is a long time to just wander around Heaven. It is totally unclear if you are simply a disincarnate spirit for this eternity or whether you are in some form of body like you had in your earthly life. If you do have a body as you had, what age will that body be? Will it be 20 years old? 35? What about children who die? Will they grow old into an older body? Will this body be allowed to enjoy food, drink, sex? Some religions ban alcohol and certain foods. Indeed if these foods are meat-based, where will this food be sourced?

If we exist 'in spirit', then there are no such problems. We will all be disembodied somethings. If we are, how can we enjoy this eternity? We will never again taste food, enjoy a drink or have any form of physical contact with others. Indeed, all our loved ones (assuming that we can find these in this disincarnate existence) will be similarly disembodied somethings. Surely we know people from their physical bodies, their voices, their scent. None of these sensory factors will be available in this forever-and-ever scenario.

3. You get reincarnated into another body.

This body will be a totally new one, and it could be located anywhere on Earth. Why assume that you will be reincarnated as a human being in your own society and geographic location? This body may not be human; it could be an animal, a fish, or even an insect.

Indeed, why restrict it to Earth? Could you not be reincarnated on another planet? Could you be reincarnated as a plant? A microbe?

What about being reincarnated at a different time, in the deep past or the far future?

But let's assume that the rebirth takes place as most advocates of reincarnation believe – that is, in a body and set of circumstances that reflect your actions in your previous life. If you have been a 'good' person (whatever that means), you will be reincarnated into a higher level of human life (viz. the Caste System) or a lower level if you have been a 'bad' person. Who or what actually 'decides' this promotion or demotion is very unclear.

Even more unclear is by what process this transfer of a soul takes place. Indeed, the advocates of reincarnation also seem to be inconsistent as to where the new body will be located in relation to your location in your previous life. Are you reincarnated in your locality or miles away?

Similarly, different belief systems have different amounts of 'time' between incarnations. Is it immediate, or does the soul exist in some kind of cosmic waiting room for an amount of time (if time can be said to exist in such an environment)? But let's ignore these logical issues. You get reborn as somebody else. When this happens, it seems that all your past life memories are wiped clean. You simply do not remember who you were before. So this new life, to all intents and purposes, is totally new. You are born as a new person in a new body. How can this still be you?

Surely what makes us us is our memories and our remembering of our life experiences. In a new body with a new brain (including new memory stores), the old you has ceased to exist. There is no part of you that 'remembers' what you were before. But, we are told, there are some individuals who remember past lives. Why do they remember when the vast majority of incarnates do not? Why are they different? Others can 'remember' past lives by being hypnotized.

How does this work? If the person's brain is a totally new one, how does it carry forward memories from any past lives? These memories are not located in the neurons, synapses, or other 'new' brain parts. Again the question has to be asked why certain people can be 'regressed' and others cannot.

But for me, the most critical issue is simply this: how can these lives ever be iterative or advancing? If I cannot remember my past lives and what I did in them and none of my life-lessons are remembered, then how can I learn from my mistakes? If every life is a new life with no continuity of memories from past lives, what is the point? Indeed what kind of system 'punishes' or 'rewards' somebody for actions they do not remember?

Surely the whole point is to learn and progress. *I will not do that again because I recall how bad I felt the last time I did it.* This does not take place in the classic reincarnation scenario. To all intents and purposes, this reincarnated entity has no relationship with the previous incarnation. They might as well be different beings.

I would like to suggest that there is a fourth alternative, one that is based on science, logic and simple common sense, one that also manages to explain a number of seemingly mysterious experiences such as precognition, déjà vu, synchronicity, near-death experiences, out-of-body experiences, doppelgangers and spirit guides. It is called Cheating the Ferryman.

But why is this concept so important to me, so important that I have devoted nearly two decades of my life and written probably in excess of a million words over 11 books and numerous articles?

Well, it all comes down to an event that took place in the winter of 2003, which focused my attention on another event that took place a few years before. This was to change my life forever and focus me to take a totally different career path, a path that has ultimately brought about this book that you are about to start reading.

So let's roll back the years to a cold winter's evening on the wild moorlands of northern England.

Following the Clues

On a Lost Highway

During the winter of 2003, I worked as a contracted compensation and benefits consultant for a national private hospital group in the UK. I had just completed a meeting at their Harrogate hospital, and I was positioning for an appointment the following day at their Chester hospital. This involved driving along the M62 motorway, one that joins Yorkshire and Lancashire. This motorway is, by English standards, at quite a high elevation and, because of this, is notorious for extreme weather conditions. This was particularly the case that evening with a heavy blanket of freezing fog covering the motorway and the surrounding moorland. Indeed, as I was driving along, I was reminded of the famous scenes from the 1980s cult film *An American Werewolf in London*. I was half expecting the signpost for the Slaughtered Lamb to appear out of the mist.

As I reached the highest point, the motorway started its decline down towards Milnrow. Driving conditions were really bad, but traffic was moving at a fair pace. I was in the inside lane enjoying my music. The music was supplied by my MP3 player, an Archos AV400 with over 16,000 music tracks recorded in its memory. Whenever I was travelling on business, I would have this on random play. It was my own personal radio station, and I always enjoyed (and, indeed, still do) the fun of not knowing what the next track will be. Because it was on random, there was a 1 in 16,000 chance that any one track would be played. So imagine my surprise when, as I started my drive down into Lancashire from the heights of the Pennine Ridge, the first few bars of the song 'Round of Blues' by the American singer-songwriter Shawn Colvin started playing. This track had never come up ever before. This was the first time. Shawn began to sing:

Here we go again
Another round of blues
Several miles ago
I set down my angel shoes
On a lost highway
For a better view
Now in my mind's eye
All roads lead to you

I was on a 'lost highway', looking for a 'better view' through the swirling banks of fog. My blood ran cold. 'This is your death song,' I heard my brain scream at me from the most profound areas of my subconscious. Suddenly, and without my own volition, my left arm pulled the steering wheel down and veered my car off the inside lane of the motorway onto the hard shoulder. As it did so, the open-backed van in front of me shed its load of crash barriers into the now empty section of motorway that my car had vacated a second before. We were driving at around 60 miles an hour. Had I not taken evasive action, the barriers would have crashed into my car, sending me careering across the motorway. I could have been killed.

I rejoined the motorway from the hard shoulder to see, in my rear-view mirror, and in the mist, the van driver and his assistant leaping out of their vehicle to, I assume, get the crash barriers out of the road and secured back in position.

During the rest of the journey, I took stock of exactly what had happened. I could easily have been killed in this incident. The crash barriers would have hit my windscreen at some speed, shattering it. Indeed, the barriers would have hit me on the head as they entered my car. Even if this had not happened, I would have lost control of the vehicle and turned right into the outside lane, with traffic going even faster. Remember, this was a foggy evening. Other drivers would not have seen my totally unexpected manoeuvre until the last second and could not have then taken evasive action. Conversely, I could have turned left at speed and with a shattered windscreen and possible injuries, which would have had me leave the motorway altogether and down into the ditch along the side of the road. All of these outcomes would probably have brought about my death.

I was curious about this event because it proved to me that an idea I had been playing around with since 1999 was more than just an ideal hypothesis. In October of that year, I had decided to write a book. I had no idea what the subject matter would be, nor, indeed, if any publisher would be interested in my writings. But something deep within me demanded that I start on this endeavour. I had enough savings to take 12 months from my career to follow my muse and create a book.

I had long been fascinated by the phenomenon popularly known as déjà vu. On numerous occasions throughout my life, I had experienced the sensation that I was reliving an event or set of circumstances. I felt I 'remembered' from a dim and distant memory what was happening to me and, more importantly, what was about to happen next. After a particularly powerful migraine-related déjà vu sensation, I decided that this would be the subject matter of my book. Furthermore, my research during that year also drew links between déjà vu and something known as the near-death experience (NDE).

This, in turn, stimulated me to join the International Association of Near-Death Studies (IANDS). I felt I needed to know as much as possible about this intriguing perceptual effect whereby individuals have reported powerful 'hallucinations' during close encounters with death throughout history.

In 2000 I invested up to ten hours every day reading up on NDEs and followed several paths of enquiry, all of which led me to conclude that a new explanatory hypothesis may be applied to the experience. This linked a number of seemingly unrelated elements. I called this hypothesis Cheating the Ferryman (CTF).

In my research, I came across several books by P.M.H. Atwater, a prolific writer on NDEs and somebody who had experienced two of these life-changing events. I took the liberty of contacting P.M.H. and asking her advice about my work. She asked to read my then completed first manuscript. After reading it, she responded with the great advice of 'you have written this book for yourself. Now write it for your readers.' I took this on board and rewrote large sections to make it less technical and more accessible for the general reader. She also advised me to contact Professor Bruce Greyson, the editor of the *Journal of Near-Death Studies*, the academic periodical of IANDS. She felt he might also be interested in Cheating the Ferryman.

This I did, and Bruce was extremely helpful. He suggested to me that I should consider writing an academic paper outlining the hypothesis. Not only that, but he offered to be my peer-reviewer. And it was with his help that, in the Winter 2004 edition of the journal, my paper was published. Entitled 'Cheating the Ferryman: A New Paradigm of Existence?', this outlined the model in some detail.

The article stimulated a flurry of interest, and several letters were written about it and subsequently published in the next edition of the journal. I had hoped that this would be the springboard for an approach by a publisher interested in taking the book. Much to my delight, Arcturus, a London-based publishing house (and the publishers of this book), took a gamble on an unknown author and offered me a contract. This involved a total rewrite of the original manuscript and the loss of 'Cheating the Ferryman' as the book title.

In October 2006 *Is There Life After Death?: The Extraordinary Science of What Happens When We Die* appeared in British and North American bookshops. Professor Greyson kindly wrote the foreword. In this, he stated that he considered that my explanation of human immortality was 'the most innovative and provocative argument I have ever seen'.

This work has proven to be a reasonably successful book with sales in excess of 50,000 copies and several foreign language editions plus an Audible audiobook version.

What was particularly interesting about the book was how it stimulated thousands of people from across the world to contact me about their own experiences that supported the central thesis proposed in the book (now affectionately known as ITLAD after its initials). Furthermore, in the following years, I continued my writings, wrote a further nine books, co-authored a tenth, and edited and contributed to an eleventh. I have also contributed chapters to several books on a broad subject matter area. The book also opened doors in that several academics and researchers became interested in my ideas and were happy to share their findings with me.

All this made me conclude that the original hypothesis discussed in ITLAD needed to be revisited in light of all the information I had received over the last 15 years. I was, therefore, delighted when Arcturus agreed to publish a new book that will pull together all the data and research I have been involved in during that decade and a half.

And this is the book you now have in your hands.

But to understand the new material, you, dear reader, will need to understand the original hypothesis proposed precisely. My advice would be to source a copy of ITLAD and read through it. But I am aware that for many of you, time is of the essence. With this in mind, I have decided to incorporate below a number of sections of the academic paper from 2004. This reading will give you a quick overview of the hypothesis, something I call 'Cheating the Ferryman'. This will allow you to dive straight into the new material and, hopefully, appreciate how the concept has been broadened and deepened. I hope you will find it of interest.

And, by the way, there is still more to come on why the M62 incident proved to me the truth of CTF. We shall return to this later.

PART 2

The Hypothesis

The Banks of the Styx

In the following few pages, I will discuss the information I presented in the 2004 paper published in the *Journal of Near-Death Studies* and peer-reviewed by Professor Bruce Greyson (Peake, 'Cheating the Ferryman: A New Paradigm of Existence?', 2004). This will introduce to you the initial ideas I had, ideas that were to be expanded upon in my 2006 book *Is There Life After Death?: The Extraordinary Science of What Happens When We Die*.

According to ancient Greek myth, the first challenge to confront the recently dead was crossing the River Styx. At the riverbank, they were met by a ferryman who would, for a payment, take them across to the opposite side. This place was the realm of the dead known as Hades. This being, known as Charon, probably expected to make a good living from the millions of coins he would receive.

I contend that Charon has been awaiting his first customer. Hades on the far bank remains empty of souls, the screeches of the frustrated harpies echoing across the quite literally soulless landscape. Charon has been cheated by a trick of subjective time perception that takes place at the moment of death. This ensures that no soul ever arrives at the riverbank. People may be perceived to die by those witnessing that death, but from their point of view they never reach that point in time where their death occurs.

To facilitate an understanding of how I come to such a conclusion, I need to review the true nature of the physical world as presented to us by the latest discoveries of quantum physics and, more importantly, what these discoveries are telling us about the central importance of consciousness in creating the physical world.

Taken in isolation, these theories are fascinating and challenging ideas. However, they are rarely placed in the context of modern neurology, perceptual studies, and the evidence for human psychic duality. Central to the Ferryman thesis is that all these seemingly unrelated areas of enquiry need to be brought together and the information reviewed in the light of what we know about near-death experiences.

We will now review a number of these and place them in context regarding the CTF hypothesis.

The Daemon and the Eidolon

In many classic reports of the near-death experience, a 'being of light' appears at the point of death, guides the dying persons through such other elements as the life review, and is usually responsible for announcing that these persons need to return, as 'it is not their time'. This being manifests in many ways, usually in a psychologically comforting form to the dying person. However, in its classic manifestation, the being is simply a presence that communicates verbally or telepathically.

To some researchers, this entity represents a projection from the subconscious of the dying person (Gabbard & Twemlow, 1984; Serdahely, 1987). This is evidenced by the seemingly culturally biased nature of its manifestation. To believers in the afterlife, it is what it seems to be: a relative, an angel, or even God. However, this entity is the single most intriguing element of the phenomenon because it may prove another long-held belief that all human beings consist of not one but two mutually independent forms of consciousness (Novak, 1997, 2002, 2003).

This idea is culturally and historically almost universal. The ancient Chinese called these two independent consciousnesses *hun* and *p'o*. The ancient Egyptians were the *ka* and the *ba*, and the ancient Greeks knew them as the *Daemon* and the *Eidolon*. In each case, the two entities shared their senses and perceptions of the external world but interpreted those perceptions from their respective history, knowledge and personality. For the Greeks, the relationship was an unequal one. The higher self, the Daemon, acted as a form of guardian angel over its lower self, the Eidolon. The Stoic philosopher Epictetus wrote:

> God has placed at every man's side a guardian, the Daemon
> of each man, who is charged to watch over him; a Daemon
> that cannot sleep, nor be deceived. To what greater and
> more watchful guardian could He have entrusted each of
> us? So, when you have shut the doors, and made darkness
> in the house, remember, never to say that you are alone;
> for you are not alone. But God is there, and your Daemon
> is there.
>
> Epictetus, 1st–2nd century CE

The belief was that the Daemon had foreknowledge of future circumstances and events and could warn its Eidolon of the dangers. It was as if in some way the Daemon had already lived the life of its Eidolon.

However, the Daemon and Eidolon are more than cultural or theological beliefs. There is compelling evidence from both physiological and psychological experimentation that we all have a duality of consciousness. The human brain has two hemispheres joined together by what is called the corpus callosum. For many years, surgeons had speculated as to what would happen to personality and consciousness if the callosum were cut and the subject survived.

In the 1960s, surgical techniques had progressed to the extent that such an operation could be attempted on human beings. Neurosurgeons Philip Vogel and Joseph Bogen concluded that certain epileptic patients would gain from such surgery and suffer no serious mental loss. Between 1962 and 1968, they performed nine such operations.

Generally, the effects of the operation were beneficial. The patients showed some short-term memory loss, orientation problems and mental fatigue immediately after the operation. Some were unable to speak for two months after the procedure. But in all cases, there was gradual recovery. Bogen and psychologist Michael Gazzaniga set up a series of tests to discover the changes in these patients. These tests were forever to change our understanding of how the human mind works. In short, they unknowingly confirmed the existence of the Daemon. The senior researcher behind the experiments, Roger Sperry, made the following observation:

> In our 'split-brain' studies of the past two decades . . . , the surgically separated hemispheres of animals and man have been shown to perceive, learn, and remember independently, each hemisphere evidently cut off from the conscious experience of the other. In man the language-dominant hemisphere further reports verbally that it is not consciously aware of the concomitant or immediately preceding mental performances of the disconnected partner hemisphere. These test performances of which the speaking hemisphere remains unaware obviously involve perception, comprehension, and in some cases non-verbal memory, reasoning, and concept formation of different kinds depending on the nature of the test task. In these and many other respects, the split-brain animal and man behave as if each of the separated hemispheres had a mind of its own.
>
> Sperry, 1975, p. 170

The work of psychologist Roland Puccetti strongly reinforced this analysis. He concluded that even without a split-brain operation there are always two independent centres of consciousness in the human brain. He appealed to the cases where a complete hemisphere was removed. In this event, and whichever hemisphere was left, there remained a person. He argued that if people were unitary, these operations or circumstances would leave only half a person. Puccetti concluded that the only way he could explain the completeness of the remaining person was by supposing that before the operation, there was not a unitary person. He wrote:

> He or she was a compound of two persons who functioned
> in concert by transcommissural exchange. What has
> survived is one of two very similar persons with roughly
> parallel memory traces, nearly synchronous emotional
> states, perceptual experiences, and so on, but differential
> processing functions.
>
> Puccetti, 1973, p. 352

Reinforcing solid evidence for the existence of the Daemon can be found in research done into deep trance states. Writing in the late 1970s, Ernest Hilgard became convinced that we all have another being sharing our lives. Hilgard termed this entity the 'hidden observer'. Hilgard described a classic test of how this hidden entity is part of our consciousness. A hypnotized blind student, while in a trance state, was told that he would become deaf. The suggestion was so strong that he failed to react to any form of noise, even large sounds next to his ear. Of course, he also was unable to respond to any questions he was asked while in his trance state. The hypnotist was keen to discover if 'anybody else' was able to hear. He quietly said to the student, 'Perhaps there is some part of you that is hearing my voice and processing the information. If there is, I should like the index finger of your right hand to rise as a sign that this is the case' (Hilgard, 1977, p. 86). The finger rose.

At this, the student requested that he be brought out of the hypnotically induced period of deafness. On being 'awakened', the student said that he had asked to come out of the trance state because 'I felt my finger rise in a way that was not a spontaneous twitch, so you must have done something to make it rise, and I want to know what you did' (p. 186). The hypnotist then asked him what he remembered. Because the trance was light, the student never actually lost consciousness; all that occurred was that his hearing had ceased. To deal with the boredom of being deprived of both sight and sound, he had decided to work on some statistical problems in his head. It was while he was doing this that he suddenly felt his finger lift. This was strange to him because under normal circumstances he was, like all of us, the 'person' who decides on how the body moves. In this case, he was not. Not only that, but 'somebody else' in his head responded to an external request that he had not heard. As far as Hilgard was concerned, the person who answered was the 'hidden observer'.

Another of Hilgard's subjects made the following interesting statement about what she experienced, making particular reference to what she sensed was her higher self:

> The hidden observer is cognizant of everything that is going on. . . . The hidden observer sees more, he questions more, he's aware of what is going on all of the time but getting in touch is totally unnecessary. . . . He's like a guardian angel that guards you from doing anything that will mess you up. The hidden observer is looking through the tunnel, and sees everything in the tunnel. Unless someone tells me to get in touch with the hidden observer I'm not in contact. It's just there.
>
> Hilgard, 1977, p. 210

It seems that the more profound the trance, the more chance there is of encountering this being, or so it appears from the work of psychologist Charles Tart. In the 1960s and 1970s, Tart was keen to see just how deep a trance state could be brought about by hypnotism. Depth cannot be described solely by the responsiveness to suggestion. Indeed, at greater depths, responsiveness can actually disappear. In Tart's experiments, the subjects were required to assign self-consistent numerical values to the depth they subjectively felt.

Tart had an excellent subject called William, who was in the highest 1 or 2 per cent of hypnotic responsiveness. He had been hypnotized 18 times previously for various reasons, often with an emphasis on depth. William usually gave depth ratings of 40, experiencing amnesia at 30. He had never gone beyond 60. It was agreed that an attempt would be made to take him much deeper than he had gone before. He was instructed that, at each 10-point interval on a depth continuum, he should remain at that depth as the experimenter had him describe what he was experiencing.

As he went through the levels, he experienced the typical effects: early relaxation followed by a sensation of distance, increased peacefulness and a gradual withdrawal from the environment. Beginning at a level of about 50 on this scale, he started to have distortions of consciousness. These distortions were similar to those reported in mystical experiences. At this stage, the passage of time became meaningless and the body seemed to be left behind, and a new sense of infinite potentiality emerged. However, at a level of 50, another consciousness was experienced, an individual that William described as being him but not him. This 'other William' showed that he was fully aware of the experiment and what was going on. What is strange was that this other being was amused by the attempts of the psychologists to understand the human mind. Tart described this event as an 'intrusion'. The other entity accompanied William from level 50 to level 90, where it disappeared. It was at its strongest at level 70 (Tart, 1976, pp. 191–200).

What is of great interest is that the 'intrusion', at the early stages of the now deeper hypnosis of the experience, was amused by William's participation in these experiments. Amusement is not something one would expect of the nondominant hemisphere of the brain. This 'intrusion' seemed to be a being who knew precisely what was going on and observed from a position of superiority, not inferiority.

Most 'normal' people can live their whole lives without ever being aware of their Daemon. This other self quietly observes what is going on. However, there is strong anecdotal evidence that the Daemon regularly communicates with its Eidolon through dreams, hunches and occasionally through direct verbal contact. These 'communications', dream or otherwise, are nearly always a warning to avoid a particular course of action. Often those who heed these warnings survive to report the fact. It is as if the Daemon knows the future and actively involves itself in preserving the ongoing existence of its lower self.

The late Julian Jaynes argued that this other entity is in regular communication with its lower self (Jaynes, 1976). His interest was stimulated by a particular vivid auditory hallucination that occurred to him when he was a student. This hallucination encouraged him to research this specific phenomenon. He was surprised to discover that one man in 12 experienced this form of hallucination among the Anglo-Saxon population. For women, it was even more common: one in eight. Indeed, this was relatively low in relation to other groups. In Russia, the figure was twice as high, and in Brazil, almost 25 per cent of the population had had or would have at some stage in their lives a similar experience. These were ordinary people, not those under mental or psychological stress. From this, Jaynes concluded that under certain circumstances, many if not all individuals might experience auditory hallucinations, the differences being purely cultural.

Jaynes believed that this vivid auditory hallucination could explain the universal religious experience of communicating with the gods. It is quite understandable how an individual, living in a culture or a historical period where the existence of gods is unquestioned, could naturally assume the voice to be the words of a god. The curiously portentous and somewhat obscure meaning of what the voice said then reinforced this belief.

However, for Jaynes, there was more to it than that. He pointed out that for 99 per cent of human evolution, men and women grouped in tightly bonded, mutually dependent groups. Each individual had no sense of individuality within these groups, no sharp sense of 'ego-self'. The concept of selfhood came about, according to Jaynes, about the first millennium BCE. Jaynes based his theory upon studies that he made of early writings such as Homer's *Iliad* (circa 1000 BCE). He noted that this book had no reference to concepts such as thought and mind, human actions being the results of the gods willing men to do things. From this, he concluded that human consciousness had split into two entities at some time in the recent past. Not only that, but it was this very process of splitting that brought about self-consciousness.

So what of modern humans? If Jaynes' statistics are to be believed, then many of us interact with our Daemon regularly. As such, the implication is that this 'other person' shares our life with us, unseen and unheard, until they decide that intervention is needed. Brian Inglis (1990) described various modern equivalents. An example is a tale told by the Italian opera singer Tito Gobbi, who wrote in his autobiography about when he was driving far too fast on a steep mountain road. As he became more reckless, he heard his brother Bruno's voice:

> . . . so distinctly that he seemed to be sitting beside me, saying 'Stop – instantly'. Instinctively I obeyed, coming to a halt on a wide grass verge, practically the only spot of any width in the whole path. A few minutes later, round the narrow bend came an articulated lorry out of control.
>
> Inglis, 1990, p. 85

In another example, the writer Philip Paul was walking to work during the London Blitz in the Second World War when a voice told him to stop. He was, quite naturally, surprised and his rational mind decided to ignore the intruder. He later wrote:

> The warning persisted. So, putting a foot on a pile of rubble, I pretended to tie a shoelace. At that moment, the high wall ahead collapsed into the alleyway, filling it ten feet high and burying walkers a few yards ahead of me.
>
> Paul, 1985, p. 25

In these cases, the 'voice' saved the life of its lower self. Indeed, in both cases, the Daemon showed an ability to see the future. Suffice to say that without these interventions, it is likely that neither Paul nor Gobbi would have survived to tell the tale.

Temporal Lobe Epilepsy

If you accept my 'Daemon hypothesis', you accept that we all have two aspects to our 'self'. The everyday self, or Eidolon, lives within time and perceives a limited amount of what we term 'reality'. The other aspect of the self, the Daemon, exists outside of time and knows not only what has happened but also what will happen. As such, any accidental access to the Daemon's perceptions will involve heightened sensory awareness and an ability to foresee the future.

Throughout recorded history, it has been believed that some of those who experience epilepsy have the gift of second sight. An example of this is found in the works of the Arabic author Ali Ibn Rabban al-Tabari. Writing in the 9th century, he discussed the illness known as *sar'un* or 'the falling sickness': 'The people call it the diviner's disease because some of them prophesy and have visions of wondrous things' (Rabban al-Tabari, 1928/9th century, p. 138).

Indeed, those who could foretell the future, the *ka˜han*, were thought to be possessed by the *djinn*, demons who caused madness and epilepsy. It was believed that another entity took them over during the epileptic attack, and that entity was responsible for the prognostications. Here we have evidence of all our suspicions regarding the duality of human consciousness.

However, there is another factor that is known by neurologists to be inextricably tied to epilepsy: déjà vu. Déjà vu is recognized as the most common psychic phenomenon (Neppe, 1983). However, it is so common among people with epilepsy, particularly as part of the pre-seizure aura, that it is considered one of the classic symptoms.

There have been various attempts to explain this experience, but none has succeeded. The reason for this failure may be that déjà vu is precisely what those who experience it claim it to be: a reliving of an event brought about by a 'hiccup' in temporal perception. But why do people experiencing epilepsy, particularly temporal lobe epilepsy, experience déjà vu with such regularity?

A seizure in either of the temporal lobes may be caused by a neurotransmitter known as glutamate. Under normal circumstances, glutamate is the primary neurotransmitter within the temporal lobes, particularly the hippocampus. When a message is transferred from synapse to synapse, this chemical brings about the transfer. Usually, this is a harmless process. However, in large amounts, glutamate can overexcite the synapses and cause a massive increase in electrical activity. Once started, this rapidly gets out of control, and a seizure takes place. However, there is a short period of time when the excess glutamate stimulates neuronal activity without loss of consciousness. This period is perceived by the person affected as the pre-seizure aura.

During this flood, there can be an immediate loss of temporal awareness. For a few seconds, the Eidolon glimpses reality as it really is and sees time as an illusion. For that period, the Eidolon's 'specious present', as psychologist William James termed it (1950/1890, p. 613), becomes longer. In its confusion, the Eidolon thinks that it is seeing a rerun of the previous few seconds of perception. This is not the case. What has happened is that the glutamate flood has temporarily nullified the usually effective censorship of regular perception. This is perceived as a déjà vu. Within a few seconds, the censorship processes regain control. Either the seizure begins, or everyday perceptions are regained.

So far, I have presented evidence that all human beings consist of not one but two interrelated entities. These entities, termed the Eidolon and the Daemon, share the same sensory inputs of sight, sound, taste, touch and smell. However, the Daemon perceives reality as a riot of swirling colours, sounds and sensations, not as the ordered world presented to the senses of the Eidolon. For some individuals – specifically, people who experience schizophrenia and temporal lobe epilepsy – access to the Daemonic worldview is facilitated by neurotransmitters such as dopamine and glutamate. The Daemon also perceives time differently from the Eidolon. For the Daemon, time does not flow from past to present but is seen as a continuum where past, present and future coexist.

Indeed, at its most fundamental level, matter itself shows this reciprocity to such an extent that physicist Geoffrey Chew called his model of reality 'bootstrap theory'. Chew was particularly interested in hadrons, strongly interacting subatomic particles. For Chew, 'each particle helps generate other particles, which in turn generate it' (Chew, Gell-Mann & Rosenfeld, 1964, p. 74). Or, to put it another way, every hadron is made up of combinations of other hadrons, including itself. And so it is with your brain in your universe, and my brain in mine. However, the suggestion that the universe is an internally created illusion implies that each consciousness carries a fully functioning, three-dimensional version of that universe within its brain. To accept such a proposition, one has to accept that there are literally millions upon millions of personal universes, each one being generated by the thought processes of a single conscious observer.

Thus far, I have presented a series of interrelated observations leavened with empirical examples from the worlds of neurology, psychology, particle physics and consciousness studies. What I am suggesting is that all self-aware beings consist of not one singular personality but two. These two entities, known from classical times as the Eidolon and the Daemon, have a curious symbiotic relationship. The less-developed Eidolon, usually known as 'I', is, except in certain psychological states, totally unaware of its more developed partner, the Daemon. However, the Daemon seems to be very aware of its twin and how their shared life will develop. Indeed, there are many well-documented cases of prophets, seers and clairvoyants whose ability to predict the future depended upon the prognostications of another being, such as Socrates' Divine Sign and Nostradamus' Divine Splendour.

By various means, including dreams, hunches and auditory halluc-inations, the Daemon ensures the ongoing survival of its Eidolon. In doing so, it may change the future timeline of its unitary self. It changes nothing as regards the perception of other consciousnesses. All it does is send itself and its partner down a different alternative version of reality, and in doing so, enters another universe, one of the trillions to choose from.

I contend that the perceptual universes we all exist within are subjective projections. I call this concept the Bohmian IMAX; by this I mean the internally created and externally projected sensory vista that we believe to be an objective, external reality. I use the term 'Bohmian IMAX' as a counterpoint to Daniel Dennett's famous 'Cartesian theatre'.

Dennett, a philosopher and cognitive scientist, is an eliminative materialist who argues that self-referential consciousness is an illusion and that we are all fooling ourselves into thinking we are conscious. Apparently, it is all a grand magical trick. Exactly how something non-conscious can be fooled by anything is, to be honest, beyond my comprehension. But then again, according to eliminative materialism, I have no awareness, so I am also trapped in his Cartesian theatre.

Dennett created the term 'Cartesian theatre' to sarcastically dismiss the long-held belief that the universe comprises two quite distinct types of 'stuff' – matter and spirit. That is, material things that have extension in space and non-physical things that do not. The body is matter, whereas the mind is not. This is known as substance dualism. This idea was discussed extensively by French philosopher René Descartes and so is also referred to as Cartesian dualism. Descartes presented his ideas in his 1641 book *Meditations on First Philosophy*. For eliminative materialists such as Daniel Dennett, this idea is ludicrous. They argue that if mind is not matter, but some kind of 'ghost in the machine', a term coined by another eliminative materialist philosopher, Gilbert Ryle (Ryle, 1949), how can it physically affect matter in any way? In mechanics, every action is brought about by a force, but spirit, as it is defined, cannot create any force. So how does it influence nerves to bring about muscular contractions? Indeed, Dennett takes this further by suggesting that the idea of a 'ghost in the machine' brings about an infinite regress.

For example, when I perceive the outside world, I imagine a miniature version of myself sitting in a small room inside my head. It has a pair of speakers on either side broadcasting the sound signals from my ears and a stereo TV screen in front of me showing what my eyes are seeing. I sit in a chair that reproduces the nerve sensations from my skin. In this way, all my senses are presented to me. All these are the contents of my consciousness, and 'I' am the audience who experiences them. But there is a problem. If I imagine this little homunculus in my head, then he, in turn, must have a little person in his head sitting in his own little room, and so on and so on. This quickly becomes an infinite regress of ever-smaller homunculi. This makes no sense. This inner auditorium is what Dennett calls the 'Cartesian theatre'. This is the place in the brain where consciousness resides and 'observes' the sights and sounds processed by the senses. But for Dennett to believe this is to fall into another version of Cartesian dualism.

I would like to argue that Dennett's Cartesian theatre is a totally outmoded model. Instead, we should suggest a Bohmian IMAX in that my model of how the observer interacts with sensory data describing the phenomenal world is far more expansive and direct.

My comparison between a theatre and an IMAX cinema is reasonably self-explanatory. But what do I mean by 'Bohmian'? This is a reference to the writings and theories of physicist David Bohm. We shall return to this in greater detail later, together with a complete analysis of the mechanism whereby what we think of as being an external reality that exists independent of us is, in fact, a vast virtual-reality simulation that is downloaded into our perceptual field in the same way that a virtual-reality computer game is uploaded into a virtual-reality headset.

I have suggested that all this takes place in a highly personalized version of reality, a version of reality projected into the consciousness of the Eidolon, who in blissful ignorance carries on with its life. For the Daemon, it is very different. It has already viewed the Bohmian IMAX, this being its second or even 10,000th viewing of this life. Sometimes there is a metaphorical 'jump' in the recording, perhaps brought about by leakage of certain neurotransmitters across the synapses. For a split second, the Eidolon accesses the Daemon's senses and feels that it has lived this event or circumstance before. This is a déjà vu.

All of my examples can be dovetailed together to give a satisfactory, scientifically based explanation as to what really happens at the point of death, an explanation that will possibly be philosophically acceptable to all within the field, from theists to atheists. Let us now look at what may happen at the point of death according to my Ferryman thesis.

Cheating the Ferryman

First, we need to understand the role of the neurotransmitters, which has to do with what I have termed the 'Chronon Zeno effect'. This is named after Zeno of Elea, who devised his famous paradox of Achilles and the tortoise to show that motion was an illusion.

Zeno suggested that a race be arranged between the fleet-footed hero Achilles and a much slower tortoise. Because Achilles can run ten times faster than his reptilian opponent, he agrees to give the tortoise a 10-metre head start. The starter's gun is fired, and Achilles swiftly runs the 10 metres. However, because we know that he can run ten times faster than the tortoise, the tortoise will have already walked 1 metre closer to the finishing line. Achilles, still behind by the 1 metre, runs that metre as fast as he can. However, on reaching the 11th metre, he discovers that the tortoise has walked a further centimetre. Achilles runs that centimetre, but in the time it takes him to do so, the tortoise has progressed a further millimetre towards the finishing line. Rushing along the millimetre, Achilles discovers that he is still a tenth of a millimetre behind. One can go on literally to infinity, but Achilles will never overtake the tortoise.

In reality, Achilles shoots past the tortoise and wins with ease, but the philosophy behind this paradox has an underlying truth when applied to time. More interesting is that neither the tortoise nor Achilles ever reaches the finishing line. They just cover smaller and smaller amounts of distance.

I would like to propose that this is what happens to dying persons as they approach the point of death. Instead of metres, we have units of time. Let us call them 'chronons'. At the moment when death becomes unavoidable, chemicals are released into the brain. These chemicals influence how the Eidolon perceives time. As regards the perceptions of the Eidolon time, it seems to slow down. The human brain is very flexible in its perception of temporal flow: drugs, mood and metabolism all contribute to time's perceived duration.

Massive chemical changes take place in the body at the point of death. The chemicals released at that point are virtually identical to those released during an epileptic seizure. Juan Saavedra-Aguilar and Juan Gómez-Jeria pointed out the link between near-death experiences and temporal lobe epilepsy, suggesting that the stress brought about by a close brush with death leads to a release of a particular class of chemical called neuropeptides and specific neurotransmitters such as endorphins, dopamine and glutamate (Saavedra-Aguilar & Gómez-Jeria, 1989). These chemicals become particularly active in the brain's limbic and temporal lobe areas and cause psychological effects during near-death trauma identical to those experienced by people with epilepsy during a pre-seizure aura. It is therefore reasonable to conclude that all the changes in perception reported by people with epilepsy, particularly in terms of time perception, are experienced, albeit in much greater intensity, at the point of death. In this way, psychological time for the dying person begins to slow down. In effect, they 'fall out of the time perspective' of any observers who may be witnessing the death. For dying persons, each second may take twice as long to pass as the previous second. As such, their consciousness moves away from the observer's, whose seconds continue to be seconds.

This is a total supposition on my part, but I propose that sometime in your own personal past, you once did live a real life in a real universe. It is that life that laid down the template by which all your other lives were lived. In that first life, your Daemon and Eidolon, like Julian Jaynes' preconscious ancients, lived as a unitary being. Your consciousness was singular, and the Daemon was unaware of itself as an entity separate from the Eidolon. Could it be that certain people with temporal lobe epilepsy or schizophrenia have the duality from the start?

Suffice it to say, the singular consciousness lived its life for the first time. Its holographic memory banks busily recorded every thought, feeling, sensation, emotion and event that happened during that life. Because these recordings were being made as consciousness perceived them, they could not generate déjà vu sensations. The analogy to use is this: you cannot watch the ending of a recorded television programme before the digital recorder has finished recording. At this stage of human development, the future simply did not exist. This is why some people have never experienced a déjà vu: they are quite literally 'first-timers', living their life for the first time.

As death approached in that first life, endogenous chemicals flooded the brain. These stimulated the Daemon into wakefulness and self-awareness. Although shocked, it quickly realized what it had to do. Imagine the scene at a road accident. The paramedic desperately tries to save a badly injured man's life and realizes that his patient is about to die. Six seconds before the man does die, the endorphins, dopamine and glutamate flood his brain and release his Daemon. As he lies on the ground, the endogenous drugs affect his psychological time.

The time between the sixth and fifth second before the injured man's death takes one second in the perception of the concerned paramedic. However, for our dying man, the very nature of time is changing. For him, that second takes two seconds to pass. The next half-second (another second for the paramedic) takes four seconds for the dying man (Chew, Gell-Mann & Rosenfeld, 1964). The next quarter-second (again, another second for the paramedic) takes eight seconds. Within three seconds of 'normal time', our two people are existing in totally different time-worlds. The dying man is still back in the first second and living in an ever-shrinking chronon of time. His subjective seconds are dividing as time progresses. In the same sense that Achilles never overtakes the tortoise, so it is that the dying man never reaches his actual point of death. The curiosity, however, is that in the temporal world of the paramedic, the man dies.

It has been well recorded that glutamate manifests itself during periods of high anxiety and stress. It is also known that glutamate in large doses can overexcite the synapses and cause a massive increase in electrical activity. Once started, this rapidly gets out of control, and an epileptic seizure takes place. Therefore, our dying man has moved out of time (and, it must be said, space) and inhabits a world within his mind. He has, in effect, unlimited time, but what is this time for? In answering this question, we must return to the Daemon.

The Daemon is now aware of what its task is to be. It is responsible for ensuring that the life review takes place, but not as it is known from the reports of near-death experiencers. The standard description of the life review is often similar to 'my life passed before my eyes in a split second'. But that is only how the life review is recalled by a person who has returned to 'normal' consciousness and 'normal' time. In an actual death situation, the review occurs at normal speed, in minute-by-minute equality. The Eidolon perceives each minute of the life record as a precise minute. Put another way, the Eidolon lives its life again in real time.

At a microsecond before death, the dying person's consciousness is flooded with new images, images of rebirth. The Eidolon finds itself coming into a virtual-reality world as a newly born baby. Its memory banks wiped clean, it remembers nothing of its previous life. It begins afresh in a world created from recovered memories. Every sound, feeling and emotion is reproduced in perfect fidelity. As far as the Eidolon is concerned, this is all new. However, this second life has one significant difference from the first one: it has a conscious and aware Daemon who knows everything that is about to take place. As the child grows in this second life, the Daemon keeps a watchful eye over its progress. It experiences everything, and in dreams, may communicate subtle changes to the advancement of this second life.

As we have already seen, as the Eidolon-child becomes older, circumstances may occur that, either by accident or design, the Daemon causes a 'glitch' in the programme. The Eidolon will be confused at these strange sensations and may feel that it has lived these events before and remembers what will happen next. These curious sensations are very common, and are called déjà vu.

There may be occasions when the Daemon wishes to change the course of action followed by its Eidolon. The Daemon may manifest itself in many ways: a voice in the head, a dream or even a doppelganger. In this way, it can manoeuvre its Eidolon into a better position or into a situation where it may learn from experience. I term these situations 'temporal mutations', and they work the same way that Darwinian mutations occur in nature.

And so the human 'soul' evolves in the same way that an animal species evolves. Equal to each Darwinian generation is a life, each one subtly changed from the last one. Note that my theory involves multiple, rather than singular, life reruns. Like the character Phil Connors in the film *Groundhog Day*, we each have endless lives to get things right. The mechanism is simply a repeat of the end of the first life. At the end of the rerun, death again approaches and is again denied by the person's consciousness slipping out of time. Psychological time again slows down exponentially, leaving Charon yet again with an empty boat.

For both the Daemon and the Eidolon, the approach of death is a stressful time. However, in terms of our own research into the possibility of the Ferryman thesis, it is also the time that the interaction between the two should be at its most intense. The evidence seems to support this contention in that the Daemon seems to become visible to the dying Eidolon. The interesting example below is taken from the work of psychologists Erlendur Haraldsson and Karlis Osis:

> A college-educated Indian man in his twenties was recovering from mastoiditis. He was doing very well. He was going to be discharged that day. Suddenly at 5 am he shouted, 'Someone is standing here dressed in white clothes. I will not go with you!' He was dead in ten minutes. Both the patient and the doctor expected a definite recovery.
>
> Haraldsson & Osis, 2012, p. 44

In this case, the patient did actually die, indicating that the 'being of light' may be seen as part of the 'real thing' as well as in 'near misses'.

Chemicals released in the brain before death appear to create a level of awareness in normal consciousness that allows perception of our Daemon, or higher self. In the case described by Haraldsson and Osis, the Daemon decided to be seen as a being that could not be recognized as another version of the self. However, there has been a long-held belief that to see one's double is a portent of death (Maack & Mullen, 1983; Rank, 1971/1925). Could this have come about when the dying reported that they could see their Daemon as a doppelganger? It is reasonable to conclude that, whereas some Daemons show themselves at this point, others take on the appearance of whatever person or religious archetype will instil a feeling of happiness and joy in the dying person.

So at the moment of death, the Eidolon is transported back to the point where the embryo becomes a person, the point where some form of consciousness enters the growing brain. If the theory is correct, this can occur as soon as the neurons have developed sufficiently for the Eidolon to attach itself. At this point, the brain 'wakes up' and becomes, if not fully conscious, at least aware in some fundamental way. Indeed, at this point, dreaming will begin. The Eidolon has the opportunity to review and reflect upon what took place in its previous life, possibly under the guidance of the Daemon. This form of prenatal dreaming is a form of what is termed 'active sleep'. According to biologist Lyall Watson, the developing foetus seems to spend most of its time doing it (Watson, 1979). The question is: what can a being who has had absolutely no experience dream about?

Could it be that during the last few seconds of our previous life, we will experience a full temporal lobe epileptic seizure brought about by a cocktail of endogenous drugs that stimulate the brain into its final activities?

The epileptic French writer Edmond de Goncourt was said to have described life as 'a series of epileptic attacks, preceded and followed by a blank' (Bourget, cited in Lombroso, 1891, p. 342). It seems more like 'a blank, preceded and followed by an epileptic attack'. Could it be that by living inside that blank, we finally cheat the Ferryman?

And that was how I concluded my 2004 journal article, 'Cheating the Ferryman: A New Paradigm of Existence?'. Little was I to know that a couple of months after the article's publication, the incident on the motorway was to prove beyond all doubt – for me anyway – that at least some of the elements of my Cheating the Ferryman hypothesis had validity. But for you to fully understand the significance of what took place that wintry evening in 2003, I have to take you back exactly 10 years further, possibly to the day, and, in doing so, fill in some more details regarding this curious event.

It was a cold December Saturday afternoon in late November 1993. I had popped into my local record shop to purchase a copy of the new Mary-Chapin Carpenter album, *Come On, Come On.* Colchester had been pretty busy that day with many pre-Christmas shoppers excitedly making impulsive purchases of gifts that probably would never be used come January. But this purchase was, for me, to become of great significance.

As I took the CD to the till, the sales assistant suggested to me that as I was purchasing a Columbia label recording, would I like to have a free publicity CD containing several tracks from forthcoming albums to be released on that label? Never turning down anything offered for free, I accepted it and took it home.

That evening, while my then partner Jenny was in the kitchen preparing our evening meal (yep, I know, very sexist, but she did enjoy doing that, and I was usually more of a hindrance than a help), I decided to listen to the publicity CD – my plan being to listen to the new Mary-Chapin Carpenter album later over dinner. I listened to the first five tracks, all of which were quite reasonable. And then track six started. From the opening few bars, I was transfixed. I knew this song, knew it to a visceral extent. Images and emotions flooded my mind. It was quite overpowering. I called out to Jenny, asking her to come into the living room. From nowhere, I found myself yelling out, 'Listen to this song. I want it played at my funeral.' Jenny looked at me in astonishment. 'Why?' she quite reasonably asked. 'I don't know,' was my confused reply. 'I just do.' The song came to an end. I grabbed the CD sleeve to discover it was a track entitled 'Round of Blues' by the American singer-songwriter Shawn Colvin.

The song itself is a happy, fun song with an upbeat, foot-tapping rhythm section. Not in any way a song that one would associate with a funeral. But this is what I wanted. The following Saturday, I had my will changed to state that this was the song that was to be played as my coffin enters the crematorium. Indeed, all these years later (I write this in March 2021), this is still part of my funeral plans.

Is this why my past self, 11 years before my close brush with death on a 'dark highway', associated this song with my death? If I had died that cold foggy night, the last thing I would have been aware of was Shawn Colvin singing 'Round of Blues'. It would have quite literally been my death-song. But how can this possibly be? How can a future event be 'remembered' before it is experienced?

But it gets stranger. It was many years later that the relevance of Shawn Colvin's lyrics really struck home to me:

> *We had our bitter cheer*
> *And sweet sorrow*
> *We lost a lot today*
> *We get it back tomorrow*
> *I hear the sound of wheels*
> *I know the rainbow's end*

'I hear the sound of wheels'. Before oblivion, my last recollection would have been, quite literally, the sound of my wheels skidding across the road. I was looking at 'the rainbow's end'.

Of course, some will say that this was purely a coincidence. Others, of a more mystical nature, will state that it is a classic example of synchronicity. I would like to argue that it is far more than either of these options. It is evidence of our potential immortality. We will now embark on a voyage of discovery that will take us across oceans of ideas to disembark onto a new continent of scientific theories which will suggest that you are an immortal being, one who will never die.

So let us set sail.

PART 3

The Ideas

THE PERENNIAL PHILOSOPHY
Introduction

Is there life after death? This is probably the most profound question that any sentient being can ask. For as long as we can remember, we have been alive, existing in a three-dimensional universe that we call 'reality'. However, death is all around us. The realization of our own impending mortality takes many years to dawn upon us. We witness the death of others, but somehow, we believe that death is something that happens to other people. Nonetheless, our own death is inevitable, and we have to face up to the fact that one day we will cease to be here and will 'move on'.

But what do we 'move on' to? Modern materialist-reductionist science is quite precise in this regard. Consciousness is simply a product of the brain. When the brain ceases to function, consciousness simply disappears. We are merely something that comes about during all these neurological interactions.

I believe that life after death is a mystery only because we confuse the relationship between *consciousness* and *reality*. Indeed, to understand the relationship between these two seemingly unrelated elements, we have to decide precisely what we mean when we use the terms.

The only thing I know with absolute certainty is that I am something perceiving something. There seems to be a world out there beyond my body that I can interface with by moving my body within what appears to be a consistent three-dimensional space. I also seem to move through time, defined by things around me, including my body, moving from a state of order to a state of disorder. With regard to my body, this process is known as ageing, and this happens in time. Other objects and entities that exist within the three-dimensional space also seem to have this gradual deterioration. Despite this, the parts of my body that I can see appear to be more part of this external world than the internal world that involves 'me'. This inner something looks out through my eyes and, in some mysterious way, wills my body to take certain actions. These may involve my manipulation of my immediate environment by picking things up, moving them around, or putting them together to create new configurations of objects.

I can also will my body to stand up and, by the use of my legs, move within the three dimensions of space. When I move from one location to another, my viewpoint changes, and I see external objects from a different angle. This suggests to me that this outside environment has an existence independent of my perception of it. If I close my eyes and open them again, everything in my visual field is where I expect it to be. I am also aware of other beings who exist within this world. In general terms, many of them look like me. They also move around in this world and seem to perceive it in the same way that I do. They react to stimuli in the same way. I can also communicate with these other beings and they can respond to me if they feel inclined. I do this by using my lungs to expel air and make specific vocalizations.

These vocalizations leave my mouth and create vibrationary waves in the air around me. These waves enter the ears of those in my vicinity and cause their eardrums to vibrate. This vibration is converted into an electric signal and sent to a part of their brains that creates a series of sounds. Without eardrums to vibrate, these sounds do not exist except as air vibrations. My associates' brains interpret these vibrations as sound, which has meaning if those around me have a mutual understanding of what these 'noises' signify. In this way, I can conclude that these other beings are similar to me and perceive the world in the same way. Indeed, I can use these mutually understandable vocal sounds to share information with regard to my perceptions.

But all of the above observations are based upon one generally accepted truth, which is that these are all my perceptions of what is really outside of me. Everything I perceive is processed and reconfigured by my brain and is then presented to whatever 'I' am. But I am not my brain, just like I am not my body. The very fact that that we describe these things as being objects we possess speaks volumes. We talk of 'my brain', 'my hands' and 'my pain' in the same way that we talk about 'my car', 'my partner' or 'my holiday'. It is clear that we feel ourselves to be something more than simply electricity reacting with chemicals in the brain. We feel we have a focus of awareness that views the world through a number of sensory inputs such as sight, hearing and smell. The biological systems that process these sensations are located in the head, giving the illusion that 'we' are located in our head. But imagine for a second that our eyes and ears were on our knees. Would we not have the feeling that we were located in our knee joint? Obviously, by following the trail of nerves that carry these sensations from their source, it is clear that the processing takes place in the brain. But the analogy still applies in that a similar false sense of location can be engendered as the eyes and ears on the knee model. So why is modern science so sure that consciousness is brain-located?

This is not what has been believed by most, if not all, cultures throughout history and across the globe. To a certain extent, this belief was supported by two crucial areas of perception: personal experience and observation of the natural world. People perceived dreams, and in these dreams, they travelled to other locations and sometimes encountered people that had died. Then, they realized that sometimes they could see the future or meet spirits or gods during waking life. For such societies, nature had two aspects, the physical and the spiritual. The first could be experienced directly with the external senses, whereas the second was perceived internally.

In 1944 the British author/philosopher Aldous Huxley wrote an essay entitled 'Vedanta and the West'. Taking the ideas of Renaissance thinkers such as Marsilio Ficino and Giovanni della Mirandola regarding universal knowledge, he argued that all traditional mystical traditions have, at their core, one universal model of reality. He called this the 'perennial philosophy'. This presents a universe that is the manifestation of one single consciousness, the Godhead or Ground. This source is both transcendent and immanent, and each individuated consciousness is part of this greater mind.

In my opinion, there is a more profound message to be found in the perennial philosophy, a model of reality that only now, with our understanding of the universe as presented to us through recent discoveries in quantum mechanics, cosmology and information technology, is becoming clear.

Huxley was introduced to this concept through his interest in the Indian Hindu monk Swami Vivekananda and his neo-Vedanta, a Western adoption of the ancient Indian philosophy of Vedanta. I will use this fascinating model of reality as our starting point regarding a review of the perennial philosophy across several spiritual/mystic philosophies before moving onto a scientifically based argument for personal immortality.

Hinduism and Vedanta

The Vedas are a collection of ancient scriptures whose collective teachings are known as Vedanta. These are the basis of the religious system known as Hinduism.

In Sanskrit, the sacred language of India, *Veda* means 'knowledge'. There are four Vedas, all written between 1500 and 500 BCE, the *Rig Veda* (Praise Knowledge), *Yajur Veda* (Sacrificial Knowledge), *Sama Veda* (Melody Knowledge) and *Atharva Veda* (Knowledge of Magic Formulae). The oldest is the *Rig Veda*. Associated with the Vedas are the philosophical texts known as the *Upanishads*. This word has a fascinating meaning in Sanskrit. It is 'sitting near' from *upa* 'near' and *ni-sad*, 'sit down'. This can be interpreted as sitting at the feet of a master or teacher. There are 108 Upanishads. Collectively, these are known as *Vedanta* ('the end of the Vedas') and were written to make understanding the Vedas easier.

According to the Vedas' philosophical teachings, all things and events that take place in this universe are all different manifestations of a singular reality known as *Brahman*. This is the inner essence of everything. When manifest within consciousness, Brahman is known as *Atman*.

The *Chhandogya Upanishad* states:

> In the beginning was only Being; One without second. Out of himself He brought forth the cosmos and entered into everything in it. There is nothing that does not come from Him. Of everything He is the inmost Self. He is the truth; the Self supreme. You are that . . . you are that.

And the *Katha Upanishad* adds, 'Can there be anything not known to That Who is the One in All? Know the One, know all.'

Brahman creates from himself the seemingly physical universe and its non-physical aspects, such as Atman, in a process of ongoing creation known as *Lila*. In this way, he brings about, by his creative power, a world of experience that is, in its pure form, an illusion. By being unaware that all perception is simply aspects of Lila, the individuated Atman exists under the spell of the most intriguing Hindu concept, the much-misunderstood *Maya*.

There are several interpretations of the meaning of the word *Maya*. *Ma* in Sanskrit is 'not real', and *ya* is 'this'; literally, 'this is not real'. This is defined more clearly in the *Isha Upanishad*, where we are told that the veil which covers the truth is golden, so rich, gaudy and dazzling that it takes away the mind of the observer from the inner contents. The *Chhandogya* and the *Bandaranayke* relate Maya directly to Atman, the former stating that Atman is the only Reality; everything else is merely a word, a mode and a name; and the latter that 'The Lord, on account of Maya, is perceived as manifold'.

That we are all one consciousness experiencing itself subjectively is suggested by the Vedanta concept of *Sat Chit Ananda*. In Sanskrit, *Sat* means 'being' or 'existence, *Chit* means 'consciousness', and *Ananda* means 'happiness' or 'bliss'. So, in effect, it is blissful existing consciousness. Although this is generally recognized as simply another variation on the concept of Brahman, it is more than that. It is the idea that Brahman is immanent in the individuation of consciousness in the guise of Atman. It is a game by which Brahman becomes lost in his own creation and forgets who he really is.

One school of Vedanta, known as *Advaita*, takes the concept of Maya even further. Advaita is literally 'non-duality' in Sanskrit (prefix *a-* meaning 'non-' and *dvaita* meaning 'duality' or 'secondness'). This means that the only thing that exists is Brahman and that everything, including human consciousness in the guise of Atman, is simply a manifestation of Brahman. We are not individuals in any way. We are quite literally all one. Maya itself is simply a dream of Brahman, and when he eventually awakens, all reality will simply disappear. This suggests that we are all part of an unconscious dream state and that Brahman is no more in control than a dreamer is in control of their dream world.

This extreme non-dualism was advocated by another school of Hindu/Vedanta philosophy known as *Trika* (or Kashmiri) *Shaivism*. There is archaeological evidence from the Indus Valley that Shaivism may go back to at least 2500 BCE. If this is the case, then it is the oldest living religion in the world. Of significance here is that the Indus Valley was home to one of the earliest urban civilizations. This shows just how far back into the past these philosophies go, possibly vestiges of even earlier beliefs. What is intriguing is that Trika Shaivism has a central tenet that contradicts Advaita Vedanta's belief that Brahman is dreaming our reality.

Trika Shaivism teaches that the phenomenal world (*Śakti*) is real in that Brahman is actively generating this reality through an act of consciousness, not through an unconscious dream state.

According to Shaivist beliefs, the fundamental stuff of the universe is a universal consciousness called *Citi*. In effect, Citi is Brahman. This universal consciousness has reduced itself to a multitude of singular consciousnesses, known as *jīvas*. This process of becoming a multiplicity of distinct points of self-awareness is called *Mala*, which translates as 'impurity'. In other words, by manifesting individuation Citi becomes tainted. Each individual consciousness can escape from this embodied existence within Śakti by spiritual practices known as *sādhana* and, if successful, achieves unity again by reaching *Moksa*, self-realization. In effect, this is the realization that we are not individual beings but emanations of Citi.

Of significance to our enquiry is a Shaivite concept known as *Prakāśa*. This is translated as the 'light of consciousness'. Also known as 'uncreated light', this form of illumination is the basis of everything. *Prakāśa* is one of several light-related concepts that are found in Kashmiri Shaivism, including *sphurattā*, *pratibhā* and *ullāsa*.

These two ancient philosophies agree that this reality is an illusion and that we are all emanations of a singular pure consciousness known as Brahman. We believe ourselves to be individuals purely because we exist in a state of forgetting. We are fooled into thinking that there is any reality outside of our own perceptions of that reality. When we die, our selfhood, what in the West we call the ego, is lost, and the soul is reincarnated in a state of forgetting in a new body.

As we have already discovered, for Hinduism, what carries through from life to life is an essence known as *chitta*. Chitta is the emotional ground, and the experiences of each life leave impressions upon this. These are like subliminal memories that are buried deep in the subconscious. This is the immortal part of the person, but one that is a higher level of reality, simply an expression of Brahman.

According to Hindu teachings, there are three other aspects of the human mind in addition to chitta: *buddhi* (intelligence), *manas* (the conscious mind) and *ahamkara* (the ego principle). At death, all aspects but the chitta ceases to exist. These are all embodied principles, and when the body returns to the earth, so do they. But the chitta does not die; it is reincarnated into another body.

It is important here to realize that the central belief of life after death in Hindu traditions is rebirth. This life is just one of a cycle of lives; we die and we are reborn, and what the chitta has experienced in this life will determine what path it follows in the next. We live a series of lives in which our chitta-essence carries forward. The body dies, and the spirit dies with it. But ultimately, all is but a mind-perceived illusion created by Brahman. As the Vedanta scholar Shantanand Saraswati stated:

> The world is a great show, which God is staging around you
> in the shape of the universe. But it is mere show. Your birth
> is a show, your death is a show. Actually there is neither
> birth nor death. Know that, and you would be happy.

This idea is that the phenomenal world, as presented to consciousness by the senses, is not what it seems. Not only that but the overwhelming sense of individuation and selfhood is also an illusion. This concept remains central to the teachings of Hinduism to this day, together with the idea that we live multiple lives and that our actions in this life will have ramifications for how the next life is lived. Hindu philosophy states that each life is different from those experienced before. The body dies and returns back to nature. This includes the brain and all it contains. With this also ends the spirit, which also exists for just one life. The significant issue here is this: What does actually carry from life to life? What exactly is the chitta?

This is a critical question, as is the relationship between chitta and the Atman. There is also the issue of why chitta-memory is not usually accessible to the reborn individual. It seems to lie dormant, surfacing only during dreams. The everyday consciousness is manifest as the manas, which is conscious just this once. Of possible significance here is that manas is sometimes described as being the recording facility in the brain. So, we have two levels of awareness according to Hindu teachings. The consciousness that is embedded within Maya, the manas, and the consciousness that exists outside of Maya, the chitta, which re-enters the Maya state multiple times and shares the experience with the manas. As we shall discover later, this has significant similarities with my own

Daemon-Eidolon Dyad, a central pillar of my overall Cheating the Ferryman hypothesis.

Sometime after 100 BCE, the *Yoga Sutras of Patanjali* were written. These sutras are a treatise explaining how the Atman can 'yoke' or integrate with the single consciousness of Brahman. The word *Yoga* literally means 'yoke' in Sanskrit. According to yoga teachings, the chitta is trapped within the realm of matter and, by implication, within Maya's illusion. In effect, the chitta is an embodied element of an intelligence that exists outside of the Maya-matter illusion. This is the immortal and transcendent consciousness that is the Atman.

Saraswati's intriguing observation, 'the world is a great show', is one that we will return to later when we discuss what may be creating this 'great show' and why our chitta-consciousness is trapped within it.

At about the same time that Hinduism in its various forms was developing in the Ganges culture of northern India, a parallel belief system was also growing. This system shared many of the basic precepts of Hinduism, but it took those precepts and interpreted them differently. This philosophy began with the search for truth by one man, Gautama Siddhartha.

Buddhism

Siddhartha was born in the year 566 BCE in present-day Nepal. His teachings focused on suffering, its cause and how to find a way out of it. He concluded that suffering was caused by a misunderstanding of the nature of self, which is not the fixed, enduring entity that it seems to be. He taught that the self is nothing more than a collection of particles that are constantly changing. These were known as *skandhas*. At any one moment in time, the relationship between these skandhas creates what we feel is our ego or selfhood. These teachings are collectively known as the *Dharma*. The Buddha died around 483 BCE, and within a hundred years, several schools had come into existence, all teaching a subtly different version of the *Dharma*. Over the centuries, these schools have evolved into two main traditions: the *Theravada*, which translates as 'the doctrine of the elders', and the *Mahāyāna*, or 'Great Vehicle', which, in turn, contains several sub-traditions such as Zen, *Vajrayana* and Pure Land.

According to traditional Buddhist beliefs, there is a plurality of universes. Each universe has three planes: the sphere of desire, *kāmadhātu*; the sphere of material form, *rūpadhātu*; and the sphere of immateriality, *ārūpadhātu*. These universes exist in *kalpas*, time cycles. Each kalpa is made up of four ages (*yugas*). Within this is a series of dharmas, instant points in continuing motion or changing states. These appear, age and then disappear.

There are five dharmas that create the transitory and illusory state of human selfhood. These are known as the *skandhas*. As these change in time, the concept of 'I' in the sense of an individual ego is an illusion. This cosmology was incorporated as a central tenet of Theravada Buddhism.

The concept of *kālacakra* defines the cycles of time discussed above and has become an essential concept within Mahāyāna Buddhism. These cycles of time are intriguing, specifically when linked to the teachings of another school of Buddhism known as *Yogācāra*.

Like all religions, Buddhism has two models. One is for the masses and involves ritual and repetition. The second form is the esoteric model, which involves seeking out meaning and symbolism within the sacred texts. The latter form can be approached only after years of training in structured and rational thought. In both Hinduism and Buddhism, this esoteric tradition is known as *Tantra*. In Mahāyāna Buddhism, this tantric school is known as *Faxiang* in China and *Hosso* in Japan, with the Tibetan Buddhist descriptor *Yogācāra* being the most commonly recognized in the West.

The original concepts of Yogācāra were outlined in 6th-century writings known as the *Saṅdhinirmocana Sūtra* (Elucidating the Hidden Connections), but these became widely distributed only in the 1st century BCE.

The Yogācāra doctrine that there is 'nothing but cognition' (*vijñapti-mātra*) focuses on cognition and perception and the role of the observer in relation to the phenomenal world of experience. In many ways, it has parallels with the Hindu concept of Maya discussed above. But it has another interesting angle, and that is that consciousness itself is not continual but arises moment by moment. Vijñapti-mātra suggests that both the perceiver and the perceived are both switched on and off. This is a total reversal of the Western idea of a 'stream of consciousness'. However, existing behind this on-off cognition exists a ground-consciousness known as *ālaya-vijñāna*, which is virtually identical to the Hindu notions of *ātman* (permanent, invariant self) and *prakṛti* (primordial substrative nature from which all mental, emotional and physical things evolve). Of course, I would argue that both these concepts are aspects of my Daemon-Eidolon model.

But most important for this discourse is how the Yogācāra teachings interpret reincarnation. Central is a doctrine of an intermediate existence experienced *between* incarnations, effectively at the instant of death. This concept is known as *antarābhava*. This literally means in-between (*antara*) existences (*bhava*). To this can be added a concept called *Gandhabba*, and it is this that lives in a place known as *para lōka*. Gandhabba is a consciousness that is awaiting reincarnation in a suitable womb. In China, this is known as *zhōng yǒu*, and in Japan, it is described as *chūu*.

To the north of India is the mountainous kingdom of Tibet. Mahāyāna Buddhism did not arrive there until the 8th century, and when it did, it was to incorporate two, much older, belief systems: the local shamanic religion and the enigmatic Bon tradition.

Tradition has it that Bon was founded 30,000 years ago by Shenrab Miwo. This suggests great antiquity to the Bon tradition. What is even more intriguing is that Bon's roots may be from the Iranian sphere of cultural influence, which, in turn, may have had a similar effect on Iranian Sufism. We shall return to Sufism later.

Of particular importance for our enquiry is that the Bon teachings regarding the afterlife suggest a great interest in the between-lives state.

This theme carried through into Tibetan Buddhism, specifically the 'Bardo State'. This is described in great detail in *The Tibetan Book of the Dead*. It is to this fascinating work that we now turn our attention.

The Bardo State

The Tibetan Book of the Dead or *Bardo Thodol* (literal translation 'liberation through hearing in the intermediary stage') was, according to legend, written by the 8th-century Buddhist sage Padma Sambhava.

This book is a guide for the 'dead' during the intermediate stages between death and rebirth. The Tibetan Buddhists believe that as soon as physical death occurs, the spirit goes into a 'trance state' during which time it is disorientated, and the person is not aware that they have died. This period is called the First Bardo. Towards the end of this period, the person sees a bright light, and if they can embrace this light without fear, they will be freed from the cycle of rebirth. Most people fear this light and enter a state called the Second Bardo. In this, they experience a past-life review whereby they are shown the things they may have done wrong, giving them an opportunity to put these things right in their next incarnation.

Now, this is very interesting when viewed in the light of Cheating the Ferryman (CTF). CTF suggests that there is a period between apparent death and actual death. According to CTF, this period is filled with a virtual-reality rerun of the person's life – something, you will recall, I term the Bohmian IMAX. This is identical to that described in the Second Bardo. Now, here is where CTF and the Thodol are amazingly similar; I suggest that the first and second Bardos happen consecutively in that the First Bardo (being in a state of trance and unknowing) is experienced by the Eidolon and the simultaneous Second Bardo is experienced by the Daemon (the aware part of consciousness that takes on board the events being experienced by the blissfully unaware Eidolon).

At the end of the past-life review, according to the Thodol, the Daemon is given the choice of entering the light and dying a second time (and in doing so move on into the Spirit World) or to again turn away from the light and return to another rerun of the Bohmian IMAX. This decision is made by the 'aware' part of consciousness (the Daemon), not the unaware part (the Eidolon). The Daemon will carry the memories of all the past reruns and will know if it is ready to move on or not. This decision may be made many times, and many times the Daemon may consider that its Eidolon is not yet ready and has more learning experiences needed.

It has been argued by several scholars that Vedanta not only influenced Buddhism, a belief which is fairly self-evident, but also that its philosophy also moved westwards and in the 5th century BCE may have arrived in Greece. This may not be so surprising. One of the great centres of trade between India and Greece was the city of Taxila, the place that tradition suggests was where the Mahabharata was first recited. The city is also mentioned in the Vedic texts, such as the *Shatapatha Brahmana*.

The major Pre-Socratic philosophers – Thales, Anaximander and Anaxagoras – were all based in the Asia Minor city of Miletus. This city had close trading relations with Mesopotamia, which, in turn, had links with Persia and northern India. It is also known that the philosophers themselves travelled extensively into Asia. Of significance here is that all three Milesian thinkers flourished at a similar time to when Buddhist and Vedanta ideas were flowing westwards. That they made the short hop from the coastline of Asia Minor to the off-shore islands is of no surprise.

Ancient Greece

The island of Samos sits just a few short miles off the shores of Asia Minor. In 570 BCE, the great Pre-Socratic philosopher Pythagoras was born on Samos and, before his death, in 495 BCE, he had introduced a number of radical new ideas, most of which had no precedents within Greek thought before that time. Many of these were mathematical, such as his Theorem of Triangles. This was uncannily similar to an algebraic function found in the Vedic *Baudhāyana sūtras* compiled at least a hundred years before. In *Baudhāyana Sulba Sūtra* is found this rule:

> A rope stretched along the length of the diagonal produces an area which the vertical and horizontal sides make together.

Kak, 2006

This is an exact equivalent of the Pythagorean theorem that many of us were taught at school, which states that on a right-angle triangle, the area of the square whose side is the hypotenuse is equal to the sum of the areas of the squares on the other two sides. Indeed, several other mathematical ideas, such as how a reduced version of the Pythagorean theorem regarding an isosceles triangle, also appear in the much earlier *Baudhāyana Sulba Sūtra*, as does the first published calculation of an accurate value of π (pi).

It is not unreasonable to conclude from this that Pythagoras was aware of Vedantic teachings. So his concept of metempsychosis, that the soul is reborn again at death, is simply a literal adaption of the Vedanta concept of reincarnation.

As we have already discovered from my IANDS paper ('Cheating the Ferryman: A New Paradigm of Existence?', *Journal of Near-Death Studies*, 2004), the Pre-Socratic Greeks believed that when a person died, they had crossed the River Styx and were taken to the land of the dead by Charon the Ferryman. On arrival, they were presented with a choice: two chalices, both containing a small amount of water. One chalice contained waters from the Spring of Memory and the other waters from the River of Forgetting, the tributary of the Styx known as the Lethe. If the person chose to drink from the Spring of Memory, they walked along the right path to heaven. If they chose the waters of the Lethe, they took the left path and were reborn with all their past-life memories wiped clean. This was known as *anamnesis*, a Platonic concept uncannily similar to the rebirth concepts of Vedanta, Hinduism and Buddhism.

But it is unclear whether the ancient Greeks believed in a transmigration of souls whereby the person is reborn in a completely new body and as a different person (or even an animal or insect) or whether they were literally reborn as themselves. This is not as strange as it may seem. Another school of Greek philosophy, known as the Stoics, presented an alternative form of rebirth related to their belief that time is cyclical and that it repeats itself over and over again.

The Stoics called this endless repetition *palingenesia*. The word has its roots in Greek: *palin* ('again'), plus *genesis* ('becoming', or 'rebirth'). Many dictionaries and web references state that this is another word for reincarnation. It clearly is not. The Stoics did not in any way believe in reincarnation as it is understood by most people – that is, after death, a person is reborn as somebody else, or even a different life-form. They understood palingenesia to be exactly how I describe it in CTF – that we are all reborn as ourselves living our own lives again. They believed in a precise return of all events and a return of those who perceived or experienced those events. As they stated, in each and every cycle, Socrates will be tried and executed.

Specifically describing this is the concept of *anakuklesis*, from *aná* ('up, completing a process'), which intensifies *kainō* ('make fresh, new'). This means that each person will live their lives again, not once, but countless times as each cycle comes round. More importantly, because in the afterlife, time is of a different quality, each life, as regards the soul's viewpoint, starts at the end of the previous life, the same way that a circle comes round and meets itself again.

So, from a Stoic point of view, the Platonic anamnesis is a forgetting that you have lived this life before. All your past-life memories are lost, and you experience this life as if for the first time, every time. This is profoundly similar to the argument I put forward in my Cheating the Ferryman hypothesis. But there is more.

Plato argued that this reality is a mind-created illusion. This has powerful echoes of the Hindu concept of Maya which we encountered earlier. Plato taught us that all things presented to us by our senses are facsimiles, copies or simulations of real objects outside of the illusion. This idea became known as *mimesis*, from the Greek *mimos* ('actor'), hence where we get our English words 'mimic' and 'mime'. This suggests something that is a copy of something original. In Book X of Plato's *Republic*, written around 375 BCE, he has Socrates describe the metaphor of the three beds. Socrates states that the original bed is created in the mind of God and made manifest. This is the 'Form' of the bed. A carpenter then makes a copy of the bed in wood, and then an artist comes along and paints an image of the bed. Plato argued that everything presented to us by our senses is mimesis, inferior copies of the pure Forms that exist outside of this 'phenomenal' illusion.

It is important here to appreciate the subtlety of this argument. For the ancient Greeks, the word *phainomenon* was 'thing appearing to view' from the verb *phainein*, 'to show'. For them, *phainomenon* meant whatever comes to the light of mind.

Earlier in the *Republic* (Book VII), Plato has Socrates in conversation with his pupil Glaucon. He asks Glaucon to imagine a group of prisoners who have lived their whole lives in a great underground cave, a cave that is open to the outside world only after a steep and challenging ascent. The prisoners are chained, so they cannot move in any way; their faces are forced to continually look at the cave's back wall. Behind them, and out of their sight-field, is a raised walkway, wide enough for other people to walk along carrying wooden cut-outs in the shape of animals, plants and other objects. Behind the raised walkway is a fire. This causes the shadows of the cut-outs to be cast on the cave wall in front of the prisoners. As they cannot look away, all the prisoners ever see are the shadows on the wall. As they have never seen anything else, their perceptual universe consists solely of the images 'shown' to them, shadow *phainomenon*, things 'appearing to view'. They believe that all that there is are shadows on the wall. It is decided to free one of the prisoners, guide him past the walkway and fire and to the entrance of the cave. Here he sees true reality for the first time, which consists of bright colours and three-dimensional objects, real plants and animals. He is taken back inside the cave and allowed to converse with his fellow prisoners. He tries to explain to them that there is a much more expansive reality than simply the shadows on the cave wall. The prisoners refuse to believe what he tells them, claiming that he is crazy.

In this way, Plato explained how the phenomenal world is a facsimile simulation of a greater, purer and far more real universe outside our everyday perceptions. Everything we perceive here is mimesis, an illusion that exists within another illusion, time.

Let us recap here precisely what the ancient Greeks, or more specifically, the Platonists and the Stoics believed. For them, the phenomenal world is a simulation, a simulation that repeats itself over and over again. In our modern technological society, we have something very similar. It is called a third-person role-playing game (RPG). We shall return to this observation in greater detail later. But now we need to move on in time to discuss how these ideas became refined by later philosophies, specifically several related belief systems collectively known as Gnosticism.

Gnosticism

The philosophies of Platonists, the Stoics and the Pythagoreans carried forward into the Christian world of the 1st and 2nd centuries AD with a philosophy known as Gnosticism. The Gnostics carried on the idea that this world is a facsimile or simulation of the real universe, which lies outside of our sensory perceptions and that time is cyclical. One of the major advocates of this cosmology was the 2nd-century philosopher Plotinus, in agreement with Plato, who taught that material objects are inferior copies of Forms that exist in an eternal reality. It is highly likely that Plotinus's philosophy was influenced by ideas he encountered when he spent time in Persia searching out the teachings of both Persian and Indian sages.

Central to his philosophy was the concept of the Monad, or the One. This is a singular pure consciousness that is the sum of all things and is pure light. The Monad has distinct echoes of Brahman from Hinduism.

The Monad is not the creator of the universe; it *is* the universe. From the Monad emerges an intriguing concept known as *Protennoia*, 'the Thought that dwells in the Light'. Also called *Barbelo*, it is the creation thought of the One. In the Gnostic scripture entitled the *Trimorphic Protennoia*, the following intriguing comment is made by Protennoia:

> I am the movement that dwells in the All . . . I am invisible within the Thought of the Invisible One . . . I am incomprehensible, dwelling in the incomprehensible. I move in every creature.

From Protennoia, a series of 'emanations' poured forth. These were known as the Aeons, one of which is a feminine entity known as Sophia. It is Sophia who wishes to create her own emanations. She succeeds only in bringing into existence a being called Yaldaboath, and this was when things became complicated.

Yaldaboath, also known as the Demiurge, believed that he was the true God. From this belief, he fabricated from the pure light that is the Monad (the One) the perceptible, phenomenal illusion that is the material universe. In doing so, he trapped 'the Light' inside matter.

This, in effect, split reality into two components: the universe of coarse matter, which is, by its very nature, inherently evil; and the non-physical universe, which is inherently good. The material world is called the Kenoma, and the non-physical world is the Pleroma. In Biblical terms, this can be mirrored in the statement, 'Then the word [Pleroma] became flesh [Kenoma]' (John 1:14). In modern terms, we may interpret this as being non-physical digital information and the physical matter that that information describes. We shall return to this idea in much greater detail later.

This idea of a universe consisting of two realities, the Pleroma and the Kenoma, both created and emanating from a singular source, the Monad, together with a mirrored psychic duality of the human mind, can also be found in two other Gnostic mystical schools, the Kabbalah within the Jewish tradition and the Islamic Sufis. This suggests that the source of the three traditions (Christian, Jewish and Islamic) must have roots far back in history to a time further back than even the ancient Greeks.

Gnostics believed that trapped within each human being is a spark of the Divine Light, an element of the Pleroma hidden with the Kenoma. This 'divine spark' is humanity's inner guiding spirit, and it gives us all a sense that there is more than just this material world.

At this point, it is of extreme importance to stress that this idea is not confined to early Gnostic thought. For example, in Plato's *Timaeus* can be found the following:

> The divine soul of God lodged in the head, to raise us, like plants which are not of earthly origin, to our kindred: for the head is nearest to heaven.

This concept of the 'divine spark' has long been considered to be the common point between all the mystic traditions that developed from Gnosticism. In 1966 the World Congress on the Origins of Gnosticism in Messina, Sicily, announced this conclusion:

> The idea of the presence in man of a divine 'spark' . . . , which has proceeded from the divine world and has fallen into this world of destiny, birth and death and which must be reawakened through its own divine counterpart in order to be finally restored.
>
> Rudolph, 1984, p. 57

I would like to argue that this 'divine spark' is what I term the Daemon. This intelligence within all of us has direct communication with the Pleroma while we, as Eidolons, are firmly rooted in the Kenoma.

This idea of human conscious duality can be found in all strands of Gnostic teachings. For example, one of the major Gnostic sects of the

3rd century onwards were the Manicheans of Persia, followers of the intriguing teachings of the enigmatic prophet Mani. Mani had a number of incredibly modern ideas regarding the true nature of matter. For example, in my book *The Daemon: A Guide to Your Extraordinary Secret Self*, I make this observation:

> For him (Mani), the purpose of religion was to release the particles of light imprisoned in matter. This is an amazing belief taking into account what we now know about matter. The mathematician Sir James Jeans suggested in the early 1930s that what we call light is really matter moving at its fastest possible speed, and that to move matter at this speed requires infinite power. As he pictured it, the moment this infinite energy is reduced and the speed of matter slows down, it ceases to be light and becomes 'matter'. He termed matter 'bottled light' and he termed light 'unbottled matter'. Can it be that Mani, writing over 1,700 years ago had awareness of the ultimate nature of matter? If this is so, then his teachings on the possible dual nature of human consciousness should be taken very seriously.
>
> Peake, 2008, p. 150

And it is. Indeed, Mani's model of human duality is of particular resonance regarding our enquiry, specifically in terms of how his model mirrors my own Daemon-Eidolon Dyad. At the age of 12, another consciousness became manifest in his mind, only to disappear again. At age 25, it returned, this time permanently. This entity told him to preach a new religion which states that the world is evil and that matter is tainted. Mani believed that this was his own 'divine spark' speaking to him from within.

This idea of human duality links Manicheanism with the other great Middle Eastern Islamic Gnostic traditions, Sufism, the mystic Isma-illiyahs and the much-persecuted Mandeans of southern Iraq.

Sufism, which is the mystical school of Islam in a similar way to which Kabbalah relates to Judaism, stresses that we must all seek unification with the 'God within'. This process is known as *tauhid* and is facilitated by working with intuitive knowledge (*ma'rifa*), in other words, *Gnosis*.

According to the Qur'an, God created the universe with the word 'be'. However, in an interesting Gnostic interpretation, the Isma-illiyahs change the Arabic imperative 'be' into the feminine aspect, *Kuni* (Halm, 1996, p. 17). In doing so, this mirrors the Gnostic creation myth of Sophia. For the Mandeans, the human soul (*nišimta*) is the part that contains the 'divine spark', whereas the 'spirit' (*ruha*) is part of the lower world. For this, read Daemon/Pleroma, Eidolon/Kenoma. For Sufis, there is a similar dyad, but the spirit (*ruh*) is related to the Daemon/Pleroma and the soul (*nafs*) taking the role of the Eidolon within the Kenoma.

The idea of two realities can also be found in the writings of the 12th-century Persian sage Yahya ibn Habash Suhrawardī who founded an Islamic philosophy known as Illuminism (*hikmat al-Ishraq*), the ideas of which were expounded in his great work, *The Philosophy of Illumination*, which he completed in 1186. This amalgamated Greek Gnostic thought with that of traditional Iranian beliefs, making particular reference to Plato.

Suhrawardī argued that there are two perceptual worlds: the world of matter, the *terrestrial*, the equivalent of the Gnostic Kenoma; and the *sidereal*, identical to the Pleroma. In Arabic, these translate as *Molk* and *Malakut*. Similar parallels can be found in the Jewish Gnostic tradition of Kabbalah.

There is a degree of controversy as to the historical source of the Kabbalistic teachings. Practitioners claim that it has a heritage that pre-dates any religion. This suggests going back at least as far as the ancient Egyptians and maybe back to ancient Sumer. Whatever the claims in this regard, it became well known within Jewish communities only in the 12th century through the teachings of Isaac the Blind. Whatever its source, it has a number of totally identical concepts mirroring the Gnostic model of reality.

The Gnostic idea of the transcendent, unknowable totality that is everything – the Monad or the One – is identical to the Kabbalistic *Ein Sof*. Both are the sources of the inner light that illuminates the Pleroma and is the 'divine spark' within all sentient beings. I will argue later that this is the information field from which everything is rendered.

The Gnostic concept of Sophia as the feminine aspect of God is reflected in Kabbalistic teachings as the Shekinah. Similarly, the ten emanations through which the Ein Sof reveals itself within the Pleroma and Kenoma, the *Sephirot*, are similar to the Gnostic's Aeons.[1]

This suggests a consistent model of reality in both traditions, and one which, as we shall discover later, closely mirrors the growing belief that the universe we exist in is a simulation.

If Huxley's perennial philosophy model is valid and my Cheating the Ferryman hypothesis has similar validity, there should be supporting evidence for my model in the teachings of all main religions, including mainstream Christianity. We have carefully reviewed the esoteric teachings of Judaism, Islam, Gnostic Christianity, Buddhism and Hinduism. But what about the mainstream Christian churches? It is to these we now turn our attention.

According to Roman Catholic doctrine, there is an immediate state that exists immediately after death. The soul is judged and sent to Heaven, Limbo (Purgatory) or Hell. This has echoes of the Bardo state in Tibetan Buddhism and Gehenna in Judaism. A similar tradition can be found in the Eastern Orthodox Church, Lutheran Church and Methodist Church, all of which suggest that some kind of 'cleansing' occurs immediately after death. This is also found in some aspects of the Anglican tradition. In Islam, the term for the intermediate state is *Barzakh*. Indeed, the word *Barzakh* means 'barrier' or 'partition' in Arabic and Persian. Here, according to the Qu'ran, it is a place where the soul contemplates the actions of its former life. Now how can it do this unless it is reminded in some way of what it did in its former life? I would like to suggest that the most effective way to do this would be a 'life review', precisely, as we shall discover later, as is reported during a classic near-death experience and as a central pillar of my Cheating the Ferryman hypothesis.

Bu now, as part of our review of the realm of ideas, we need to move swiftly on from theology to philosophy. Does classic philosophy also support my model?

Reality as a Mind-Creation

There are clearly many overlaps between philosophy and theology. Therefore, it should be no surprise that arguments regarding the possible dualistic nature of reality will be found in both areas of enquiry. Indeed, many theologians are also recognized as philosophers. One of the most interesting of these was George Berkeley (1685–1753).

George Berkeley was the Bishop of Cloyne in Ireland. He published two works between 1710 and 1713, *A Treatise Concerning the Principles of Human Knowledge* (1710) and *Three Dialogues Between Hylas and Philonous* (1713). In these, he detailed his attack on the belief that material things are mind-independent. For Berkeley, everything perceived is mind-created and the external world is a form of illusion or ongoing hallucination. Ordinary objects are simply ideas; hence his model became known as Idealism.

His motivations were simply to prove the existence of God as what is known as a 'necessary being'. That is, God has to exist because if he didn't, nothing would. His argument was simple but also profound. He pointed out that we interface with the world outside of ourselves only through our senses. He asks us to make the distinction between ideas and minds. An idea is anything that we perceive, be it a sensation like heat, a taste of a strawberry or even the viewing of a setting sun. Everything we perceive is through sensations. What brings these sensations into reality is when a mind perceives them. An earlier philosopher, John Locke, had argued that all objects have primary and secondary qualities. Primary qualities, such as the object's position or shape, are independent of any mind observing it, whereas secondary qualities such as its colour or smell are mind-dependent. Berkeley countered this by stating that one cannot imagine an object with only primary qualities. He writes:

> But I desire any one to reflect and try whether he can, by any abstraction of thought, conceive the extension and motion of a body without all other sensible qualities. I see evidently that it is not in my power to frame an idea of a body extended and moving, but I must withal give it some colour or other sensible quality, which is acknowledged to exist only in the mind.
>
> Berkeley, 1710

Of course, the problem is that if I now decide to walk out of my study into my kitchen to make myself a cup of coffee, how is it that my laptop remains in the same position when I return? During my time away, my laptop has not been observed by anybody, but, by implication, it has continued to exist in my absence. How can this be if all objects need an observing mind to create them?

Berkeley had a solution for this. Indeed, his solution was the reason for the essay in the first place. As a believing Christian – indeed, as an Anglican clergyman – he was keen to prove the existence of God. And it was God who provides the solution for my continuing laptop. While I was making my coffee, God was observing from an omniscient location outside space and time. God is always 'observing', so the universe continues to exist. This argument is not new, and it again shows the influence of Plato.

Over the years, Berkeley's argument has attracted ridicule and derision and continues to do so, but only from those critics blissfully unaware of the experimental findings of modern quantum physics. As we shall discover later, Berkeley has been proven right. Reality and the act of observation of that reality have a direct and consequential relationship.

Twenty-eight years after the death of George Berkeley, his ideas would be taken into a fascinating new direction by the publication of a book that was to have a profound effect on Western philosophy.

The book in question, *The Critique of Pure Reason*, proposed that the human mind, far from being a passive recorder of the world, was the formulator of the world. The author was Immanuel Kant, professor of Logic and Metaphysics at the University of Königsberg, Germany.

Like Berkeley, Kant argued that we can never perceive the true nature of anything that is presented to us by our senses. He called this true nature the thing-in-itself (German: *Ding an sich*). As we attend to things, they become the subject of our enquiry or *noumena*. When noumena are manifest within our perceptions, they become phenomena or representations (*Vorstellung* in German). However, we can never actually know the true nature of noumena. This does not mean that Kant agreed with the extreme Idealism of Berkeley. For Kant, the phenomenal world has an existence independent of the observer, but the actual thing-in-itself can never be really known.

Kant called his new philosophy Transcendental Idealism to differentiate it from the somewhat solipsist idealism of Berkeley.

Many years later, American philosopher William James Durant summed up Kant's philosophy in one pithy statement: it 'rescued mind from matter'.

Kant was a curious character who had few friends. However, there was one young philosopher who not only impressed him but whose work he helped get published. This was Johann Gottlieb Fichte (1762–1814). In 1792 Kant paid in part for the publication of Fichte's first work, *Attempt at a Critique of All Revelation*. It was published anonymously, giving the reading public the impression that it was another work by Kant himself.

The association between the two philosophers was not surprising, because in his later works Fichte took Kant's Transcendental Idealism to its logical conclusion in suggesting that if reality is beyond all possibility of apprehension, as Kant claimed, then we have no grounds for claiming that there is anything out there at all. Therefore, the entire phenomenal world is not an independent reality but the creation of the individual ego that creates this world for itself. Fichte argued that at his death, his world will cease to exist with him. His world needs him as its observer to continue being. However, he also argued that other people also live in their own worlds, and somehow, we all exist independently and interrelated.

In 1794 he elaborated his idea of *Wissenschaftslehre* (theory of knowledge) in his hugely ambitious book *Foundations of the Entire Science of Knowledge*. In this, he suggested that all knowledge resides in something he called the absolute ego, his term for God. The goal of *Wissenschaftslehre* was to be able to relate the individual ego to its source, the absolute ego. This suggests that for Fichte, there resides in all of us an independent source of consciousness that is both us and not us. In my terminology, this is the Daemon and is yet another reflection of the Gnostic idea of 'the divine light', the shard of the Pleroma that is embedded deep within the Kenoma.

Another classical philosopher influenced by Kant's Transcendental Idealism was Arthur Schopenhauer (1788–1860). What made Schopenhauer's works somewhat different to the philosophers of the time was that he was also fascinated by Eastern thinking, specifically the teachings of Hinduism and Buddhism.

In 1808 Friedrich Schlegel published *On the Language and Wisdom of the Indians*, which seeded a fascination for Indian and Iranian philosophy within German intellectual circles.

In 1818 Schopenhauer's major work, *The World as Will and Representation*, was published. In this, he took the Kantian model in which the world is a projection of the mind and expanded upon Kant's concepts of phenomena and noumena; the world as we experience it as opposed to the world as it is in-itself. Schopenhauer adapted these and called them 'will' and 'representation'. But it is important to realize that for him, the ground-state of everything is will with representation being created out of will. In effect, representations are mental images that are projected outwards. He wrote:

> . . . things and their whole mode and manner of existence
> are inseparably associated with our consciousness of them.
> . . . the assumption that things exist as such, even outside
> and independently of our consciousness, is really absurd.
>
> Schopenhauer, 1966, p. 25

But 'behind' the representations is another world that exists when it is not being observed. This world exists outside of space and time. This is pure Will. I have capitalised this to differentiate it from the will that is manifest in human behaviour.

I would like to suggest that Schopenhauer also considered that consciousness had two elements, similar in many ways to my Daemon and Eidolon. He called these the 'knower' and the 'known'. Indeed, he also proposes that individuality (like my Eidolonic consciousness) is lost at the point of death, but that some awareness (like my Daemon) continues:

> Death is sleep in which individuality is forgotten; everything
> else awakens again, or rather has remained awake.
>
> Schopenhauer, 1966, p. 695

Here is the idea that behind individuated consciousness is another consciousness which is, in turn, a part of the greater universal consciousness.

Due to space constraints, I have selected only a few great philosophers of the 17th, 18th and 19th centuries who were fascinated by the idea that perceptual reality is a form of mind-created illusion. But there are a number of others who took this further and argued that reality may also be cyclical in nature and that we will repeat our perceptions over and over again. This concept is popularly known as the 'eternal return' or 'eternal recurrence', and it is yet another element of my Cheating the Ferryman hypothesis, indeed probably the most critical part. It is to this intriguing and, for some, disturbing idea that we now turn our attention.

THE ETERNAL RETURN
Louis-Auguste Blanqui

When the term 'eternal return' is brought up in educated circles, the controversial German philosopher Friedrich Nietzsche will inevitably be cited as the creator of this idea. However, although Nietzsche may be the philosopher automatically associated with this idea, he was far from being its originator. We shall return to Nietzsche's interesting angle on the eternal return, but first, let us review his possible inspirations.

For example, a possible but unacknowledged influence upon Nietzsche is the French political activist Louis-Auguste Blanqui (1805–81). Although generally known for his political theory and the concept of Blanquism, he was also an intriguing philosopher. In his little-known work, *Eternity by the Stars*, written in the winter of 1871 when he was imprisoned in Fort du Taureau in Brittany, he stated that when an infinity of time contains a finite number of possible events, one inescapable conclusion presents itself; every series of events will be repeated an infinite number of times.

In his opening chapter Blanqui cites his own influences, quoting Blaise Pascal, who once wrote:

> The universe is a circle, whose centre is everywhere and its circumference nowhere.
>
> Pascal, 1670

He observes that the concept of a limited universe is absurd because this suggests the existence of space outside of the universe. From this, the only rational conclusion, however incomprehensible it must be to our human intellect, is that the universe is infinite both in time and in space.

Blanqui concluded that all of history was cyclical and that we would all relive the events of our lives again. In *Eternity by the Stars,* he wrote:

> Men of the nineteenth century, the hour of our apparitions is fixed forever, and always brings us back to the very same ones.[2]

The implications of Blanqui's model is that of a universe populated with countless versions of Earth, and on countless of these would be a set of circumstances in which a version of each human being who had ever lived, and ever will live, will live a life – from a virtually identical life to countless lives that were different in a tiny way, right through to lives that would be totally different. In effect, each possible outcome of every decision, both minor and substantial, will be played out repeatedly. This is far more than simply an eternal return; this is a universe that follows up on every single possibility in precisely the same way that particles in an enclosed box will, given sufficient time, locate themselves in every point location in the box. Blanqui offers a model whereby:

> . . . the entire life of our planet, from birth to death, with all its crimes and miseries, is being lived partly here and partly there, day by day, on myriad kindred planets. What we call 'progress' is confined to each particular world, and vanishes with it. Always and everywhere in the terrestrial arena, the same drama, the same setting, on the same narrow stage – a noisy humanity infatuated with its own grandeur, believing itself to be the universe and living in its prison as though in some immense realm, only to founder at an early date along with its globe, which has borne with deepest disdain the burden of human arrogance. The same monotony, the same immobility, on other heavenly bodies. The universe repeats itself endlessly and paws the ground in place. In infinity, eternity performs – imperturbably – the same routines.[3]

Could it be that Nietzsche may have read this work and incorporated it into his own ideas on the eternal return? In a footnote in his book *Constellation: Friedrich Nietzsche and Walter Benjamin in the Now-Time of History,* James McFarland suggests that Nietzsche was aware of Blanqui's speculation. It seems that both the book title and Blanqui's name appear in his notebook N VI 6 from autumn 1883. This suggests nothing more than a name reference, so it is evident that although Nietzsche knew of Blanqui's theory, he did not acknowledge this in his published works.

Why he did this is a mystery. It could simply be that he forgot to, or was it that he wished to claim the idea for his own? So what were these ideas?

Friedrich Nietzsche is probably one of the most misunderstood philosophers in history. Much maligned for his supposed seeding of Nazism through his concept of the Superman, he is an author whose writings are usually approached with trepidation and fear. But Nietzsche was, in fact, one of the most original thinkers of the 19th century and one whose positive and negative influences have carried through well into the 21st century. It is also fair to point out that his association with Nazism was not through him but through his sister, Elisabeth Förster-Nietzsche, who, after his death in 1900, took control of his literary estate and remoulded much of his writings to appeal to the Nazis. In fact, Friedrich detested both anti-Semitism and German nationalism.

It is no coincidence that he was educated at the famous German boarding school of Pforta, the same school attended by Johann Fichte many years before. Fichte's philosophy was a significant influence on the young Friedrich.

It may also come as a surprise to discover that Nietzsche was a disciple of Schopenhauer in his early years and used a variation of Schopenhauer's concept of 'Will' in his own idea of the 'will to power'. Legend has it that the young Nietzsche accidentally came across a copy of Schopenhauer's 1818 book *The World as Will and Representation* while browsing in a bookshop. It is also reported that he read it in one sitting. From this, he was to develop his unique philosophy. His first book, *The Birth of Tragedy*, published in 1872, had him reject much of Schopenhauer's philosophy, calling it a 'Buddhist negation of the will'. However, his intention was to refine Schopenhauer's concept of Will to accommodate the seeming pointlessness of life. As the son of a Lutheran minister who had become an avowed atheist, he had a deep need to replace the religious model of life after death with something more scientific and non-theistic. After 1879, when he resigned from his university position on the grounds of ill health, he received a small pension which freed him to focus exclusively on his writings. He lived in utter solitude in Sils Maria in Switzerland, where he used to take long walks in the forests and lakelands of this beautiful area. On one of these walks in August of 1881, he received a massive revelation about the true nature of human existence which presented him with a model of life after death, one that had no need for religion. As he walked beside the Silvaplana Lake, he felt the need to stop and rest next to a huge pyramidal block of exposed rock. It was then that an idea appeared in his mind, fully formed and complete. He realized that life just repeats itself over and over again for all eternity. He was so excited by this he included a section on this idea in his 1882 book *The Gay Science* when he described it thus:

> What if a demon were to creep after you one night, in your loneliest loneliness, and say, 'This life which you live must be lived by you once again and innumerable times more; and every pain and joy and thought and sigh must come again to you, all in the same sequence. The eternal hourglass will again and again be turned and you with it, dust of the dust!' Would you throw yourself down and gnash your teeth and curse that demon? Or would you answer, 'Never have I heard anything more divine?'
>
> Nietzsche, 1882

Nietzsche considered that his model was scientifically valid, stating that it was 'the most scientific of all possible hypotheses'. In *The Will to Power*, he makes his logic quite clear:

> In infinite time, every possible combination would at some time or another be realized; more: it would be realized an infinite number of times. And since between every combination ānd its next recurrence all other

possible combinations would have to take place . . . a circular movement of absolutely identical series is thus demonstrated.

Nietzsche, 1901

In effect, in an infinity of time, all possible outcomes of our decisions, made across a whole lifetime, will come to pass, not just once, but an infinite number of times. This is not how Nietzsche's 'eternal return of the same' is interpreted by many writers. For them, his argument is that if you knew that you were going to live this identical life innumerable times in an infinity of timelines, then you would try your best to make this life the best it could possibly be. In doing so, you ensure that all your lives are similarly the best possible life.

In the late 20th century, a number of philosophers such as Gilles Deleuze (1925–95) argued that what Nietzsche was suggesting here is not an 'eternal return of the same' as it is generally termed, but a 'return' of the different. In his 1968 book *Difference and Repetition*, Deleuze states:

> We can thus see how the eternal return is linked, not to a repetition of the same, but on the contrary, to a transmutation. It is the moment or the eternity of becoming which eliminates all that resists it. It releases, indeed it creates, the purely active and pure affirmation.

Deleuze, 1968

In his fascinating short book *Nietzsche: The God of Groundhog Day*, Michael Faust's description of Nietzsche's model of the eternal return sounds very similar to my own Cheating the Ferryman hypothesis. He writes:

> Amongst these possible lives will be ones where everything goes right for us, every decision we take is the right one, and we get everything we desire. The eternal recurrence

then becomes a promise of a heavenly afterlife. Nietzsche's 'demon' would be whispering, 'This life hasn't worked out well for you, but don't worry, the eternal recurrence will grant you the life of your dreams. You can take comfort that at some point you will lead a perfect life, and indeed you will get to repeat it an infinite number of times.' In this form, eternal recurrence is little short of a Christian promise of a better life in the next world.

Faust, 2011, p. 27

As referenced earlier, this link with Christianity is an interesting one. Although a self-proclaimed atheist, Nietzsche came from a family of devout Lutherans, and he never successfully shook off the influence. As Faust points out, Nietzsche was still searching for a model that suggested life after death and which used science as its starting point. The eternal return, as described in *The Will to Power*, was precisely this. This book is an attempt to place Nietzsche's philosophy on an even broader and deeper scientific basis, a subject we will be returning to in much greater detail in the second half of this book.

Walter Benjamin

Another thinker who was influenced by Blanqui was German philosopher Walter Benjamin (1892–1940). Sadly, this was to come very late in his life. In late 1937, as the clouds of Nazism began to obscure the sun of reason and humanity across Europe, Benjamin read *Eternity by the Stars*. As a Jew, Benjamin had been forced to leave Germany many years before and was, at that time, living in exile in San Remo in northern Italy. He was researching material for a project he described as an *Urgeschichte der Moderne* (an archaic history of modernity). This involved him reading up on obscure texts from the mid to late 19th century, and so a copy of *Eternity by the Stars* came into his possession.

In the previous 40 years, science – specifically cosmology and physics – had been revolutionized by the discovery of quantum mechanics and relativity. Benjamin was able to apply his knowledge of these developments to the ideas of Blanqui, and in doing so, he was able to refine and adapt them.

This was not Benjamin's first introduction to the idea of the eternal return. Earlier in 1938, at the author's suggestion, Benjamin read Theodor Adorno's personal copy of Karl Löwith's *Nietzsche's Philosophy of the Eternal Recurrence*. In this, Löwith noted that the original title of *Also Sprach Zarathustra* was to be *Noon and Eternity*, an apparent reference to Schopenhauer. With regard to Nietzsche, Löwith argued that this is the 'eternal moment' where time stands still and eternity can be perceived. It may be more than just coincidence that at the same time, a Russian philosopher-mathematician was coming to similar conclusions regarding the circular nature of life, the fascinating Pyotr Ouspensky.

Peter Ouspensky

Pyotr Demianovich Ouspensky was born on 5 March 1878. His family had a tradition of calling each generation of sons either Pyotr or Demian. I am intrigued about the odd similarity between my use of the word 'Daemon' and how one of the significant writers on the eternal return ended up with the middle name 'Demian'. The latter originates from the Greek word *damazo*, 'to conquer, master, overcome, tame'.

Ouspensky was a very serious child. Many years later, towards the end of his life, he reflected upon this and concluded that it was because, at that time, he was actually 'remembering' his previous life. For him, this was not a prior life as somebody else, which would be the case in classic reincarnation, but a previous life experienced as himself. He believed that some people subliminally recall their previous lives and that early childhood is simply an extension of the last years of their last life.

But Ouspensky's viewpoint was more elegant than this. He proposes that we live our own life again, and in doing so, we can, with great effort, realize that our actions will have outcomes. This suggests extreme solipsism whereby other people are simply players in a huge drama that evolves from actions made by the 'observer' consciousness. However, what Ouspensky fails to explain is the mechanism by which this 'remembering' works. If each of us will, after death, be reincarnated into the past to live our lives again, what can be the agent of change? If we are ignorant of the fact that we are living our life again, how can we possibly change anything? All the other 'minds' that we encounter will blindly follow the same plot as they did last time. We are doomed to act a role in the same extended 'formation novel' or *bildungsroman* of literature. We are ignorant of the fact that this is a 'rerun', and as such, we will react in the same way to the lines as they are fed to us by the other 'actors' in the drama. He described this life by using a Russian term called *Byt*. Ouspensky described this as a 'deeply rooted, petrified, routine life'. For Ouspensky, this was the lot of the vast majority of humanity. They are simply trapped in an endless cycle of repetition.

However, Ouspensky believed that certain 'advanced' human beings can break out of this mindless repetition. By a process that he never explains, these people become aware that they are living their lives again. Not only this, but they remember what happened last time. In this way, they can correct any errors they made last time and follow that outcome to its conclusion. This theme of 'self-awareness' is central to his 1905 novel *Kinemadrama* and its subsequent rewrite, *The Strange Life of Ivan Osokin*. In this intriguing book, we find a theme that has been explored by several modern writers. These include novels such as Kate Atkinson's 2013 book, *Life After Life*, Audrey Niffenegger's *The Time Traveler's Wife* from 2003, and *Replay*, a much-overlooked but quite extraordinary work by the late Ken Grimwood from 1986, and films such as *The Butterfly Effect*, *Vanilla Sky*, *Edge of Tomorrow* and *The Fountain*.

In Ouspensky's novel, a 26-year-old man, the eponymous hero, loses the love of his girlfriend, Zinaida, through a series of decisions he makes.

In desperation, he decides to commit suicide. He allows himself one last night of hedonism before killing himself when he meets a magician who offers to send him back to relive the previous 12 years of his life. But there is a catch. The magician explains that these 12 years will be different because Osokin will remember what happened to him in his previous journey through these years.

The young Osokin should now have a wonderful opportunity to correct all the errors of his previous life. However, this is not to be. He makes the same decisions and falls into the same traps. By the time he meets Zinaida again, his life has followed such a predictable path that he has even forgotten that he is reliving it again. He makes precisely the same mistakes that led to him losing the love of Zinaida and finds himself, again, contemplating suicide and meeting the magician. At this point, he has an overpowering sensation of déjà vu and realizes that he has lived this life many times and, more importantly, is doomed to experience it many more times.

In his non-fiction writings, Ouspensky argued that time was similar to space in that it consisted of three dimensions. These are duration, speed and direction. This makes time a cube rather than a single line. Indeed we see the straight-line element only because we are stuck in time. We perceive time flowing from one event to another, always in one direction going into the future. For Ouspensky, this meant that life is full of unfulfilled potentialities or, as he describes them, 'non-actualised potentialities'. When life comes to an end, it just starts again, and we go on living the same life over and over again. However, in the Eternal Recurrence chapter in his book *New Model of the Universe*, he stated that only lazy people live exactly the same life. For most of us, each life changes ever so slightly, and in this way, we do progress.

Towards the end of his life, Ouspensky would always announce the ending of a meeting of his study groups with the Russian term *ne zabuyvayte*, which means 'don't forget'. This was an instruction to his followers that it is only by 'not forgetting' that any advantage can be gained from living one's life over and over again. Indeed, in the final months before his death, he spent a great deal of time visiting locations from his past as a way of preparing himself for his rebirth. On 2 October 1947 he completed his circle and, if he was right, 5 March 1878 would reappear, and Pyotr Demianovich Ouspensky would be born again.

As we shall see later, the British playwright J.B. Priestley overtly acknowledged Ouspensky's contribution to the world of ideas. But for now, we will continue our roughly chronological review of philosophers whose ideas preceded those I have presented in my Cheating the Ferryman hypothesis.

THE MODERN PHILOSOPHERS
Edmund Husserl (1859–1938)

Edmund Husserl was the originator of the philosophical movement known as phenomenology. In this, he suggested we must study objects that are presented to consciousness without any preconceptions about them. Just perceive them in their purest sense by reducing them to their pure form. He called this reductionism *epoché*, a term borrowed, yet again, from Plato's academy.

For Husserl and his phenomenology, to discover ultimate consciousness, we must use epoché to bracket out any mere particulars about perceptual objects and focus on their existence in consciousness rather than in the external world. In effect, he is suggesting that we do not focus on Kant's thing-in-itself (*Ding an sich*), a noumenon, but on its phenomenal representation within our consciousness. We then need to focus on studying what is taking place that makes these representations appear in the mind. Husserl called these mind-created representations *noemata*. But the acts of consciousness which conjure up these noemata have none of the attributes of the actual external objects. What mind does to create an internal image is mix together a series of acts of consciousness – for example, 'analyzing', 'judging', 'measuring' and 'remembering'. Husserl calls these acts *noeses*. But it is only through this internalization of objects that we can ever know anything. In this respect, the only thing we can know with certitude is that something is 'observing' the contents of consciousness. That observer is what Husserl calls the Transcendental Ego.

Of linguistic interest here is that this suspension of any preconceptions of an object of study is called *eidetic reduction*. This uses the Greek word *eidos*, meaning 'essence' or 'form', as in the term 'Eidolon'. I would argue that Husserl's Transcendental Ego is an absolute equivalent of my own Daemon concept. His particular use of the term 'consciousness' is equivalent to my concept of the Eidolon.

From 1916 onwards, it was his investigations into the Transcendental Ego which took up much of his attention. He later argued that although the real world exists outside of perception, it still needs the Transcendental Ego to bring it into existence. In effect, what he means here is that it is the 'observer' who draws forth the phenomenal world from a deeper informational source. As we shall discover later, this is exactly what modern quantum physics tells us is taking place. Furthermore, we have a reasonably good idea of what this ground-source is.

His writings suggest that Husserl was not aware of the advances made in quantum physics, but he certainly was thinking in precisely the right direction. And it was his academic assistant at the University of Freiburg in southern Germany who was to take this model even further towards the model of reality I am presenting in this book.

Martin Heidegger (1889–1976)

It was in 1909, while studying at the University of Freiburg, that theology student Martin Heidegger first encountered the philosophy of Edmund Husserl. Such was his interest that Heidegger opened up correspondence with Husserl in 1914 and, in 1916, when Husserl moved to Freiburg, they became close friends.

What drew them together was one of the central themes of this book: how we perceive things within time. In 1927 Heidegger, with the direct help and assistance of Husserl, published his book *Being and Time (Sein und*

Zeit). This was reflected in Heidegger's dedication page, which read 'to Husserl with friendship and admiration'.

Curiously, Heidegger makes little reference to the time theories of Friedrich Nietzsche in *Being and Time*. In the whole work, there are only three references to Nietzsche, and these are extremely marginal and only concerning his analysis of history. But this was all to change in the mid-1930s. It was then that he became interested in the implications of Nietzsche's 'eternal return', which he considered to be one of the three most important parts of Nietzsche's writings (the other two being the will to power and revaluation, neither of which concern us with regard to our present enquiry).

In *Being and Time*, Heidegger argued that consciousness is always proceeding from its past and existing in a present that is forever changing into the past as it moves into the future. And in this future lies one certain inevitability: death. Consciousness does not choose to be born and has no control regarding its own death.

During this process of perceiving consciousness, a point of perception exists in a world of sensory experience. It is literally 'in-the-world'. Heidegger called this concept *Dasein* – 'being-in-the-world' ('there' [*da*], 'being' [*Sein*]). By this, he meant our everyday process of thinking and perceiving deflects us away from the fundamental truth about consciousness, and that is what it means to exist, to literally 'be in time'. Dasein points out that we are both in-the-world as part of a body but also outside of the world as a consciousness that views the world from somewhere else. We have no control over the fact that we are in the world. When we are born, we are 'thrown in', and we simply have to deal with it. This concept of 'thrownness' (*Geworfenheit* in German), is a powerful image of a confused consciousness just having to deal with life.

However, if we apply the Daemon-Eidolon Dyad to this model, we are not actually 'thrown in' at all. At the start of each life (or run through the Bohmian IMAX), we are accompanied by a 'game player' (Daemon) that remembers all previous experiences of this life. The state of *Geworfenheit* is only actually experienced by each unique iteration of the Eidolon. It feels like it is 'thrown in', but it still has subtle guidance from its Daemon.

One of the major factors that attracted Friedrich Nietzsche to the eternal return was that it was supported by science. It was an application of French mathematician Henri Poincaré's recurrence theorem. In simple terms, Poincaré argued that if there is a vast but finite number of particles in the universe and that the universe is infinite both with regard to space and time, then every possible configuration of particles will occur an infinite number of times. So every set of circumstances will reoccur an infinite number of times.

There is an analogy here to a pack of cards. If the pack is initially placed in suit and number order and then shuffled, it will be in a less ordered state than before the shuffling. However, because the pack has only a finite number of states, continued random shuffling must cause any order to appear and reappear infinitely more often.

Like Nietzsche, I believe that however far we can go with philosophy and theology, they will never present us with objective evidence of a hypothesis. Objective proof can be supplied only if science supports it. My Cheating the Ferryman hypothesis is not exempt from this rule. I have presented considerable supporting material from the world of ideas, but I now need to present to you the science.

PART 4

The Proof

PROOF FROM QUANTUM PHYSICS
The Problem

In 2006 Bruce Rosenblum, Professor of Physics at the University of California and his associate, Dr Fred Kuttner, published a book entitled *Quantum Enigma: Physics Encounters Consciousness*. In their opening chapter, they head it with a quotation. This reads:

> Though what you're saying is correct, presenting this material to nonscientists is the intellectual equivalent of allowing children to play with loaded guns.
>
> Rosenblum, 2006, p. 3

This was an actual objection from one of their academic colleagues to Kuttner and Rosenblum's plan to set up a course for nonscientists that would explore the fundamental mysteries of quantum mechanics. Why was there such fear? Well, the answer was clear for these two brave scientists; there is a massive skeleton in the closet, and those 'in the know' would rather like to keep it there. This skeleton is that although modern quantum mechanics is by far the most successful scientific model of reality ever conceived by the human mind, it simply makes no sense. It has been said that the level of mathematical accuracy with regard to what quantum theory describes and the observed behaviour of how the universe works is accurate to the breadth of a human hair in measuring the distance across the Atlantic Ocean. But it is built upon a series of fudges, compromises and, it has to be said, 'just-so stories' that would have Rudyard Kipling giggling into his moustache.

There is something not quite right about reality as it is revealing itself to our science. All the evidence points to a conclusion that in some very profound way, the universe, and everything in it, is part of a greater reality. Not only that, but what we perceive to be our reality seems to have been designed. This does not mean that there is a creator-god as such, but it does suggest that we exist in a universe that is programmed. Why can such a conclusion be drawn?

The first real issue is matter itself, the seemingly solid material that makes up everything that physically exists, including your body and brain. Modern quantum physics has discovered that what we think of as solid material is mostly empty space. Let's look at this in greater detail.

To understand any working system, be it a machine or a human body, the component parts have to be isolated. A house is built of bricks; a body is made up of cells. The universe is made up of matter, which in turn is made up of molecules. So far, so good. This is as far as 19th-century science had delved, and it all made perfect sense. Each molecule was a collection of more primary particles called atoms. These atoms were the indivisible 'bits' of matter. This was evident from the fact that each type of atom was the smallest possible piece of an *element* and that these atoms joined together to form new, more complex forms of matter, termed *compounds*. An example of a compound is water. This consists of three atoms joined together to form a molecule. There are two hydrogen atoms and one oxygen atom (H_2O). Water is quite different to both hydrogen and oxygen, but that is all it is made of.

Hydrogen and oxygen are examples of elements. These basic substances that we see (of which 118 have been discovered) are made up as perceived by humans of billions upon billions of identical atoms. Water, as a compound, is made up of billions and billions of water molecules. It can be broken down to molecule level, but breaking down even further would leave hydrogen and oxygen; the water would cease to exist.

All chemistry is based on this knowledge, and Victorian scientists happily created new substances by mixing different atoms together.

However, one question had to be asked; what were atoms made of? In the late 19th century, it had been discovered that atoms, always with a neutral electric charge, were found to have within them smaller sections that were negatively charged. For the overall atom to be neutral, this discovery implied that the atom itself had a negative part and a positive part (a negative and a positive giving the observed neutral charge). These newly discovered packets of negative charge were termed *electrons*.

The Victorians visualized that these electrons sat in the solid surface of the atom like plums in a plum pudding. In this way, the apparent solidity of the atom, which in great numbers contributes to a solid world, was preserved.

This cosy world of tiny, solid bits of matter joining together to make up a solid universe is how the vast majority of people see the world even today. Like the Victorians, they are comfortable knowing that the chair they sit upon is made up of trillions of solid 'bits'. It makes sense and is confirmed by common sense and observation. The problem is that this view is totally wrong. The man on the Clapham omnibus can, if he wishes, pick up any book on science, and he will be informed to the contrary. However, received wisdom simply cannot accept the new science. As such, most people see the universe, and therefore reality, through Victorian eyes.

In 1900 a 42-year-old German physicist called Max Planck was to shatter this illusion, at least for the scientists. The problem he tried to solve was incredibly mundane: why it was that a poker, when heated, became red hot. It was a question of how energy (heat) was transferred from one object to another. Planck had a solution, but it was revolutionary. He suggested that energy was transferred between objects in discrete packets. He termed these packets *quanta* from the Latin for 'how much'. The problem was that at that time, energy was a highly abstract concept. That it had a physical presence, implied by the fact that it came in little packages, was totally new. Nineteenth-century science understood solidity and the idea that matter had mass and weight. Mysteriously, energy had been shown to have neither of these things.

Put simply, as far as the 19th-century scientists were concerned, it is not possible to weigh light or heat. Energy, whatever it was, was carried in some way by particles such as atoms or the newly discovered 'particles' of electricity, electrons. Planck proposed that the carriers of these *quanta* were themselves *quanta*. Victorian science was reeling but was still standing. Even Planck himself hoped that he was wrong. However, five years later, a young, Zurich-based patent clerk named Albert Einstein was to prove that energy had mass and that energy and mass were the same thing. Nineteenth-century science crashed to the floor with this knockout blow pulling all the carefully positioned jigsaw puzzle pieces with it. But things were to get worse, much worse.

In 1909 British-based New Zealander Ernest Rutherford discovered, horror of horrors, that the atom was not solid. He found that what was thought to be a solid ball was, in fact, a very tiny central particle, which he termed the *nucleus*, with even smaller particles, the electrons, revolving around it. It was subsequently found that the nucleus itself consisted of differing numbers of two types of particles stuck together; the positively charged protons and the neutrally charged neutrons. Rutherford's image of a tiny solar system is the one that has taken hold of the public imagination. Suffice to say that this is also wrong as well, but it is comfortable and easily visualized, so we shall continue to use it for the time being. However, what is not fully appreciated is the relative sizes of these subatomic particles in relation to each other and the empty space around them.

The two particle types in the nucleus contain more than 99.99 per cent of the atom's mass, and each individual proton and neutron have almost the same mass. In turn, the electron is 2,000 times smaller in terms of its mass. As such, the atom's weight (its 'atomic weight') is really made up of the joint mass of all the protons and all the neutrons. For example, a sodium atom has 11 protons and 12 neutrons, so its relative atomic weight is 23. However, and this is where the empty space comes in, the nucleus is only one ten-thousandth the size of the whole atom. This is equivalent to a soccer ball in the centre circle at Wembley Stadium, where the stadium is the atom. The electrons in this model would be particles the size of a pea whizzing around the terraces at thousands of miles a second. Now in your mind's eye, take away the stadium and replace it with totally empty space. That is an atom. Trillions of these 'bits' of mostly empty space join together to make a solid object – for example, a chair. However, less than one ten-thousandths of the chair you are sitting on is made up of solid mass; the rest is empty space. And remember, each nucleus sits in the centre of each atom surrounded by empty space populated by the occasional minute electron rushing past. So when two atoms are locked together in a molecule, remember that vast distances filled with nothing in relative terms separate the two solid nuclei. And yet, you perceive a solid chair. How?

This is where things become strange. Reality is received by each of us through our senses. 'We', in the sense of that consciousness which inhabits our brain, never actually make physical contact with the outside world. We 'see' through a chemical process generated by particles of light hitting our retina. We do not 'see' the object. What we perceive is the light waves bouncing off the object. We do not 'feel' the chair under our buttocks. We 'perceive' pressure via electronic impulses that travel from our backside to our brain. When you have a 'numb bum', you cannot feel the chair, so has it disappeared? No, because you can see it. Well, not quite. All you are seeing are light waves that cause an image on your retina which your brain recognizes as a chair. And remember, it is not only the chair that is made up of these empty atoms. You, your buttocks, your retina and your brain are also made of atoms. And what about the light waves? Oh yes, the light waves. Well, they are not quite what they seem either.

What we call 'light' waves are simply electromagnetic waves that bring about an electrochemical reaction in our eyes. As their name suggests, electromagnetic waves consist of two measurable effects that we can all observe: magnetism and electricity. In the 1860s and the 1870s Scottish scientist James Clerk Maxwell noticed that electrical 'fields' and 'magnetic' fields could be coupled together to create 'electromagnetic' fields. Carrying on from Maxwell's work, a German physicist, Heinrich Hertz, discovered a particular type of wave that could transmit a signal from one location to another. These became known as 'radio waves'. The word *radio* is taken from the verb 'to radiate' from the Latin *radius*, which means the spoke of a wheel. So, spokes 'radiate' from the centre of a wheel in a similar way to how radio waves radiate from their source in all directions. Maxwell had suspected that there was a link between electromagnetic 'radiation' and light. It was Hertz who proved that Maxwell's suspicions were correct. He found that radio waves propagated at precisely the speed of light, proving that electromagnetic radiation and light were identical. More importantly, he found a way to detach these waves from wires and go free and become a method of communication across vast distances.

It is now known that electromagnetic radiation has three elements: frequency, wavelength and energy. These have a mathematical relationship, so if you know one, you can calculate the other two. Frequency is the number of wave 'crests' that pass a given point in one second. The distance between each crest is the 'wavelength', and a full revolution of a wave is, not surprisingly, called a 'cycle'. This is measured as Hertz in honour of Heinrich Hertz. For example, a wave that travels past a particular point at three cycles per second has a frequency of 3 Hz. The shortest wavelengths are fractions of the size of an atom, and the longest so far measured is larger than the diameter of the earth.

What we know as 'light' is the part of the electromagnetic spectrum which can be found between a wavelength of 380 nanometres for the colour violet and 700 nanometres for the colour red. Light with a wavelength greater than 700 nanometres is infrared, and light less than 380 nanometres is ultraviolet (UV). Both are invisible to the eyes. However, a bee can see UV light. A nanometre is a billionth of a metre, so these wavelengths are very small but sit in the middle of the whole spectrum. Although we cannot see infrared light, we can feel it as heat.

So how small is this visible spectrum in relation to what can be seen? Imagine a reel of film representing the entire electromagnetic spectrum stretching from the Oval Cricket Ground in London to the Aswan Dam in Egypt. The section containing the visible spectrum would fall somewhere in the middle, the old cricket pitch at Spianáda's Lawns on the Greek island of Corfu. The visible spectrum would be a single frame of film, around one inch. This would be less than the length of one cricket chirping happily in the trees surrounding the pitch. And this is all the human eye can see with regard to the whole 'light' spectrum. This is how we 'see' the universe, and indeed, for most people, this is what the universe actually looks like. We see the sun as a yellow ball and the moon as a grey disc. What they truly look like we can never really perceive; even using the word 'true' in this respect is pointless. We shall return to this subject in much greater detail later when we examine the mysteries of vision. But for now, we need to delve deeper into the nature of light itself.

In the same way, a wave in water consists of water, a sound wave travels in air, and so do light waves. So how do light waves travel in outer space? Get ready for a surprise. Scientists have no clue what light is for one simple reason; sometimes it acts as a wave, a disturbance spread over a distance in space, but sometimes it acts like a particle, a point located in one specific place. How can one thing be both?

The Mysterious Double-Slit Experiment

This mystery was discovered by a series of curious experimental results involving light and its observed behaviour in an experiment that has now become known as the 'double-slit experiment'.

Imagine dropping a pebble into a pond. The waves form a series of ripples moving out from the point where the pebble entered the water. Now imagine what would happen if a barrier were placed across the pond. As the waves hit the barrier, they bounce back in the direction they came. Now we place two holes in the barrier, both much smaller than the wavelength of the ripples. On the other side of the barrier, we will quickly see two sets of waves, starting at each hole, spread out as if two new pebbles were dropped in the water at the same place as each hole. As the two new sets of ripples move out, they begin to 'interfere' with each other, disrupting the flow of the two sets of semicircles. In some places, the two sets of ripples add up to make extra-large ripples; in others, the two sets of ripples cancel out, leaving little or no wave motion in the water.

The same exercise can be done with electromagnetic radiation. Light, the visible part of the electromagnetic spectrum, is shone through a single hole in a barrier. As the light flows out, it encounters a second barrier, this time with two holes. The light acts like a wave in that each hole then starts its own wave pattern the other side of the second barrier. Immediately the two waves begin to interfere with each other. A screen is then set up after the second barrier. When the light hits this screen, it shows a pattern of light and dark stripes. These stripes are called *interference fringes*. They correspond to where the light waves add together (*constructive interference*) and where the waves cancel each other out (*destructive interference*).

By using this process Thomas Young, in 1800, proved to most people's satisfaction that light functions as a wave. But in 1905 Albert Einstein suggested that light was also made up of individual particles. He even gave them a name, photons. As far as Einstein was concerned, it was the only way a particular puzzle for early 20th-century science could be explained.

It had been observed that when light was shone on a solid object, it seemed to 'kick out' electrons from the surface. This phenomenon, known as the 'photoelectric effect', was a mystery. However, as Einstein said in his 1905 paper, if light is made of particles, each particle hits the surface and then knocks out the electrons. This supposition was subsequently supported by experimentation, and in recognition of this discovery, Einstein was awarded the Nobel Prize for physics.

One problem solved, many opened. This dual nature of light (wave and particle) was to cause a radical review of our perception of electromagnetic radiation. If light was also made up of discrete packets, how can this be squared with the fact that light is also a wave? It is for this reason that we need to revisit the double-slit experiment.

We need to understand what would, or should, happen if photons were sent through the two slits. As an analogy, imagine that the two holes were holes in a barn door, the holes being about three times the size of a soccer ball. Now we kick balls against the door. After a few dozen balls are kicked through the holes, we stop the exercise. We will then find two piles of balls on the other side of the barn door. We would expect to find the pattern (two piles of balls) to be exactly the same if, instead of both holes being open at the same time, each hole was open on its own for half the time and then the other hole for the other half. What you would not expect would be a group of balls centred halfway between the two holes, right behind the solid door. Single footballs should not interfere with one another as they individually go through the open slit one by one.

Now let's imagine that the single footballs are replaced by single photons of light fired from a photon gun towards the double slits. To get through to the other side of the barrier, each photon has to go through one or other of the slits. We place at a short distance behind the barrier a screen made up of light-sensitive film. This can register each photon's arrival after it has made its journey from the photon gun through either of the slits and hit the screen. As billions, then trillions of photons arrive at the plate, a pattern emerges on the screen. Common sense would lead you to assume that there would be two circles of white light coinciding with the trajectory of each photon through whichever hole it selected, just like our piles of footballs in our barn door analogy. But this is not what we see. We get the interference fringes again. How can this be? Each photon has gone through either one of the slits with no other photons around it. Any form of interference is impossible. And yet, the interference fringes show that this is precisely what has happened. So how can a single photon interfere with itself? It seems that each photon leaves the gun as a particle and then, on encountering the barrier, changes into a wave. This wave goes through both slits and, on arrival on the other side, causes the interference pattern. It then turns back into a particle, and that is what arrives on the screen. But how does the photon know in advance where to place itself on the photographic plate to ensure that ultimately, and with all its fellow photons, a perfect pattern of light and dark stripes can be created?

This question, even today, has not been satisfactorily explained. This in itself is strange, but subsequent discoveries relating to the double-slit experiment suggest that this universe is far stranger than we can ever imagine. To move on, we need to spend some time in the capital of the Danish state, the wonderful, wonderful Copenhagen.

The Copenhagen Interpretation

As we have seen, the term *quanta* was coined by the German physicist Max Planck in 1900. The term was then used to cover all events at sizes below that of an atom. This differentiation is because classical, Newtonian physics simply does not work in this microcosmic world. As well as the duality of light, it was discovered that particles such as electrons can move from one point to another without crossing the intervening space. They disappear from one orbit around the nucleus and appear in another. The Danish physicist Niels Bohr discovered this phenomenon, now known by the much overused (and misunderstood) term 'quantum leaping'.

An associate of Bohr, Max Born, suggested that electrons do not actually exist as individual entities but are merely statistics. By this, he meant that scientists can calculate with great accuracy the behaviour of trillions of electrons, but they have no way of predicting the behaviour of any single electron. We have only a statistical chance of finding an electron in a particular place. He termed this the 'probability amplitude'. Born then proposed that an electron's 'wave function' is a statistical wave, similar to a crime wave. As such, a crime wave itself has no actual existence. A person cannot be affected by a crime wave but only by an actual crime taking place. Thus, the electron 'wave' becomes a solid, real electron only when measured and found to be in a particular location. Before the measurement takes place, the electron does not exist except as a probability. The act of observation makes the wave function 'collapse' into a solid object – in this case, an electron. It is essential that this concept is understood: before an observer detects the quantum particle, *it does not exist.* Consciousness brings the object into reality. Without conscious observation, no reality. We create our own universe!

Earlier, you will recall that we discussed the much-ridiculed philosophy of Idealism as proposed by George Berkeley and Immanuel Kant. Even today, the idea that consciousness creates reality in some way is rejected out of hand. And yet, nature itself does not dismiss such a proposition. It seems that this may be the way the universe works.

Born made this staggering proposal in 1926. At that time, the wave-particle nature of electrons was suspected only because it explained the more bizarre behaviour of quantum particles. This solution has become known by two alternative titles: the Statistical Interpretation of Quantum Physics and the better-known Copenhagen Interpretation. Named after the city to which many of the followers of Niels Bohr decamped, the Copenhagen Interpretation was to be the cause of a total schism in the world of particle physics. Bohr and his associates were convinced that they were correct. In contrast, Einstein and the other great scientist Erwin Schrödinger could not accept that there was not a reality underlying the quantum world in which logic and order were restored, a reality that became known as the 'hidden variables'.

Of course, electrons and photons are extremely small particles. We perceive these bits of matter and energy only when they are collected together in their trillions upon trillions. Indeed the bizarre behaviour of such tiny things, when individuated, is of no concern with regard to the secure reality we perceive around us. This strange wave-particle duality disappears as more and more of these particles aggregate, in a similar way as to how wetness appears with large numbers of hydrogen and oxygen atoms getting together to create water molecules. There is no 'wetness' in small numbers of H_2O molecules. It just magically appears as more and more of them come together. Well, this is what those locking the skeletons away in the cupboards would have you believe. But there is far more to this than simply electrons and photons, much more.

Why? Because the strange wave-particle duality of subatomic particles has now been witnessed with atoms and molecules, large molecules.

For example, in my previous books and talks, I have cited 'Buckyballs' with 60 atoms as being the largest molecule to show this direct link with 'observation'. These are around a millionth of a millimetre across or 10 nanometres.

Austrian physicist Anton Zeilinger and his team at the University of Vienna have shown that even larger molecules, such as the interestingly named C284.H190.F320.N4. S12, which consists of 800 atoms, show wave-particle duality. This huge advance in the size of particles showing this 'consciousness-effect' pushes the barrier between weird quantum behaviours ever closer to the nice, safe world of Newtonian physics, closer towards a very interesting barrier ... that of viruses.

One of Zeilinger's associates, Markus Arndt, subsequently created a carbon-based molecule consisting of 430 atoms which, in turn, showed wave-particle duality. This molecule was 6 nanometres across. This is large enough to be seen in an electron microscope.

A nanometre is one-billionth of a metre. In general number notation, this is expressed as 10^{-9}. A sheet of paper is about 100,000 nanometres in thickness, and a human hair is between 80,000 to 100,000 nanometres wide. To really put this into perspective, if the earth's diameter was 1 metre, then the diameter of a marble would be 1 nanometre. A single gold atom is a third of a nanometre in diameter. To put this in perspective, your fingernail grows at about 1 nanometre a second.

But there is more. In September 2019, in the journal *Nature Physics*, it was reported that a large molecule known as an 'oligo-tetraphenylporphyrin enriched with fluoroalkyl sulfanyl chains' was shown to go through both slits in a double-slit experiment. Yes, I did mean to write this. *One* molecule went through *both slits* at the *same time*!

So how big is this magical molecule? It has 2,000 atoms! Its mass is 25,000 times that of a hydrogen atom. I have yet to find a source to confirm the actual size of this molecule, but it is fair to conclude that if it consists of 2,000 atoms, then it must be at least four times the size of Arndt's molecule. This would be 24 nanometres.[4]

Now let's look at life at its smallest size. DNA is 2.5 nanometres in diameter; an antibody is around 10 nanometres and a virus is about 100 nanometres. A virus is basically a particle made up of DNA or RNA packaged inside a protein covering. The smallest known viruses are 20 nanometres across. If I am right in my suspicion that the dual-natured oligo-tetraphenylporphyrin will be around 24 nanometres, then it is larger than the smallest viruses. If this is the case, a virus could theoretically be created by an 'act of observation'. It has to be stressed that the upper limit on size regarding wave-particle duality has yet to be reached, so much larger molecules may show this effect. The much-discussed coronavirus is 125 nanometres in size. Imagine that it could be demonstrated that the COVID-19 virus is, in a very real sense, a mind creation, then how incredible will that be?

But the implications of wave-particle duality do not stop here. Have you ever wondered how the sun shines? How it has been emitting energy in the form of heat and light for over 4.6 billion years? This was a massive mystery for 19th-century and early 20th-century scientists until April 1938, when Hans Bethe came up with a solution suggesting that it was all to do with wave-particle duality.

Quantum Tunnelling

Earlier, when discussing the mysteries of the Copenhagen Interpretation, we discovered how electrons seemingly disappear from one 'orbit' around the atom's nucleus to another without crossing the space between. This is called 'quantum leaping', but it does not involve leaping at all. The electron disappears from one 'orbit' (or shell) and instantaneously appears in another. To do so, it has to eject or accept a particle of electromagnetic energy, a photon. When a photon is emitted, it is of great importance to our appreciation of the universe around us because what we perceive as light, that which illuminates the cosmos, is made up of countless photons being ejected from countless atoms. Without quantum leaping, we literally could see nothing. Of course, as every electron is absolutely identical to every other electron, we have no way of knowing if the electron that disappears in one orbit/shell is the same one that appears in the higher or lower shell/orbital. Actually, as an aside, at what 'speed' does it do this appearing/disappearing trick? Is it at the speed of light, or is it instantaneous? If it is instantaneous, then it contravenes Einstein's light-speed limitation. So, where does it go when it disappears? How can something do this? As I wrote in a previous book, this is like a car disappearing on the South Circular Road in Tulse Hill, London, and instantaneously appearing on the M25 at Reigate in Surrey.

In a similar fashion, subatomic particles have been shown to be able to move from one side of a barrier to another. This is, incorrectly, known as Quantum Tunnelling. They do not 'tunnel' anywhere. They simply disappear from one side of the barrier and reappear instantaneously on the other side of the barrier. Ponder on precisely what these words mean. What takes place during quantum tunnelling is absolutely bizarre and cannot in any way be explained by our modern understanding of scientific processes, but this is what our experimentation tells us is taking place. And without this totally weird occurrence taking place, life of any form could not exist on Earth or, indeed, anywhere in the universe. Why? Well, because without quantum tunnelling, the sun, and by implication, all stars, could not shine.

In simple terms, the sun releases energy by converting hydrogen into helium in a process known as nuclear fusion. This creates a great deal of energy which, in turn, is what we perceive as heat and light. Fusion happens when lighter elements are forced together to become heavier elements. The hydrogen atom is the simplest element possible; it consists of one proton in its nucleus and one electron. The proton has a positive electrical charge, and the electron has a negative charge which makes the hydrogen atom's total charge to be neutral. All atoms are neutral, so this is not unusual. But other atoms also have particles called neutrons in the nucleus. These are neutral in charge. As you may recall from your school-day physics, like charges repel and opposite charges attract. A proton will attract an electron, whereas two electrons or two protons will repel each other. And here lies a problem.

To create helium from hydrogen, two hydrogen nuclei must 'fuse' together to create a helium nuclei which has two protons and two neutrons. But the nucleus of a hydrogen atom consists of a single, positively charged proton. So how can two positively charged particles get close enough to each other to fuse? The repulsion is known as the Coulomb Repulsion Force, and even the intense pressures found within the sun's core are not sufficient to overcome this repulsion. So how can two hydrogen nuclei ever get close enough to fuse and create a helium nucleus? Well, it all comes down to our friend 'wave-particle duality'. As we have already discovered, all particles can be both a wave and a particle. And so it is with the hydrogen protons. They are also waves, and waves have very different properties to particles. For example, they spread over space, so the 'wave function' of two protons may overlap, which is where quantum tunnelling comes into the equation. The wave is such that some hydrogen nuclei spontaneously appear close enough to each other to be captured by the short-distance attraction of the Strong Nuclear Force. As soon as this is done, the energy brought about by the fusion, in the form of gamma photons, is released and makes its way from the core of the sun to the surface, which then spreads out into space. This journey takes around 100,000 years. So the heat you feel when basking in the sun was created 100,000 years ago (plus the eight minutes the light takes to get from the surface of the sun to the earth) by quantum processes. This is powerful evidence that quantum mechanics, however counter-intuitive it is, is very real.

There is also something extraordinary about quantum tunnelling. It has been shown by experimentation that the tunnelling process takes place in zero time. The particle disappears in one location and appears instantaneously in the new location (Nimtz, 2003). Interestingly, a subsequent experiment in 2008 has shown that what was actually transferred instantaneously was information (Eckle, 2008).

Let this sink in: all stars shine because of quantum tunnelling. This means life on this planet, and I assume all other planets that may have life, depends upon the fact that particles can also be waves. These particles/waves can disappear in one location and reappear instantaneously in another *without crossing the intervening space*. This is how reality works.

Quantum tunnelling and virtual particles are fascinating, but these effects seemingly take place without an active observer. But other particles apparently come into existence *only* for one observer and not another.

The Unruh Effect

According to Einstein's theory of relativity, time starts to slow down as we accelerate through space. In effect, what is really happening is that space is being converted into time. The faster we go, the more this happens until a point is reached. When we are at the speed of light, that time stops altogether. But even weirder is the 'fact' that if we travel through empty space at a constant speed, there would be no particles present. However, as soon as we begin to accelerate, particles just pop into existence, particles that do not exist in the perceptual universe of a person travelling at a constant speed. This strange set of circumstances is known as the Unruh-Davies-DeWitt-Fulling effect or, for short, simply the Unruh effect.

This suggests, in effect, that the notion of a vacuum depends upon the path of the observer through space-time. By vacuum is meant space that contains the lowest possible quantized-energy state.

From the viewpoint of the accelerating observer, the vacuum of an inertial observer will contain many particles in thermal equilibrium, effectively a gas. But from the perspective of the inertial observer, there are no particles. The moving observer will perceive radiation that *does not exist* in the conceptual universe of the inertial observer.

The gas 'observed' will have a temperature directly related to the observer's acceleration.

To put this another way: in one frame of reference, there are particular objects (structures made of particles), while in another frame, all of this 'disappears', and there is nothing but the vacuum (fluctuations). What one observer sees as a vacuum, another describes as being riddled with particles. These are opposite states, and yet both are absolutely correct. This suggests that both observers are perceiving different realities.

Another curious result of the Unruh effect is that when somebody is travelling at a constant acceleration away from a pursuing photon travelling at the speed of light, that photon, although travelling far faster than the person receding away, will never reach the person, even though it is travelling far faster than the person. This is technically known as an Asymptote, a value that you get closer and closer to but never quite reach. This comes from the Greek *asumptōtos*, meaning 'not falling together'. This has direct relevance to my Cheating the Ferryman hypothesis.

In my first book, *Is There Life After Death?: The Extraordinary Science of What Happens When We Die*, I used something known as the Zeno Bisection Paradox to explain how subjective time can expand infinitely when experienced as a series of lifetimes, each one taking half the objective (consensual) time to be lived than the one preceding it. In effect, an infinite number of lives can be lived as each subsequent life is lived in half the amount of objective time as the last one. I argued that the actual moment of death would never be arrived at in objective linear time. I subsequently discovered that adding an infinite number of terms together as each one gets smaller does give a finite result. The answer lies in calculus. But this seems to apply only to distance, not time. If the scenario is purely time-related, then the calculus escape does not work.

But the Quantum Zeno effect suggests something just as strange. As we have already discovered, before the state of a quantum object is measured, it exists in a quantum superposition of all possible states, while immediately after the measurement, it is observed in one and only one state. It has been discovered that if an object receives repeated measurements (or 'observations'), the actual act of measurement (or observation) prevents the object from changing to another state.

This is all to do with transition states. Subatomic particles can transit from one state to another. But like in Zeno's paradox, there are an infinite number of steps to take in order to transition from one state to another, which means the second state is never reached. Here is an example couched in terms of classical physics. Imagine a pot of freezing water. As it is heated, its temperature makes its way to boiling point. If we measure the state of the water, we discover it is, for example, 50 per cent on the way to boiling. After it is measured, it is still at 50 per cent. But if it were a quantum particle, it can only have two states – in this example, freezing or boiling. In effect, if you find that it isn't boiling, then you have to start heating it again.

In 1977 two researchers at the University of Texas, Baidyanath Misra and George Sudarshan, were intrigued by how it seemed that subatomic particles were affected by 'the act of observation'. They continually monitored an unstable quantum system in a fascinating experiment to see if it decayed while under observation. Much to their amazement, it did not. It continued in an unstable situation in defiance of all known physical laws (Misra & Sudarshan, 1977).

A more sophisticated experiment took place at the National Institute of Standards in Boulder, Colorado, in 1989. Wayne Itano and his team observed the behaviour of 5,000 charged beryllium atoms trapped in a magnetic field. The atoms all started at one energy level, although they could be 'boiled' by exposure to a radio-frequency field for 256 thousandths of a second. After exposure to this field, the atoms all occupied a higher energy state – so long as no measurements were made in the interim. By probing with a laser at intermediate moments, the team found that the more often they recorded the state of the atoms, the fewer reached the higher energy level; with observations made every four-thousandths of a second, no atoms boiled at all. It seems that a watched quantum kettle never does boil (Itano, Bollinger & Wineland, 1990).

But there is more – much more. Other scientists have approached the mystery from a different angle, and their conclusions were, and remain, extraordinary. Welcome to the truly bizarre 'sum over histories' model. Tighten your seat belts because this is going to be an incredible ride.

Wave-Particle Duality and the Sum over Histories

Regarding the mystery of the double-slit experiment (which slit the electron goes through), the answer may be a 'simple' one: the electron does not go through both slits simultaneously but in different versions of history. In one history, it went through the left slit, and in another, it went through the right slit. This avoids the seemingly impossible situation whereby it goes through both at the same time, and is another solution suggested by Richard Feynman, considered by many to be the greatest physicist of the late 20th century. According to Feynman, if there are alternative ways in which a set of circumstances can come to pass, then each alternative does happen. He called this model the 'sum over histories'. In his book *The Fabric of the Cosmos*, Brian Greene described it as showing that:

> . . . a probability wave embodies all possible pasts that could have preceded a given observation and illustrates well that to succeed where classical physics failed, quantum mechanics had to substantially broaden the framework of history.
>
> Greene, 2005, p. 180

Let us consider here the implications of what Greene (and Feynman) suggest: within the probability wave can be found the information describing all the other possible routes the electron could have followed in arriving at either slit. If every probability wave carries this information, then every possible outcome of every quantum event is encoded within the information field associated with each subatomic particle. We witness one outcome, but every other outcome also has potential existence. This is a remarkable statement. It suggests that we exist in a universe in which one outcome has been drawn from potentiality to actuality, but a universe that accommodates the outcome of every other route the particle could have taken also has existence; it is just that we exist in one of these universes and act as the 'observer' of that universe. To be clear here, this suggests that there are countless universes, all of which contain different histories and, by implication, different futures. To coin an often-used phrase, everything that can happen does happen.

And this is precisely the solution to the double-slit experiment that was suggested by physicist Hugh Everett III. If your brain is reeling at the moment, get ready for the Many-Worlds Interpretation.

Schrödinger's Cat and the Many-Worlds Interpretation

We discussed earlier the discovery by Anton Zeilinger and Markus Arndt at the University of Vienna, that very large molecules turn from a probability wave to an actual physical particle when measured (or 'observed').

This is an extraordinary discovery. It means that there is no such thing as objective reality, including the human brain and everything it perceives. Reality, and all it contains, is not determined until it is observed. In 1925, the Austrian physicist Erwin Schrödinger had created a mathematical formula describing how quantum matter-waves evolve in space and time. He argued that there is no 'collapse' of the wave function; it just continues. He found the idea that consciousness was involved in bringing about this supposed collapse to be preposterous.

And to show how illogical it was, he proposed a thought experiment to highlight the 'quite ridiculous' implications. In an article published in the science journal *Naturwissenschaften* he imagined that:

> A cat is penned up in a steel chamber, along with the
> following diabolical device (which must be secured against
> direct interference by the cat): in a Geiger counter, there is
> a tiny bit of radioactive substance, so small that perhaps in
> the course of one hour one of the atoms decays, but also,
> with equal probability, perhaps none. If the atom decays,
> the counter tube discharges and through a relay releases a
> hammer which shatters a small flask of hydrocyanic acid. If
> one has left this entire system to itself for an hour, one would
> say that the cat still lives if meanwhile no atom has decayed.
>
> Schrödinger, 1935

During the hour, there is a 50/50 chance that the radioactive substance
will decay at some time in those 60 minutes, bringing about the cat's
death. But there is also a 50/50 chance that it will not decay and the
cat remains alive. But if the atom is unobserved, then it is in a state of
superposition in which its wave function does not collapse and there exist
two cats: one alive and one dead. Only when the box is opened does
the observing scientist bring about the collapse that results in a dead
(or alive) cat. In effect, this means that one set of circumstances simply
disappears while the other spontaneously comes into existence.

Could it be that everything we perceive around us is being brought
into existence as we observe it? This is the only conclusion that can
be drawn from the Copenhagen Interpretation. Without conscious
observers, the universe, and everything in it, is simply a statistical wave
function, a mathematical construct with no actual reality in itself.

Or is it? In 1957 Princeton student Hugh Everett III submitted his PhD
thesis suggesting a solution. He agreed with Schrödinger that the wave
function never collapses but continues. So far, so good, but he then argued
that the wave function splits into two at the point of measurement, one
to accommodate a universe containing a dead cat and one containing a
live cat. He then argued that as the box is opened, the observing scientist,
and his whole universe, also splits into two versions, one in which a dead

cat is observed and one containing a live cat. This has become known as the Many-Worlds Interpretation (MWI). And so consciousness and the collapsing wave function are taken out of the equation.

In effect, this means that there will be a version of you and every other consciousness that will experience every possible outcome of every decision that you can and will make. Not only this, but all decisions made by your ancestors will also create new versions of you. And this is of great importance for the question being asked in this book. You may die in one universe, but a version of you will always survive. Let us review this in more detail.

Firstly, MWI suggests that the wave function never collapses but continues with all possible outcomes coming into existence. In doing so, the outcome of every possible wave function involves the creation of a number of new universes to accommodate the evolution of each wave function. And in each universe, there will be an observer who will 'measure' the outcome of each quantum event. In effect, this means that there are countless universes, some virtually identical to this one and some totally different. In some universes, life will have evolved, and in countless others, the conditions will be hostile to life. This hypothesis explains all of the 'coincidences' that brought about life in this universe and, as such, destroys the idea that in some way, the universe was hard-wired for the evolution of life. We just happen to exist in a universe whose wave-function evolved to facilitate life and, ultimately, conscious observers. This universe was not 'designed' for life; it is simply one of a number whose chance conditions coincided to create life.

This may seem to invalidate my carefully structured argument for CTF. But it doesn't. Indeed, it offers an alternative scenario that also supports the hypothesis. Why? Well, if there are countless universes, then there are innumerable versions of every conscious observer within the 'megaverse', and each one will experience numerous times every possible outcome of every decision they can make in their lives. Not only that, but there will be in existence a universe that will accommodate the consequences of every decision that the ancestors of that consciousness will have made in the past. This can also be extended into the future. What is more, all these universes may be existing concurrently, so, at this moment in time, all outcomes of all decisions already exist waiting to be experienced. And this is exactly what cosmologist Professor Stephen Hawking argued in his very last academic paper.

PROOF FROM COSMOLOGY
Hawking and Hertog's Top-Down Hypothesis

Ten days before he died, Stephen Hawking sent to his publishers a paper he had been working on with his associate author, Thomas Hertog of the CERN research centre in Switzerland (Hawking & Hertog, 2018).

In a variation on Feynman's 'sum over histories' discussed above, the paper proposed that the outcome of every event was encoded into the fabric of the universe from the first femtoseconds of the Big Bang. In this model, known as the Top-Down Hypothesis, Hawking and Hertog ask us to visualize a universe with trillions upon trillions of films all running on top of each other. This is the 'real' universe. All we do is perceive one slice of this mega-reality. But what is crucial to understand is that for Hawking and Hertog, this multiverse exists in a different form of time from the nice linear time of the Newtonian universe. He calls this 'imaginary time', but this does not mean that it is not real. Hawking describes it this way:

> One can think of ordinary, real time as a horizontal line.
> On the left, one has the past, and on the right, the future.
> But there's another kind of time in the vertical direction.
> This is called imaginary time, because it is not the kind of
> time we normally experience. But in a sense, it is just as real
> as what we call real time.[5]

This is similar to the fact that the outcome of every decision in a virtual-reality simulation game is already programmed onto the DVD or encoded within a computer hard drive. This is also crucially important regarding my Cheating the Ferryman hypothesis and yet more proof that it has validity.

With regard to this idea, in 2011 the hugely popular British TV scientist Brian Cox published a book with the title *The Quantum Universe: Everything That Can Happen Does Happen*, which he co-authored with Jeff Forshaw. Cox is known for being somebody who ridicules and dismisses writers like myself, describing us as 'woo-woo merde-merchants' whose writings are a 'pit of drivel' in an article he wrote for the *Wall Street Journal* in February 2012 (Cox, 'Why Quantum Theory Is So Misunderstood', 2012). But note the title of the book. Indeed, the reason for his writing the article was that he came under a fair degree of criticism for stating on a BBC TV lecture that according to quantum theory, 'everything is connected to everything else', and he wished to distance himself from the 'pit of drivel' that writings such as the contents of this book are sourced from. But he cannot escape from the fact that this is precisely what quantum physics tells us about the universe. Indeed, although Cox and Forshaw carefully avoid citing Hawking and Hertog's earlier paper ('Populating the landscape: A top-down approach', 2006), the title of their book is an accurate description of what Hawking and Hertog were suggesting. Everything that can happen does happen. If this is the case, then the greatest mystery of cosmology, how life seems to have evolved against all the odds, may be explained. Either the universe is one of countless universes, as is suggested by Everett's Many-Worlds Interpretation and its many variations, or it is the only universe that has ever existed. If MWI is correct, then it is not at all surprising that life and consciousness evolved here. It had to happen somewhere in one of the countless universes and this, not surprisingly, is the one we are in.

The Anthropic Cosmological Principle

But what if MWI is incorrect and this is the only universe that has ever existed? Well, then things become quite strange, suggesting that this universe has been 'hard-wired' for the evolution of not just life but also self-reflecting consciousness, the kind of consciousness that can collapse a wave function. This 'teleological' model suggests something most scientists find totally unacceptable – that this universe has been *designed*. The problem scientists have is that in a singular universe, the evidence for design is overpowering. This hypothesis is known as the Anthropic Cosmological Principle. It is to this fascinating idea that we now turn our attention.

It has long been suggested that the human mind, facilitated by the human brain, is singularly the most amazing component found within the known universe. However, this remarkable device is trapped inside the consciousness of a being who will exist, at most, for 115 years on a small planet revolving around a very average star in the outer reaches of a medium-sized galaxy. Within the vastness of space and time, the sheer waste of such a complex and wonderful result of natural selection seems almost gratuitous. If, as it appears at the present time, life has evolved only in this small corner of the cosmos, then the pointlessness of it all beggars belief.

So why are we here? Religion attempts to answer these questions, but the answers all seem to contradict each other. As such, it is not beyond the bounds of reason that one religion may be correct, but we have no way of telling. For those of us with an enquiring but rationalistic mind, religion can offer no solace.

And what are the variables that seem to have conspired so well together to ensure that I am here to write these words and you are also here to read them? This is not such a strange statement. The chance of life developing in the universe has come about by a series of amazingly fortuitous events and circumstances. In this chapter, I will endeavour to present evidence that life, particularly intelligent life, is such an unlikely event that one can only conclude that it was, in some way, inevitable. Those scientists involved in research into cosmology and life sciences continue to be staggered by the complexity and the sheer consistency of it all.

It therefore comes as no surprise that, in 1974, astrophysicist Brandon Carter commented upon how it seemed that the universe had engineered a large number of variables to coincide in such a way that self-conscious life was evolved. He called this the Anthropic Principle. Carter has subsequently admitted that he wishes he had used another term. *Anthropic* suggests a uniquely human focus, whereas he argued that the universe was hard-wired for intelligent life, human and non-human. On reflection, he considers that the *biophilic* principle would have been a much more accurate descriptor.

Carter's principle has evolved into two variations: the Weak Anthropic Principle (WAP) and the Strong Anthropic Principle (SAP). WAP proposes that to have evolved intelligent carbon-based life-forms, the universe has to be the size and age it is. In addition, it has to have the mixture of elements that is observed because without this structure we would not be around to observe the fact. SAP, on the other hand, is far more revolutionary. It proposes that the universe has been, in some way, 'hard-wired' to develop the way it has for us to evolve. This is not a simple chance. The evidence, when reviewed in detail, is simply overpowering. There are many of these coincidences, but as I am focusing specifically on the evolution of consciousness, I would like to focus on two essential contributors to life: carbon and water.

In the first milliseconds of the Big Bang, temperatures were so high that only subatomic particles existed. There was far too much electromagnetic energy around for them to join together to form atomic nuclei. There was a hot, dense plasma full of an almost equal amount of matter and anti-matter in the guise of protons and anti-protons, neutrons and anti-neutrons, electrons and positrons, neutrinos and anti-neutrinos, all existing in a sea of photons (the 'carriers' of electromagnetic energy). And it is here, at this early stage of the universe, that the first evidence of the 'fine-tuning' took place. It is logical to conclude that there would be precisely the same amount of matter as anti-matter. After all, one is simply the mirror image of the other. Each proton has an anti-proton, and each electron has a balancing positron. But for some very mysterious reason, there was a tiny amount more matter than anti-matter (how this could be has never been explained). When matter and anti-matter come into contact, they annihilate each other in a flash of electromagnetic energy. However, because there was slightly more matter than anti-matter, what was left after all this energy release was a universe made almost entirely out of matter. If this slight imbalance had not been factored into the initial blueprint, matter and anti-matter would have disappeared in a flash of electromagnetic energy, leaving nothing but photons (which do not have their own anti-particles). What actually remained were the photons, protons, electrons and neutrinos.

Having survived its initial potential destruction, the universe survived to create something called the strong nuclear force. This is one of the four basic forces of nature (the others being gravity, the electromagnetic force and the weak nuclear force). How this was formed from the Big Bang is totally unknown, but it did. It has an exact strength which, we assume (if we deny any form of design being involved), came into existence with this precise value just spontaneously and quite by chance. It could have had any strength, but it arbitrarily 'chose' the one it did. This is profoundly fortunate for the evolution of life and consciousness, because life would never have happened if it had been 2 per cent weaker or 2 per cent stronger.

Three minutes after the Big Bang, when the temperature had dropped to around 1 billion degrees, the strong nuclear force was able to attract single positively charged protons and neutrally charged neutrons into something known as a deuteron. When two deuterons stuck together, they created helium nuclei (two protons and two neutrons) because there were not enough neutrons available to allow all protons to find a home, leaving six out of every seven protons flying free. These single protons are, in effect, hydrogen nuclei in their own right. And this is where the strong nuclear force also created hydrogen, lots of it. Each free proton was able to attract a single electron and, in doing so, become a hydrogen atom. In this way, the amount of hydrogen in the universe is three times the amount of helium.

Here, the precise strength of the strong nuclear force came into its own with regard to the evolution of consciousness. Had the strong nuclear force been 2 per cent weaker than it is, hydrogen would have been effectively the only element in the universe. This is because, as we have already discovered, hydrogen is converted into other gases when the strength of the nuclear force is precisely strong enough to crush the free protons together. The strong force is just powerful enough to overcome the electromagnetic repulsion of similarly charged particles such as protons and, in doing so, crushes them together.

Conversely, if the strong force had been 2 per cent stronger, the hydrogen molecules would have been fused quickly into another form of hydrogen known as deuterium. As such, all of the hydrogen in the universe would have disappeared in the first few minutes after the Big Bang. Without hydrogen, stars would not have formed, meaning that galaxies would have similarly never existed.

Gravity is another crucial factor. It has a fine-balanced relationship with the strong nuclear force. If, in the early stages of the Big Bang, gravity had been very slightly weaker, matter would have dispersed too quickly for stars to have formed. However, if gravity had been slightly stronger, the universe would have reached a maximum size and then recollapsed in a big crunch before carbon-based life had had the time to evolve. Indeed, carbon, and associated heavier elements, are absolutely crucial to life. It is only the heavier elements that can form complex atomic structures among themselves. The lighter elements cannot do this. But the Big Bang created only the lighter elements which, by the exact amount of gravitational force needed, were pulled together to create nebulae and, in turn, the first stars. Only when these stars exploded at the end of their lives were these heavier elements created.

Another of the heavier elements created within the first stars is oxygen, and, together with hydrogen, this creates another of the curious 'coincidences' that have led to the creation of life and consciousness from a seemingly inanimate universe. When two hydrogen atoms link with a single oxygen atom, something magical is created that has no similarities with its parent atoms; it is called a water molecule. The atoms form in a triangular molecule whose electrical charge is unequally distributed. It is 'polar' in the sense that the oxygen side of the triangle is negative and the opposite side, with the two hydrogen atoms, is positive. This structure means that water is particularly crucial in the development of life. For example, it creates surface tension which supports the formation of cell membranes. As it is less dense in its solid state than in its liquid state, water freezes from the top down, not the bottom up. This means that the oceans have never frozen solid. If they had have done, all marine life would have been killed – and life started in the oceans. Other important properties of water include its solvency, cohesiveness, adhesiveness and other thermal properties.

But life needs certain other substances if it is to come into being. The most crucial of all these elements of life is carbon. Without carbon, all of nature would be inanimate. So, where does carbon come from?

Within all stars, chemical processes are taking place at all times. Atomic nuclei are colliding with each other, bonding with each other or smashing each other apart. Massive amounts of energy are thus released and, together with the energy within the star, assist in the creation of new compounds. It is within stars that carbon is created, vast amounts of it. An example of this is a type of star classified as an *R Coronae Borealis Variable*. These stars are variable because, on occasions, they suddenly lose brightness like an electric light being dimmed. This is caused by huge concentrations of carbon. The carbon vapour condenses into soot, and the star is hidden under a vast cosmic smog. So there is lots of it. However, without the most amazingly fortuitous set of chemical circumstances, carbon would simply not be.

Carbon is formed by the rare triple collision of three separate helium nuclei (alpha particles). When two helium nuclei collide, they immediately create new, larger, nuclei. This new nucleus is an isotope of the hard white metal beryllium. This is known as beryllium-8. Now, beryllium-8 is a very unstable isotope that has been created artificially on Earth. It is so unstable that it spontaneously fissions (splits) into two alpha particles in less than 10^{-15} seconds after it is formed. The third helium nucleus has to collide with the newly created beryllium-8 nucleus within that short 10^{-15} second period for carbon to be created. But this is not the end of the story. The third helium nucleus has to hit, and therefore contribute, precisely the right amount of energy to ensure that the new newly created nucleus of carbon (actually the most common isotope of carbon, carbon-12) is stable. If the new nucleus has too much energy, it must either divest itself of any excess kinetic energy that it does not need or eject a particle. As such, in many cases, the two colliding nuclei will fail to stick together, resulting in a very swift ricochet and a continued existence of a quantum singularity. However, if the amount of energy resulting from the collision is exactly right for the new nucleus's natural level, then the conversion of lighter nuclei to heavier nuclei has worked perfectly. This set of conditions is called 'resonance'.

To ensure that the newly formed isotope of carbon-12 does not suffer fission, it has to be in total energy balance with the two contributing isotopes, helium-4 and beryllium-8 and, fortunately, this is the case. However, our newly formed carbon-12 has other potential hazards to overcome.

The carbon-12 molecule has been created by the impact of three helium-4 nuclei. Obviously, there are a lot of these flying around. Therefore, it is logical that our new carbon-12 molecule will collide with another helium-4 alpha particle within a short period of time. When this occurs, and if there was the appropriate resonance, the carbon-12 and helium-4 will fuse into oxygen-16. Now, this is where the whole process seems to be designed to ensure that carbon survives. The nearest oxygen-16 resonance has 1 per cent *less* energy than helium-4 plus carbon-12. But this 1 per cent is all it takes to ensure that resonance does not occur. So, in simple terms, if the oxygen energy level were 1 per cent lower, virtually all the carbon made inside stars would be processed into oxygen and then much of it into heavier elements still. As such, carbon-based life-forms like ourselves would simply not exist.

Indeed, equilibrium and balance affect stars in another crucial way: the equality of electromagnetism and gravity. Bigger stars, those with high mass, throw out heat at such a vast rate that they become 'blue giants'. Smaller stars suffer from the same symptom, heat loss, but because of a different cause. This time it is the responsibility of convection currents. They, in turn, become a star type called 'red dwarfs'. Both these extremes are inherently unstable. Between these two groups is a small area of stellar stability where both electromagnetism and gravity are in balance. If gravity becomes stronger, all stars would be blue giants, and if nature preferred electromagnetism, then the whole universe would be filled with red dwarfs. As we have seen, both options would have excluded life on Earth developing, so, yet again, humanity would not exist.

I have given here only a small number of the many, many facts that suggest that this universe is, in some way, designed for life, consciousness and, ultimately, conscious observers. But are these not simply an error of logic, that we can exist as observers only in a universe that is coincidentally fine-tuned to our evolution? Following on from the theme of water is a popular analogy cited by critics of the cosmological anthropic principle regarding a sentient puddle, used initially by author Douglas Adams in his book *The Salmon of Doubt*.

This is a clever and amusing critique of the seemingly egocentric thinking of advocates of the cosmological anthropic principle. But a moment's reflection will show just how weak this critique is. Our planet is full of millions of holes that can create puddles. Rain falls across vast areas of the globe. Therefore, puddles occur thousands of times a day in countless locations. Each puddle perfectly fits the hole it finds itself in. But what if there was only one puddle on our planet, and our planet was the only one in the universe? The puddle would, quite rightly, consider the chances of it finding itself in the one and only puddle in the universe, to be an amazing coincidence. Why is this of significance? Well, unless we accept the idea of multiverses, this is the *only* universe that has ever evolved. So 'nature' got it exactly right at the first attempt for conscious life to evolve. One fortunate chance occurrence seemingly quite by accident led to another, and then another. At each event, probability becomes stretched until random chance ceases to be a viable option. This is not like evolution. In natural selection, each mutation is one of many mutations available. Only one survives to carry forward the genetic code. Even one chance mutation failing would ensure that humanity and consciousness never took place, and, it seems, consciousness is an essential element regarding the existence of anything. It seems that something had planned for consciousness to evolve.

But why is consciousness so crucial to a seemingly impersonal and, in places, actively hostile universe? Could the answer be simply that the universe needed consciousness to evolve for that consciousness to create the particles that make up the universe?

Wheeler's Delayed-Choice Experiment

We now need to return our attention to the 'measurement problem' discussed earlier. You will recall that experimentation has shown a direct relationship between atoms, molecules and all the subatomic particles that constitute these structures, and the 'act of measurement' or 'observation'. If not observed, these objects are simply a mathematical wave function that has no actual existence. When measured (or observed), this wave function 'collapses' into a particle found in a specific location.

The implications of this 'measurement problem' are profound. If true, then we all create the reality around us by observing it. Suddenly consciousness is central to the creation of the physical world rather than something periphery. The universe needed to evolve self-referential consciousness to bring itself into existence.

If this is correct, how is it that the universe has existed for at least 13.8 billion years? How could consciousness, which evolved around a million years ago, collapse the wave function of matter billions of years ago? Physicist John Archibald Wheeler believed he had the answer. It is all to do with something he called the 'delayed-choice experiment'.

Wheeler was a hugely respected Princeton University cosmologist. He was fascinated by the implications of the Cosmological Anthropic Principle and, in the late 1970s, suggested an even more intriguing version, something he called the Participatory Anthropic Principle (PAP).

By this, he meant that consciousness is somehow responsible for the observed universe that we perceive now and the universe as it was billions of years ago. In other words, the 'act of observation' of a sentient intelligence is responsible for bringing into existence a universe that existed aeons before that intelligence existed. This profoundly questions our concept of time as a linear process, and, even more importantly, actions taking place now can directly affect the past. Being the outstanding theoretician he was, Wheeler suggested an experiment by which the already discussed double-slit phenomenon could be applied to prove his PAP hypothesis.

Wheeler asked us to reconsider an experimental setup for a classic two-slit experiment encountered earlier. He suggested that the experimenters wait until after the photon has passed through the two slits before deciding whether to turn on the special photon detectors.

This is the delayed-choice version of the experiment. We find that when the detectors are not turned on, an interference pattern is registered, and when they are turned on, the interference pattern is lost, and we can determine through which of the two slits the photon emerged.

There are two common explanations for such effects. One is that the choice made by the experimenter causally affects the events that occurred earlier, a phenomenon called *retrocausation* or *retrocausality*. The other explanation is that the choice made by the experimenter occurs in a universe that necessarily matches the earlier events, so that time is always moving forward, in at least two different universes in which different choices are made that match different prior events. Until a choice is made, such an experimental system is said to be in a state of *superposition*.

Some of you may, not unreasonably, consider that the delayed-choice experiment, although interesting, is simply a thought experiment and is therefore of no real importance. But it is far more than this. In February 2007, the academic journal *Science* reported that John Wheeler's delayed-choice thought experiment had been successfully performed in an actual laboratory experiment (Jacques & Roch, 2007).

This incredible experiment proved that photons 'decide' to be a wave or a particle in response to a later decision made by the experimenters. This may also suggest that the underlying intent of the experimenters is more critical in this respect than their actual observations. The French team fired photons at something known as a 'beam splitter'. This is a 'half-silvered mirror'. In effect, this mirror splits the photon beam in two, sending one group of photons in one direction and the rest in another. The first group of photons were reflected in the direction of a second beam splitter located 50 metres (164 ft) away. The second beam splitter was attached to a computer that switched it off or on in a random fashion. If it was turned on, it recombined the split waves and sent them to a detector. The resulting interference pattern was what would be expected if the particles were acting as waves. The experiment also had a second detector. However, when the second beam splitter was switched off, both detectors showed a pattern known to be created by particles. When counted, it was shown that an equal number of particles were hitting each detector. This showed that, as each individual particle could not have been split, the light taking *both* paths was in particle form from the start of the experiment. This means that the beam had decided whether to behave as a particle or a wave for its full journey not at the start but when the 'observer' (system) decided later.

Here is experimental proof that the 'observer effect' is not time-dependent. The act of observation creating our reality can be applied to the deep past, a past that did not contain sentient beings. This can be used to suggest that the universe at its inception needed to evolve consciousness to bring itself into existence. So if the universe is integrally linked to a conscious observer, then what is the 'observed universe' actually created from? Is it really out there in three-dimensional space, or is it simply another aspect of consciousness?

Wheeler first presented his 'thought experiment' in 1978. Five years later, in 1983, he turned this into a truly stellar, or more literally, quasar, version of the double-slit experiment. He suggested that the tool to use would be a known cosmological phenomenon known as gravitational lensing.

In 1959 Cyril Hazard of the Parkes Radio Telescope in Australia had discovered a radio source emitting vast amounts of energy. When optical telescopes finally viewed the source, they found not a galaxy but a star-like object. This was named '3C 273'. Later calculations showed that this object was over 4 trillion times brighter than the sun. By the early 1960s, hundreds of these objects had been discovered. They were initially described as 'quasi-stellar radio sources' which, in 1964 at the suggestion of Chinese-American astrophysicist Hong-Yee Chiu, was shortened to 'quasar'. When looked at with light telescopes, it was discovered that some of these objects were in groups of two or four light sources.

In 1979 an astounding discovery was made. These seemingly multiple quasars were actually a single quasar whose light had been bent in such a way that it created an illusion of multiplicity. This observation proved a relativity-related phenomenon that Albert Einstein had first suggested in April 1912. In an obscure academic paper, Einstein suggested that light beams would be bent by any very large gravitational source such as a galaxy. According to relativity theory, the space around a galaxy will be literally warped by the galaxy's gravitational field. Any light passing by would have to follow a deflected course as it negotiates its way through the depression space-time. In practice, this means that any light source located in a direct line from Earth with a galaxy between Earth and the source would have its light bent around the galaxy. This was precisely the effect being observed by the astronomers. Gravitational lensing was real. And it was this phenomenon that Wheeler believed could be used to prove that the act of observation creates everything, including events in the distant past.

Wheeler's thought experiment has a group of Earth-based astronomers decide to observe the quasars. In this case, a telescope plays the role of the photon detector in the two-slit experiment. If the astronomers point a telescope in the direction of one of the two intervening galaxies, they will see photons from the quasar deflected by that galaxy. They would also get the same result by looking at the other galaxy. By carefully arranging mirrors, the astronomers could make photons arriving from the routes around both galaxies strike a piece of photographic film. Alternating light and dark bands would appear on the film, identical to the pattern found when photons passed through the two slits.

Here's the odd part. The quasar could be very distant from Earth, with light so faint that its photons hit the piece of film only one at a time. But the results of the experiment wouldn't change. The striped pattern would still show up, meaning that a lone photon not observed by the telescope travelled both paths towards Earth, even if many light-years separated those paths. And that's not all.

By the time the astronomers decide which measurement to make – whether to pin down the photon to one definite route or to have it follow both paths simultaneously – the photon could have already journeyed for billions of years, long before life appeared on Earth. The measurements made now, says Wheeler, determine the photon's past. In one case, the astronomers create a history in which a photon took both possible routes from the quasar to Earth. Alternatively, they retroactively force the photon onto one straight trail towards their detector, even though the photon began its jaunt long before any detectors existed.

Wheeler's idea that time was not relevant to how an act of observation collapses a wave function was experimentally proven by physicists at the École Normale Supérieure de Cachan in 2007. This showed that photons 'decide' to be a wave or a particle in response to a later decision made by the experimenters. This may also suggest that the underlying intent of the experimenters is more important in this respect than their actual observations. The French team fired photons at a beam splitter. The first group of photons were reflected in the direction of a second beam splitter located 50 metres (164 ft) away. The second beam splitter was attached to a computer which in a totally random fashion switched it off or on. If it was turned on, it recombined the split waves and sent them to a detector. The resulting interference pattern was what would be expected if the particles were acting as waves. The experiment also had a second detector. However, when the second beam splitter was switched off, both detectors showed a pattern created by particles. When counted, it was shown that an equal number of particles were hitting each detector. This showed that, as each individual particle could not have been split, the light taking *both* paths was in particle form from the start of the experiment. This means that the beam had decided whether to behave as a particle or a wave for its full journey, not at the start but when the 'observer' (system) decided later.

Here is experimental proof that the 'observer effect' is not time-dependent. The act of observation creating our reality can be applied to the deep past, a past that did not contain sentient beings. This can be used to suggest that the universe at its inception needed to evolve consciousness to bring itself into existence. So if the universe is integrally linked to a conscious observer, then what is the 'observed universe' actually created from? Is it really out there in three-dimensional space, or is it simply another aspect of consciousness?

Another possibility regarding Wheeler's delayed-choice experiment is that we misunderstand what time actually is. Or, more importantly, what we understand to be with regard to the flow of time. Earlier, you will recall that we discussed how Scottish physicist James Clerk Maxwell discovered that electricity and magnetism were physical manifestations of the same underlying phenomenon. This became known, not unsurprisingly, as electromagnetism and that electromagnetism had wave-like qualities. In 1862 Maxwell had applied a series of equations describing the propagation of waves to both magnetic waves and electrical waves through space. He discovered that both phenomena travelled at precisely the speed of light. This suggested to him that light, electricity and magnetism were all related in some way. In 1864 he announced his discovery that 'light is an electromagnetic disturbance propagated through the field according to electromagnetic laws' (Maxwell, 1864).

This is all quite well known. What is less known is that Maxwell's equations for electromagnetism had two solutions describing two different types of electromagnetic waves: retarded waves, which are the ones we experience, and advanced waves, which travel backwards in time from target to source. Yes, you did read that correctly, light waves that travel *backwards* in time. Because this is so in conflict with our present model of science, this curious anomaly has simply been ignored and is usually omitted from nearly all forms of scientific education. But some scientists have argued that advanced waves and their reversal of time-flow actually exist. Not surprisingly, one of these scientists was John Wheeler, and another was one of Wheeler's graduate students, Richard Feynman, whose extraordinary 'sum over histories' model we also encountered earlier.

Feynman suggested that the reality of advanced waves could explain a real issue regarding a central part of quantum theory, the emission of light photons by an electron. According to the conservation of energy laws, when this happens, there should be a recoil reaction similar to what happens when a gun fires a bullet. But this does not occur. In attempting an explanation, Wheeler and Feynman proposed that not one but two photons are produced at the instant of ejection: an 'advanced' photon and a 'retarded' photon. The 'advanced' photon travels backwards in time, while the 'retarded' photon shares our timeline moving forward. Each photon would have half the energy of the one observed. In doing so, the laws of the conservation of energy are followed. This has become known as the Wheeler-Feynman absorber theory.

But if this model is true, then we have two forms of electromagnetic energy, one going forward in time and one going backwards. And this is exactly what physicist John Cramer argues in his intriguing Transactional Interpretation of Quantum Physics.

John Cramer's Transactional Interpretation

John G. Cramer, a professor of physics at the University of Washington, first introduced his intriguing solution to the observed interference patterns in a paper published in the *Review of Modern Physics* in January 1986 and followed this up with several subsequent papers.

Cramer explains the interference patterns observed in the twin slit experiment by forwards-in-time particles encountering backwards-in-time particles coming in the opposite temporal direction. He suggested that waves travelling forward in time, known as retarded waves, make up our observed universe. However, there are other waves that travel backwards in time. He calls these advanced waves. Because of how our perception of time functions, we only ever perceive what is known as 'now', that instant in which the future becomes the past. It is only at this shrinkingly tiny sliver of time that the advanced waves show themselves to us by interfering with the retarded waves travelling in the other direction. We can easily perceive retarded waves because they continue with us as we travel forward in time.

As an analogy, imagine travelling on a train with another track running parallel. If a train running in the same direction starts to go past your train at a slightly faster speed, you will, by looking out the window, have it in view for a considerable amount of time. If the second train slows down to match the speed of your train, your view of the other train will become subjectively static. Both trains will be concurrently sharing the same general location in space (and time). However, imagine that the second track has trains running in the other direction. In this scenario, the two trains will encounter each other for only a very short time. You may be looking out of the window as the other train thunders past, and it will be in view for only a second or so.

This is how it is with time. On our temporal railway, objects that share our overall speed-through-time will remain in our perceptions continually. This is why the observed world remains consistent for us. Everything that we can observe in this universe must be travelling with us. Even travelling a micro-second faster will place an object outside of our perception. It will be perceived as simply being there for a tiny amount of time and then disappearing as if into thin air. Indeed many subatomic particles do this constantly. From our point of view, they seem to flit in and out of reality in a flash. This does not mean they cease to exist; they simply move outside of our temporal frame of reference.

Now imagine the shared timeframe of an observer and a particle travelling backwards in time. This will be like two trains travelling in different directions at virtually infinite speed. The amount of 'time' they will share as they encounter each other will be 10^{-43} of a second, the smallest amount of time that physicists believe can exist. Any other quantity of time will be too large. This is known as 'Planck time', and we will encounter it again later in our enquiry.

So is the reality that is presented to us by our senses actually an interference pattern created by the interaction of retarded and advanced waves? This is an intriguing idea and supports another hypothesis that we will discuss later; that our phenomenal world is holographic in nature.

M-Brane Theory

One of the major mysteries of the Big Bang is when time was created. To overcome this problem, Paul Steinhardt of Princeton University and Neil Turok of the University of Cambridge propose a scenario in which time did not start at the Big Bang because all that happened was that the Big Bang was just one of many cosmological cycles.[6]

To really understand Steinhardt and Turok's model, we need to go back to our school days and some basic geometry and remember what we mean by the dimensions of space. Look around you. You are surrounded on all sides by space – that is, an area or arena whereby other objects can be perceived. Space stretches out in all directions. But what is it? Well, firstly, we have to define it. We can imagine space as being a receptacle that contains everything, like a huge box. Of course, from our knowledge of the Big Bang, we know that space is actually the inside area of a huge, ever-expanding, sphere; a sphere that has been expanding like an inflating balloon for 13.8 billion years. But for the moment, let us imagine it to be a box, a vast container with height, width and depth. The best way to imagine this is to visualize a point. Extend that point out in one direction, and you get a line. This gives you width. Then, at right angles to the line and at the start and finish of the line, extend out two other lines. This will give you height. Now join the ends of the two new lines by creating a mirror line like the first one. You have created, in effect, a square. This is two-dimensional in that it has height and width. Now, if you follow the same procedure from the four corners, moving out at right angles again, you end up with depth as well as height and width. You now have three dimensions, and you have created a box. So, to recap, one dimension is a line, two dimensions is a square, and three dimensions is a cube. These are the three dimensions known to geometricians since ancient times. In the early part of the last century, Albert Einstein added a fourth dimension, time.

As the cube moves through space, it needs time to do so. Objects in space, therefore, exist in four dimensions. But why only four? What would our cube look like to a consciousness observing our four dimensions from a fifth dimension, effectively from outside of space-time? There was an attempt to do this in the film *Interstellar* where the central character, Cooper, finds himself in what the director, Christopher Nolan, called 'the Tesseract'. This choice of term is quite precise. A tesseract is the technical name for a hypercube, a cube in which all the intersecting points have another projection at right angles – in effect following the process described above into the fifth dimension.

So, returning to Steinhardt and Turok's model, they envisage a number of extra dimensions of space and time. Our perceived universe is actually a 3D sheet that they call a 'membrane', usually shortened to a 'brane'. This brane is floating in four-dimensional space. Floating nearby is another 3D brane with different physics. These branes can affect each other and sometimes collide. When they do, our brane heats up to 1,023 kelvin. This is 1,023 degrees above absolute zero. Some of this energy condenses into matter. From our point of view, within our brane, it will seem like a Big Bang.

There can be a limitless number of 'membranes', each containing a differently evolved universe. In effect, this means that countless alternate universes are surrounding us at all times, like incredibly thin layers of an onion. The question is, can these other 'universes' be accessed during dreams, out-of-body experiences, near-death experiences or when experiencing the effects of entheogens and psychedelics?

In which case, the communication channel may be the brain, the organ that manifests consciousness within this 'brane'. To make an awful pun, this could be described as a 'brane from brain' theory. Indeed, could it be that by 'downloading' information from brane to brain is how we collapse the wave function of our own personal reality? In my last book, *The Hidden Universe: An Investigation into Non-Human Intelligences*, I proposed a model called the Egregorial Hypothesis. In this, I suggested that each of us, as an observer, individually collapses the wave function of our own universe. Then, by linking in with other minds, we collectively create a much broader sensual universe. This is known as 'consensual reality'. I refined this and called it the 'egregorial' – a reality that we collectively create continually. Is this possible?

Egregorions

As we discussed earlier, how can it be that mathematics, which is, after all, a creation of the human mind, be applicable across the whole known universe? Furthermore, could it be that the anticipation of discovering a subatomic particle actually brings that particle into existence? That our science creates the universe around it by thinking about it? This is not so weird as it sounds. Throughout history, scientists have come up with bizarre theories that subsequently proved to be true. Indeed, after the discovery of the muon in 1936, Isador Isaac Rabi exclaimed, 'Who ordered that?' I would like to call these mind-created particles 'egregorions'.

I would like to propose that these 'discoveries' can be presented as robust evidence for the Anthropic Cosmological Principle and suggestive that consciousness actually 'creates' reality.

American-based Swedish quantum physicist Max Tegmark, whose work has been and will continue to be referenced in this book, is fascinated by the way in which what is in essence a human-created abstraction, mathematics, can be used to explain the deeper workings of the universe. In his 2014 book *Our Mathematical Universe: My Quest for the Ultimate Nature of Reality*, Tegmark asks some really profound questions about this relationship.

This book had as its source the February 2008 paper Tegmark wrote entitled 'The Mathematical Universe', published in the journal *Foundations of Physics* (Vol. 38, Issue 2, pp. 101–150). It was his response to a long-standing personal issue with the 'observer' implications of the collapse of the wave function, as suggested by Copenhagen. Tegmark is keen to prove that the external world exists independently of any observers. The only actual reality are mathematical structures, and all structures that exist mathematically exist physically as well. He points out that maths seems to be a human creation, yet it also exists independently.

Historically there are also many incidents whereby theoretical mathematicians have arguably created a theory simply for the fun of it. This piece of theoretical doodling is subsequently discovered to be of profound importance in our understanding of how nature actually works. For example, Einstein himself was to add something called the 'cosmological constant' to his own equations, something he considered to be needed to counterbalance the effects of gravity in order to achieve a static universe. He was later to describe to fellow physicist George Gamow that this was his 'biggest blunder'. Intriguingly, what Einstein considered to be a fudge to make his figures work is now known to be an integral part of the mathematical structure of the universe. How can this be?

This concept that mathematics would exist even if humans had never evolved is known as Radical Platonism and has its roots in ancient Greek philosophy. And, as has been described above, this is the position taken by Max Tegmark.

Tegmark calls his updating of this idea the Mathematical Universe Hypothesis (MUH). He argues that all the physical properties of a subatomic particle, such as an electron, are described mathematically; therefore, as far as he is concerned, an electron is a mathematical structure, a 'pattern in space-time'. Now, this is where it gets very interèsting. Subatomic particles cannot be observed directly. For example, we can see the trails they leave in cloud chambers, but these are no more the subatomic particle than a vapour trail in a clear summer sky is an aircraft. It is just evidence of where the aircraft has been. These particles are described by mathematics. Tegmark makes a logical jump to state that these objects *are* mathematics, not just described by mathematics. Without the maths, they would not exist. He then goes further, pointing out that everything in the physical universe, including the human body and its brain, are simply structures made out of subatomic particles. We too, are all just 'patterns in space-time'.

Of course, if self-referential consciousness is simply an epiphenomenon of brain processes, then it too is simply a mathematical structure. In this regard, Tegmark states in his paper 'On Math, Matter and Mind':

> I think that consciousness is the way information feels when being processed in certain complex ways.
>
> Tegmark, Hut & Alford, 2006

Tegmark calls embodied consciousnesses within this model 'self-aware substructures'. He argues that if the mathematical structure is sufficiently complex, then self-awareness will somehow appear out of nowhere (presumably the same place that all the 'matter' appeared from in the Big Bang) or where virtual particles flit in and out of existence from. He calls these units of consciousness 'self-aware substructures' (SASs). As he states in the paper, these entities:

> . . . will subjectively perceive themselves as existing in a physically 'real' world.
>
> Tegmark, Hut & Alford, 2006

This can be referred straight back to the theory of the Platonic Forms, the abstract mathematical structures that exist outside of space and time and create imperfect reflections of themselves in 'reality'. This states that nothing really exists but these structures. This is known as ontic structural materialism. *Ontic* means a statement about an entity, and ontological is a statement concerning the being of such entities. This is a scientific application of the philosophy of Martin Heidegger, something we discussed earlier.

On a number of occasions in our enquiry, we have acknowledged that according to modern quantum mechanics, particles, be they electrons, photons, atoms or molecules, have no actual reality before they are observed. They are statistical abstractions. These exist in a sea of forces which in themselves have no existence other than their effects upon these statistical abstractions. In his book *Alien Information Theory: Psychedelic Drug Technologies and the Cosmic Game* (2019), Andrew Gallimore adds to this mystery by explaining that electrons, and all other elementary particles, have no actual size or volume. They are literally 'point particles' in that they will remain a point in space however much you zoom in on them. The only actual properties they have are four abstract mathematical concepts known as quantum numbers. These numbers define the particle's energy level (N), its angular momentum (L), the direction of the angular momentum (M-L) and its spin (M-S). That is it: the particle is just a point in space tagged with a set of values. As Gallimore states:

> . . . a particle is not an object, but only the information generated by its particular arrangement of quantum numbers … And, since, of course, all matter is composed of these particles, this means that all matter can be defined by a finite amount of information. In fact, everything within the Universe is nothing more than quantized – digital – information.
>
> Gallimore, 2019, p. 19

Of course, one can reasonably argue that subatomic particles come together to create the seemingly solid universe of our experience. Tables and chairs, planets and stars seem very solid and real. At the subatomic level, that they may disappear into a haze of mathematical abstractions is of intellectual interest but has no bearing on our everyday lives. To all intents and purposes, these things exist. If I am hit by a car, I may break a limb or even die. That the car is ultimately created out of the four quantum numbers is of no real consequence, and my injuries are real and painful. But are they? What exactly is 'real', and what is pain? I 'feel' the pain, and I 'see' the car. I smell the odour of burned rubber. But all these are simply sensations created by my brain. They have no actual existence other than my sensing of them. At this point, we can return to the ideas of the great philosophers we discussed earlier. From Berkeley to Kant and from Husserl to Heidegger, they all argued that what seems like a real, solid universe is created out of 'mind stuff'. So, is this simply an intellectual exercise for philosophers, or is it really true? Well, modern neurology suggests that it is.

PROOF FROM NEUROLOGY
Introduction

One of my major weaknesses is that I have a very sweet tooth. I just love the taste of table sugar, or, to be more precise, sucrose. I keep myself going by regular cups of sweet coffee and tea. Sucrose adds a very distinct flavouring to these drinks. I also put sucrose on my breakfast cereal, so I am very aware of what sucrose tastes like. But where, exactly is that flavour?

Let us break the sucrose down into its component parts. You will recall that all physical objects are made up of tiny objects known as atoms. Elements such as hydrogen and oxygen are made up of just one sort of atom. More complex substances, known as compounds, are made up of two or more different elemental atoms, which come together in tiny structures known as molecules. Sucrose is a compound of billions of identical molecules. Each of these contains 12 carbon atoms, 22 hydrogen atoms and 11 oxygen atoms. This is written as $C_{12}H_{22}O_{11}$.

Hydrogen, the major component of the sucrose molecule, has no taste or smell. Similarly, oxygen is odourless and tasteless. When two hydrogen atoms come together with one oxygen atom, they create the incredible compound we have discussed extensively – water. At room temperature these elements magically create water. In effect, two gasses suddenly turn into a liquid. As you will know, pure water has no taste or smell. Not surprising because neither oxygen nor hydrogen has this quality. Put an additional 20 atoms of hydrogen into the structure together with ten more oxygen atoms, and you create an organic chemical bicyclohexyl, also known as dicyclohexyl or bicyclohexane $(C_{12}H_{22})$. As far as I can ascertain, bicyclohexyl is tasteless and odourless. If we add the 12 carbon atoms, we create sucrose. Carbon is another tasteless and odourless element. So why do I taste anything, let alone the sweet taste of sucrose? Why, if I add this amalgamation of tasteless elements to my cup of coffee, does it taste sweet? In no way can the various atoms or their configuration within the sucrose molecule bring about the taste of sucrose.

In his fascinating 2019 book *The Case Against Reality*, Dr Donald D. Hoffman, Professor of Cognitive Sciences at the University of California, Irvine, makes an even more effective case than I do. He points out that a particular red berry known as *Richadella dulcifica* contains a fascinating molecule called miraculin. This does something very peculiar with regard to how we taste certain flavours. For example, if you eat this berry, then lemons and other sour foods taste sweet. Normally a lemon has a strong sour taste, but miraculin changes this to the complete opposite. Hoffman explains that the generally accepted scientific position is that the veridical – that is, the objective reality of the taste – is exclusively in the lemon. If a person subjectively tastes something different, then their perception is in error. But as Hoffman quite rightly observes:

> Which taste is illusory? The veridical-perception theory
> says it's the taste that's not veridical, that's not objectively

true. So, what is the veridical taste of a molecule of citric acid? If we say it is sour, what is the ground for this claim? What principle requires a particular molecule to truly be a particular taste? The burden is on the veridical theorist to provide a scientific justification. None has been offered. Any claim of veridicality for any taste is, for now, thoroughly implausible.

Hoffman, 2019, p. 89

The same goes for visual information. We have already discussed in great detail the mystery of light as part of the electromagnetic spectrum. We know that it consists of tiny particles known as photons and that depending upon whether they are 'observed' (measured) or not, will have them perceived as waves or point particles. When I use the word *observed* here, I am effectively describing the process of vision, the way in which the brain recreates the outside world inside your head and presents that image to your consciousness.

Most people assume that the eyes act as a pair of cine cameras that 'photograph' external reality and present these images to our consciousness, which is sitting in a form of cinema in our head. How far away this description is from what actually takes place is astounding. Approximately one-third of the human brain's cortex is involved in creating our visual world. This is a massive amount of processing power. Cine cameras have been recording moving images for over 100 years, more than a century before any form of computing power was available, and as Hoffman states, whatever is going on in the brain during vision processing is far more complex than simply what happens in a cine camera, or even a video camera. The process taking place in the brain involves not the recreation of moving images but the digital processing of the trillions of photon impacts on the retina. As Hoffman states, each eye has around 130 million photoreceptors, and each one does one thing: it records how many photons of light it has just captured. He makes his point with powerful elegance:

There are, at the photoreceptors of the eye, no luscious apples and no dazzling waterfalls. There is just a stupefying array of numbers, with no obvious meaning. To endow this hill of beans with meaning, to understand what these lifeless numbers say about a living world, is such a daunting task that billions of neurons, including many millions within the eye itself, are conscripted into service. It's not like translating Greek to English. It's more like detective work: the numbers are cryptic clues, and the brain must sleuth like Sherlock.

Hoffman, 2019, p. 41

I would like to argue that it is even more complex than Hoffman states. Earlier, we discussed how light has a direct relationship with the 'observer'. If the light is unobserved, it is a wave, and if it is observed, it is a particle. Indeed, when unobserved, light, like any other physical presence in the phenomenal world, doesn't really exist except as a potential. It is a statistical wave with no actual reality. In a very real sense, we bring the phenomenal world into existence by looking at it. But without light, in either form, we have no way of 'seeing' the external world. And light is even stranger than we can possibly imagine. For example, a photon can only ever travel at the speed of light. This means, from its point of view, there is no time. This is because, according to Einstein's theories, at the speed of light, time stops. But if there is no time from the viewpoint of the photon, how does it manage to travel anywhere? It needs time to move from one location to another.

Furthermore, if time does not exist for a photon, this means that everything happens in a continual 'now'. For it, there is no past, present or future. For example, if you look through a telescope at the Andromeda Galaxy, located 2.5 million light-years away, your retina is being stimulated by light photons that left the galaxy millions of years ago. But for them, the leaving of the galaxy and encountering your retina are simultaneous events happening in the same instant. For the photons, your retina and the stars in the Andromeda Galaxy occupy precisely the same location in space and time.

This relationship between vision and time perception is a crucially important one concerning our enquiry. One of the most revolutionary thinkers in this area is the British mathematical physicist Julian Barbour. His model, discussed in his books *The End of Time: The Next Revolution in Physics* and *The Janus Point: A New Theory of Time*, has profoundly influenced my own ideas on time and is central to the hypothesis being expounded in this book.

In his 1999 book, *The End of Time*, Barbour introduced his concept of Platonia, a location outside of space and time which will echo with those of you already intrigued by the philosophical ideas of Plato and his followers, discussed much earlier in this book.

Barbour argues that time is an illusion and that the universe is, in reality, timeless. His theory is somewhat complex, but in essence he suggests a universe similar to Hugh Everett's 'Many-Worlds' encountered earlier, but with one crucial difference; for Barbour, the universe splits not into an identical copy of itself at each quantum event but only into a probability in the same way that Schrödinger's cat has an equal probability of being alive or dead.

As particles exist in a mist of probability before they are observed, so it is for Barbour's idea of outcomes. Actual events are more likely to take place where the 'probability mist' is at its densest. Some 'nows' have a higher probability of taking place in the same way that the chance of finding a subatomic particle in a particular place is higher, where the likelihood of that particle being found in that location is higher. In Platonia, the 'nows' that are experienced are the ones with the higher probabilities. Barbour acknowledges that this is counter to our everyday experience. For example, in this model, what happens to history, both our personal history and the history of mankind in general? He calls these perceived histories 'time capsules', 'a set of mutually consistent records that suggest we have a past'.

Barbour argues that these 'time capsules' exist within our own minds and have no objective reality. These records exist now, not in the past.

We all live in an ongoing present. On first encountering Barbour's proposition, it seems easy to disprove by simple observation. If time does not exist, then how is it that we perceive motion? After all, motion can only exist in time. At one point in time, an object is in one position. Then it moves to be found in another position at a later point in time. However, he shows in a reasonably convincing way that motion may not exist external to our perception.

Barbour argues that time is just a large collection of 'nows', the physical events as they occur. These 'nows' are just piled in a big heap from which they emerge one by one as determined by some probabilistic rules. The idea that there ever was a past results from the occurrence of 'nows' that contain references to a past, but no such past exists. Neither does the future. Nor, according to this approach, does time exist as an actual reality. Indeed, earlier, we discussed in some detail John Wheeler's delayed-choice experiment and how this can be used to show that even events in the distant past can be brought into an existing 'now' by the act of observation of a conscious mind. But if time itself is part of the illusion, then no 'now' has precedence over any other 'now'. There is no cause and effect, no before and after. Just the present moment frozen in time and space.

It is important to realize that what we 'see' is a light-stimulated image on our retina. Within this statement, the critical term is 'image', a singular image like a photograph. We perceive motion in precisely the same way that cinema film gives the illusion of movement. A series of static images are flashed across the field of vision at such a speed that they 'fuse' into a single image. This single image has a duration in time which gives an illusion of motion. However, it must be stressed that it is precisely that, an illusion. A series of static images are perceived as a single moving image. The retina works in the same way. The preceding images are held in the brain and superimposed upon the next image.

As Barbour explains:

> I suggest that the brain in any instant always contains,
> as it were, several stills of a movie. They correspond to

different positions of objects we think we see moving. The idea is that it is this collection of 'stills', all present in any one instant, that stands in psychophysical parallel with the motion we actually see. The brain 'plays' the movie for us, rather as an orchestra plays notes on the score.

Barbour, 2000, p. 28

This is supported by a case cited by the neurologist V. Ramachandran. A woman he identifies as 'Ingrid' suffered bilateral damage to an area of her brain called the middle temporal area. Her eyesight was fine as long as the object she was looking at remained stationary. However, as soon as the object began to move, she would perceive it as if a strobe light was illuminating it. She was, as Ramachandran describes it, 'motion blind':

> She said that talking to someone in person felt like talking on the phone because she couldn't see the changing facial expressions associated with normal conversation. Even pouring a cup of coffee was an ordeal because the liquid would inevitably overflow and spill on the floor. She never knew when to slow down, changing the angle of the coffee-pot, because she couldn't estimate how fast the liquid was rising in the cup.
>
> Ramachandran & Blakeslee, 1998, p. 72

And this is where physics and neurology begin to overlap. We have already discovered that the act of observation has a direct influence on subatomic particles. But could there be more to this than, quite literally, meets the eye? Could the observer modulate the phenomenal world of experience and its source outside of either mind or matter?

For example, perceptions such as the Zeitraffer phenomenon are a total mystery to neurologists or perception scientists. But if the visual world, and its associated other sensory fields, are within rather than outside of the brain, and if all time is a unique series of quantized 'nows', then, by applying implications from Barbour's model, we can create a much broader explanatory framework. So let's look at this group of sensory mysteries in greater detail.

Zeitraffer Phenomenon

One of the world's major researchers exploring the neurology of time perception is Stanford University's David Eagleman. Whilst working at Baylor College in Houston, Texas, in 2007, he conducted a series of experiments involving volunteers experiencing a form of extreme sport known as Suspended Catch Air Device Diving (SCAD). This process dropped the volunteers 150 feet into a catch net. Of crucial significance regarding the theme of this book, all of the volunteers reported that as they were falling, their sense of subjective time duration slowed down (Stetson, Fiesta & Eagleman, 2007). Eagleman et al. announced that this proved that objective time did not change and that it was a neurological effect. Indeed this also seems to prove that any extremely stressful situation will facilitate a subjective slowing down of time, and dying is probably the most stressful scenario imaginable. So, the question has to be, why have we evolved to have such a perception? If it is entirely subjective, then what evolutionary advantage does it give? The person does not objectively move any quicker, so evasive action to avoid danger will be no more effective because the body will move only at 'normal' speed.

If the brain can slow down subjective time perception under certain neurological conditions, can it also speed it up? This suggests that what we consider perceptual reality is more like a recording that we are experiencing than something that objectively exists outside of us. In German, a *Zeitraffer* is an apparatus that can accelerate or slow down the speed by which the individual frames of a cine film are processed. Significantly this apparatus has given its name to a neurologically induced perceptual anomaly, first reported by Ferdinand Binkofski of the Department of Neurology of the Heinrich Heine University in

Germany and Richard A. Block of the Department of Psychology at Montana State University (Binkofski & Block, 1992).

Binkofski and Block report that a right-handed, 66-year-old retired clerk with no history of neurological disease was driving his car along a German road. The man (known as BW) was horrified to discover that suddenly external objects started rushing towards him at great speed. As he described it, it was as if somebody had pressed a fast-forward button. He also found that his car was also running at a fantastic speed. He could not control the vehicle because his reaction time remained 'normal'. He found himself driving through a set of red traffic lights because he simply could not stop. He slammed on his brakes and stopped the car. He watched in horror as the world around him moved at super speed.

This state continued for him, and two days later, in a state of great stress, BW was admitted to the Heinrich Heine Neurological Hospital. He described what was happening as an 'accelerated motion of events, like a time-lapse film'. He complained that he could no longer tolerate watching television because the progression of events was too quick for him to follow. He also described that life had begun to pass too quickly for him.

On his admission to the hospital, a CT scan showed a lesion on his dorsolateral prefrontal cortex. He was then given a series of tests. He showed no problem with time orientation. However, when asked to decide how long a 60-second period was for him, some strange things were discovered. BW was told to say when he wished to start and then remain silent until he felt that a minute had gone by. At that point, he was to say 'stop'. The test was repeated many times, and BW's subjective average 'minute' was 286 seconds.

It was then discovered that BW had a glioblastoma tumour centred in a 'Brodmann area' in the prefrontal cortex of his left hemisphere. Sadly, he died soon after without ever regaining normal time perception.

What is intriguing about this paper is that the two scientists suggest some interesting possible explanations, including the idea that we all have an internal 'pacemaker' which controls how we subjectively perceive time duration. However, they finish off by writing, 'It is unclear how best to explain the phenomenon'. In recognition of the similarities with the speeding up of film frame-rate, this illness is known as the Zeitraffer-Erlebnis Effect.

The first report of subjective perceptions of accelerated motion was reported in Germany in 1919 (Tonkonogy & Puente, 2009), and several cases have been reported since. In 1959 neurosurgeon Wilder Penfield and his associate S. Mullan recorded three instances, including one patient who described their sensory world as being like 'a movie going slow motion' (Mullan & Penfield, 1959).

Fred Ovsiew of the Feinberg School of Medicine in Chicago reported a case in 2014 in which a 39-year-old man described that while in the shower, he perceived the water droplets suddenly 'hanging in mid-air'. He likened this to the way the bullets travelled in the *Matrix* films. He was diagnosed with a hematoma in his right temporal lobe and subsequently developed temporal lobe epilepsy (TLE) (Ovsiew, 2014).

A closely related neurological condition to Zeitraffer-Erlebnis is akinetopsia, which is a defective perception of moving objects. This has the patient see objects as being freeze-framed or jumping from one location to another as if some frames were missing (Cooper, et al., 2010). This is believed to be caused by damage to cells in an area of the brain known as the extrastriate visual cortex (area V5) (Anderson, Holliday, Singh & Harding, 1996).

There seems to be a clear link here between electrical impulses in the brain and perception, both visual and aural. It appears that when disrupted, the brain's ability to process the data being presented to it through the senses, is compromised and a somewhat different reality appears.

The link here to temporal lobe epilepsy and associated issues brought about by strokes is of extreme importance. I have focused on TLE as a facilitator of NDE-like experiences in non-near-death situations in my various books. I have presented these cases as robust neurological evidence for my Cheating the Ferryman hypothesis (Peake, 2006;

Opening the Doors of Perception: The Key to Cosmic Awareness, 2016). I believe that there is compelling evidence that the 'doors of perception' are opened by such conditions. I would now like to present this evidence.

Temporal Lobe Epilepsy and Strokes

As we have discovered several times in our discussions on the physics of time, there is something of great significance regarding our overall enquiry into the true nature of perceived reality. I use the word 'perceived' here quite deliberately because time, or more accurately, time flow, is, in a very real sense, a perception processed by consciousness rather than an objective something that exists outside of our awareness of it. Time changes its duration depending upon our mood. An example of this is the famous quip made by Albert Einstein reported in the *New York Times* in March 1929:

> When you sit with a nice girl for two hours you think it's
> only a minute, but when you sit on a hot stove for a minute
> you think it's two hours. That's relativity.[7]

By this, Einstein meant that time duration is *relative* to a person's internal processing of the passing of time. But it is more complex than this. The brain does the processing in question. If the brain becomes damaged somehow, this inner perception seems to impose itself on the visual and auditory signals being received from external 'reality'.

As we discovered earlier, British mathematician Julian Barbour, in his ground-breaking book *The End of Time*, suggested that time is not at all as it seems to be when presented to our consciousness via the visual system. In support of this, there is growing evidence from quantum physics suggesting time may be quantized in the same way that matter and energy are.

An important example was a little-recorded case of a German woman admitted to a hospital in the early 1980s. She was suffering from a severe headache and nausea, and, on examination, it was discovered that she had suffered a stroke in her visual cortex, specifically an area known as MT. Her ability to perceive movement had been badly impaired. The consultants involved subsequently wrote a paper describing what she was perceiving:

> She had difficulty, for example, in pouring tea or coffee into a cup because the fluid appeared to be frozen, like a glacier. In addition, she could not stop pouring at the right time since she was unable to perceive the movement in the cup (or a pot) when the fluid rose. Furthermore, the patient complained of difficulties in following a dialogue because she could not see the movements of the face and, especially, the mouth of the speaker. In a room where more than two other people were walking she felt very insecure and unwell, and usually left the room immediately, because 'people were suddenly here or there but I have not seen them moving...'. She could not cross the street because of her inability to judge the speed of a car, but she could identify the car itself without difficulty. 'When I'm looking at the car first, it seems far away. But then, when I want to cross the road, suddenly the car is very near'. She gradually learned to 'estimate' the distance of moving vehicles by means of the sound becoming louder.
>
> Zihl, von Cramon & Mai, 1983

This is significant because it can be directly related to an incident I have described a number of times over the last two decades, one that directly relates to the subject matter of this book.

One afternoon in early 2000, I received an unexpected phone call from a recruitment agent – we'll call her 'Margaret' – who wanted to discuss a vacancy she was handling. She asked me whether I was working, and I explained that I was driven to write a book. 'What about?' she asked. 'I don't really know at the moment,' I truthfully responded. I then explained that I was reading a good deal about temporal lobe epilepsy (TLE) and was making some fascinating links.

She became somewhat reticent and suggested that we should meet up to discuss the vacancy. Three days later, I met her at a coffee shop nearby. As soon as she had sat down, she explained that she had to meet me because she wished to discuss something she could not mention in her office where she would have been overheard.

Margaret informed me that she had recently been diagnosed as having temporal lobe epilepsy. She described to me how she had first discovered that something unusual was happening in her brain.

She had been having lunch with a work associate in a crowded café. As her associate started to pour a cup of tea from a teapot, she suddenly felt a snap over her right ear. Surprised by this, she looked at her associate, assuming that she too would have heard the noise. One look told her that her lunch companion had heard nothing. This was because she had stopped moving. The stunned recruitment consultant looked around the café, and every person was frozen in time and space. It was as if she had suddenly found herself in a three-dimensional photograph. She could hear a low humming sound that seemed all around her. She then looked back at her companion to notice that she was not frozen at all; she was moving incredibly slowly.

Margaret then realized that the low hum she could hear was, in fact, people's voices! Her metabolic rate had increased to such an extent that time had slowed down to a crawl. She watched in amazement as the tea slowly appeared from the spout of the teapot and slowly fell into the cup. Margaret assured me that this took hours to take place in her mind.

At that point, she made a fascinating comment. She said that she could have been in this state for days, months, years, 'even a lifetime'. Then, after what seemed like many hours, Margaret felt another snap over her right ear, and her associate finished pouring the tea and sat back. 'Are you okay?', she asked. 'I am not sure,' replied Margaret. Her friend then explained that Margaret had suddenly stopped moving and had stared into space for about 20 seconds. As Margaret explained to me, those 20 seconds had been hours for her. She went on to tell me that she feared she had a brain tumour, but after a series of scans, she was told that she was experiencing temporal lobe epilepsy.

I then found myself asking Margaret if she ever experienced déjà vu sensations. 'I get déjà vus to die for', was her reply. 'Not only that, but when I am in this pre-seizure aura state, I know what is going to happen next. I do see the future!'

This link between precognition and temporal lobe epilepsy is intriguing. I have discussed this extensively in a number of my books, most recently in *Opening the Doors of Perception: The Key to Cosmic Awareness* (2016). I am aware of this ability to slip out of time for myself, and it was one of the most intriguing events of my life.

When my first book, *Is There Life After Death?: The Extraordinary Science of What Happens When We Die*, was published in 2006, I was approached by scores of individuals who had experienced circumstances supportive of my Cheating the Ferryman hypothesis. The vast majority of my correspondents were located at vast distances from where I lived at that time, so I could not meet with them. I was living on the Wirral, close to the city of Liverpool. One day I received an email message from Jayne Burton, a member of the Epilepsy Action charity's Council of Management. Jayne had been a nurse on a paediatric intensive care unit. In 1997 she was diagnosed with temporal lobe epilepsy and, in 1999, had radical brain surgery, which involved the removal of part of her frontal temporal lobe. This was quite successful but did not eradicate her simple partial seizures (also known as petit-mal absences, the same TLE-related neurological state that slowed down time for 'Margaret'). These led to her retirement from nursing in 2002, which allowed her to focus entirely on her volunteer work. Jayne contacted me to let me know that she enjoyed my book and was keen to meet me to discuss her experiences of TLE. We met a few times in Liverpool, and she shared some fascinating details about her surgery. For example, in preparation for her radical brain surgery, she had the Wada Test applied.

This involves the effective shutting off of the dominant hemisphere of her brain. When this took place, she had a distinct sensation that she was a totally different person. This other version seemed to take over her consciousness while the Wada chemicals were doing their job. As their effect faded, so did the personality. This, for me, was evidence that my Daemon-Eidolon Dyad had some validity.

I subsequently secured a contract at a company based in Speke on the outskirts of Liverpool. Across the road from the business park where I worked was a popular shopping centre. I was delighted to discover that not only did this have a huge Borders bookshop, but also a pleasant coffee shop located at the back of the store on a raised mezzanine floor. From there you had a fantastic view of the huge glass-fronted entrance area.

One lunchtime Jayne and I agreed to meet for coffee at the bookshop. I arrived early, and she was slightly delayed. On arriving, she explained that because of her epilepsy, she was not allowed to drive. She had travelled into the city centre on the bus with her son and his friend and then caught a bus out to Speke, a distance of about six miles. She told me that she had arranged to meet her son and his friend in the city centre later that afternoon and they would travel back home together.

I got her a coffee, and we settled down to chat. We had one of the tables right at the edge of the mezzanine and had a perfect view of the shop floor. Jayne took one sip of her coffee, placed the cup back down and just stared at me. I immediately knew that she had entered into a spontaneous TLE 'absence'. I knew it would pass quickly, having witnessed this once with another of my readers. She turned her head and looked out towards the entrance. She then suddenly exclaimed, 'Why is he here? He shouldn't be here!' I looked down and could see nothing. She then blinked twice, and she was back. I began to explain to her that she had just had an absence and had verbalized something to me, but I was cut short when she turned and looked towards the entrance. 'Why is he here? He shouldn't be here!' she exclaimed as her son and his friend walked through the entrance below us. I was stunned; I had just witnessed a classic case of precognition.

On discussing this subsequently, Jayne explained to me that déjà vu sensations had been a regular part of her 'aura' state.

So what is taking place here? I have absolutely no doubt that I witnessed a genuine precognition that afternoon. The question is, was Jayne monitoring the contents of her immediate future or was she, in some way, 'remembering' the incident from her past? Or was it that specific individuals can view time from a location in the fifth dimension when in such altered states of consciousness? What facilitated this? Was it Jayne's experience of epilepsy? If so, have we any evidence that these neurological 'storms' can open the doors of perception? A series of experiments which took place in 2013 suggest that this may be the case.

Jimo Borjigin's Rats

One of the major arguments against survival after death is that without a functioning brain (and a dead brain is very non-functioning), consciousness ceases to exist. But CTF overcomes this problem by showing that post-mortem perceptual continuity happens while the processing brain is still alive. This seeming contradiction can be accommodated by the simple fact that time dilates at the point of death. For the observing consciousness, the moment of brain death in objective, consensual time is never reached. The person is seen to die in other Everett Universes/ Instantiations as perceived by other consciousnesses, but not in their own. (Instantiation is the process by which an abstract object is turned into something real, and is discussed in detail in the next part of the book.)

Interestingly, in 2013 a research team based at the University of Michigan were intrigued to observe that during experiments when rats were humanely killed, there was a surge in the production of certain neurochemicals in the brain at the point of death. Intrigued by this, the team set up brain scans on eight anaesthetized rats. The team then stopped the rats' hearts, bringing about a cardiac arrest. They were stunned to discover that all the different regions of the rats' brains became synchronized. All the different wave frequencies across the brains showed a phenomenon known as *coherence*. This is an astonishing finding. Rats are selected for these experiments because the neurochemical processes are similar in all higher mammals, including human. Therefore if it happens in a rat's brain, a similar process is possible in a human brain. As the team stated in the abstract of the paper:

> High-frequency neurophysiological activity in the near-death state exceeded levels found during the conscious waking state. These data demonstrate that the mammalian brain can, albeit paradoxically, generate neural correlates of heightened conscious processing at near-death.
>
> Borjigin, et al., 2013

So, something extraordinary happens in the brain at the point of death, something that involves it needing to generate 'neural correlates of heightened conscious processing'. Could this be the massive uploading of the information required to create the virtual reality-like perceptual environment needed to 'cheat the ferryman'? This may be pure speculation on my part, but something definitely takes place, and it does not seem to give any evolutionary advantage.

Can Borjigin's discovery be presented as supporting evidence for my CTF hypothesis? I believe so. The dying brains of the rats are seemingly creating a set of perceptions similar to a temporal lobe seizure. We know that during such states, the subject experiences visions, flashbacks and time dilation. Could it be the processing of the life review? Indeed, there is evidence that this activity carries through into the 'next life'.

Of possible significance here are the similarities between the surge of brain activity recorded in the dead rats' brains and a temporal lobe seizure. The rats' brains showed a vast increase in electrical activity in the brain, specifically in the gamma-wave frequency. Gamma waves are the fastest brain waves possible, oscillating from 35 Hertz up to

100 Hertz. This would mean that everything perceived by the rats during such brain activity would be hyper-real. Their sense of time would slow down profoundly in relation to the temporal flow perceived by an observer experiencing standard brain-wave frequencies. In effect, this means that for the rats, if they were capable of perceiving anything in this seemingly 'dead' state, a second of 'normal' time would be perceived as a much longer period, possibly hours, weeks or years. As we shall discover later, this is precisely what is reported during near-death experiences and by individuals with other neurological conditions. These are also the perceptions reported by individuals experiencing temporal lobe epilepsy aura states. It has been discovered that gamma wave activity in the brain is directly related to TLE seizures (Hughes, 2008). This presents a direct link between Borjigin's findings, TLE and NDEs.

Of even more significance is evidence that not only do we die with the brain hyper-activated by super-fast gamma waves linking all the areas of the cerebral cortex, but we are also born with a similar activity creating super-awareness and the effective stopping of subjective time-flow. You will recall that this was one of the themes I focused in on in my original 2004 IANDS essay discussed at the start of this book. Here is proof that my ideas were somewhat perceptive.

Indeed, in an even more intriguing academic paper published in July 2021 in the prestigious research periodical *Science*, a group of neuroscientists at the Department of Neuroscience at Yale University Medical School presented evidence that baby mice dream about the world they are about to enter while still in the womb (Ge, et al., 2021). The researchers suggested that the dreaming was for the mice to negotiate the visual world that they would encounter after they were born. They further suggested that this may be the case for all mammals, including human beings. What was not made clear was how the developing brains of the baby mice were receiving the information to create their dream scenarios. Modern material-reductionist science is quite precise in that all living creatures experience just one life and then die. So what could possibly be the source of the 'memories' that create the dreams? I would like to apply Occam's famous razor to this discovery. In simple terms, Occam's razor states that the simplest solution is usually the correct one. In this case, the source of the information for the dreams is one of two possibilities, which support the model I am presenting in this book. The first is that the mice remember their past lives and that my Cheating the Ferryman hypothesis can be applied to all sentient creatures. Secondly, it is probably more likely for (possibly) non-self-referential consciousnesses such as rodents that the information is drawn up from the Information Field. Indeed, it is of possible significance that we have already discovered that a form of near-death experience may be experienced by another group of rodents, Jimo Borjigin's rats (Borjigin, et al., 2013).

Can these results be extrapolated to human beings? Many researchers think so. Indeed, rodents such as rats and mice are used in neurological experiments because of the similarities between the chemical processes in the rodent brain and that of the human brain (Ellenbroek & Youn, 2016).

Therefore, it is of no surprise to me to discover that several experiments involving the attachment of electrodes to a woman's abdomen in late pregnancy have given extraordinary results. The brainwaves of the foetus are usually recorded as slow delta waves at a frequency of fewer than three cycles per second. However, this regular pattern is sometimes interrupted by more significant discharges similar to the spike recordings obtained from adults in an epileptic attack. As the baby approaches full term, these convulsive spikes become more frequent until they are almost continuous at birth, as the child thrashes its way into the world. The implication seems to be that we are all born with something like epilepsy. If my theory is correct, then we die in a state of epilepsy, and we are born in the same condition.

But there is one intriguing puzzle regarding this gamma wave NDE model: the observed effects of Alzheimer's disease. The full-brain connectivity facilitated by gamma waves is compromised by the amyloid plaques, cell-like deposits of proteins that destroy the inner structure of brain cells. Indeed, it has been discovered that an increase in gamma activity can be facilitated by having Alzheimer's patients view flickering light technologies (Iaccarino, et al., 2018). This, in turn, stimulates the generation of gamma waves and helps slow down the disease's progress. In my earlier books, I have written extensively about how flicker technology can bring about an accessing of the greater information field, in effect duplicating the effects of entheogens like dimethyltryptamine (DMT) and ayahuasca.

However, there is strong anecdotal evidence that this loss of communication may simply focus the brains of Alzheimer's patients into a more focused and less outward-facing perception of the underlying reality. I know because I witnessed this personally a few years ago.

PROOF FROM EXPERIENCE
Alzheimer's

In 2016 I received an extraordinary phone call. My mother, who was in her early 90s and sadly sliding into the final stages of Alzheimer's disease, had been living in a specialist care home for several years. Her contact with the outside world had been diminishing day by day, and she had reached a semi-catatonic state. Therefore, I was surprised to have the care home manager call me and request that I speak to my mother. Now she and I had not had a proper conversation for many months, our exchanges being me explaining in effect who she was and where she was. Her memory had disappeared, as had, seemingly, her sense of personal identity. On taking the call, I could hear in the background my mother's voice, a voice of a much younger woman. A voice that was precise and carefully enunciated. 'I will not stand for this,' I heard her state, 'just wait until I tell my husband!' This was from a woman who had barely spoken a complete sentence in months, and what she had said was jumbled and unclear.

The manager told her that her son was on the phone and would like to speak with her. To my astonishment, my mother grabbed the phone and immediately launched into describing what had taken place as far as she was concerned. She told me that she had been sitting at home with my father on a Saturday evening watching the popular television programme *The Morecambe and Wise Show*. She felt slightly tired and closed her eyes and dropped off to sleep for what she was adamant was a few seconds. She then added, 'and then I wake up in this place!'

I was quite stunned by this response. My father died in 1988, and the last time *The Morecambe and Wise Show* went out prime time was in the late 1970s. But what she said next astounded me. 'Who are you? You are not my son. My son is away at university. You sound much older. You are part of this conspiracy. I will sue you and all these people.' And she slammed the phone down.

I phoned back immediately and spoke to her again. She was still very suspicious of me, but I managed to calm her down. I tried to explain her circumstances. I told her that she was in a safe place with people who cared about her and that she was an elderly lady in her 90s. Again her response was denial. 'No, that cannot be true.' I asked her to look at her hands. She refused. But she did seem to calm down, and her much younger self faded away, and the confused person lost to the tragedy of Alzheimer's reappeared.

That was the last time my mother engaged in any form of conversation with me. Over the final two years of her life, I watched her revert back to being a baby, curled in a foetal position and then cease to have any form of response to the world. That evening in 2016 was her final attempt to rise above the Alzheimer's. In parapsychology, this is known as 'terminal lucidity'.

But this 'lucidity' was the upwelling of a mind that was experiencing a convivial Saturday evening with her husband in 1974, not one ravaged by dementia in a 2016 care home. What was taking place here? Could it be that an earlier 'version' of my mother found herself trapped in the body of a frail old lady?

This presents several intriguing questions. Did my mother perceive the past from the future or the future from the past? Which of the two ages was she? Was she a 50-year-old woman dreaming she was a 92-year-old woman or a 92-year-old woman hallucinating that she was a 50-year-old woman? In this regard, I am reminded of the Vedantic concept of the *liṅga śarīra* or 'long body'. This is a compound Sanskrit word from *liṅga*, 'image'; and *śarīra*, 'body'. The concept of the *liṅga śarīra* suggests that the human body extends not just in space but also in time. It is a singular object perceived as an individual body that moves from one location in space to another on a moment-by-moment basis. But this division into unique moments is a perceptual illusion facilitated by Maya. As we have already discovered from our discussions on time and space, these are both relative concepts.

As discussed earlier with regard to the theory of Steinhardt and Turok, the perceptual moment can, when viewed from the fifth dimension, be extended into hours, weeks and years, possibly even to eternity. This is the 'reality' perceived by those individuals discussed earlier who experience the Zeitraffer phenomenon. For them, a series of images merge into a singular unity running through time. Was my mother actually *both* a 50-year-old and a 92-year-old? Indeed, could she actually be all of her 'selves' throughout her long life?

Indeed, and not surprisingly, this possibility intrigued J.B. Priestley himself. In 1937 he wrote a play entitled *Time and the Conways*. In this, he has one of his characters make the following observation:

> But the point is, now, at this moment, or any moment, we're only cross-sections of our real selves. What we really are is the whole stretch of ourselves, all our time, and when we come to the end of this life, all those selves, all our time, will be us – the real you, the real me. And then perhaps we'll find ourselves in another time, which is only another kind of dream.
>
> Priestley, 2000, p. 61

Is this 'another time' where my mother found herself that strange evening in 2016 (or was it actually 1974 as far as she was concerned?).

But there is an even more intriguing aspect to this incident.

I was aware of something called the Babinski reflex. Also known as the plantar reflex, this was first documented by French neurologist Joseph Babinski in 1896. The physician strokes the patient's sole. If the Babinski reflex is present, the big toe will move upward as the other toes fan outward. I had read that the reflex is found in around 75 per cent of infants under two years of age but that it then usually disappears. Doctors consider a Babinski reflex response that appears in adults or children over 24 months to be an abnormal reflex response suggestive of an underlying neurological condition or nervous system disorder. It is important to note that Alzheimer's is not one of these associated conditions.

In a fascinating series of experiments, Czech-American psychiatrist Stanislav Grof showed that adult volunteers showed positive Babinski reflexes when hypnotically regressed to early childhood states. When the same volunteers were brought forward in time to later childhood, the response disappeared. This mirrored exactly what the response would be had they actually been these ages. When brought out of the hypnotic state, the volunteers displayed normal Babinski responses (Grof, 1993, p. 39). This intrigued me, and I wondered what response I would get from my mother if I tested her Babinski reflex. Soon after her 2016 'terminal lucidity' incident, she stopped speaking, and within a year, she was bed-ridden and showing only autonomic sensory responses. She also seemed to be shrinking in size and locked in a foetal position. It was as if she was going back to the womb. If this were the case, I suspected that she would show a positive Babinski response, as would a newly born baby. I stroked the underside of her foot with the blunt end of a knitting needle, following the precise instructions from a medical book. I watched as her big toe extend up towards the top of her foot while, at the same time, her other toes fanned out away from each other. This was absolute proof that she had a positive Babinski reflex. As far as her brain and nervous system were concerned, it seemed as if she were not a 92-year-old but an embryo in the later stages of gestation.

And this is not as crazy as it may first sound. In a paper published in 1999, researcher Barry Reisberg applied the term 'retrogenesis' in specific relation to Alzheimer's Disease (Reisberg, Franssen & Hasan, 1999). He and his team argued that Alzheimer's is a reversal of the developmental processes during infancy and childhood. In effect, the Alzheimer's patient is going backwards in time and approaching birth from another direction. In his patients, he noted an almost perfect reversal-mirroring regarding the development of an infant and the decline of a dementia patient, specifically in cognition, coordination, language, feeding and behaviour. Such was the power of Reisberg's retrogenesis that a process of caring for Alzheimer's patients has been devised in which the carer applies the mother-infant relationship to the patient, and this has been very successful.

The most curious thing is that the decline of dementia does not stop at the point of birth regarding the mirroring effect of infancy. It continues reflecting a reversal of the embryo's development in the womb. Like my mother, the person becomes silent and unmoving and starts to echo the foetal position of hands and legs curled in and the back bent forward. This seems to suggest a journey back to birth, an overlapping of two states that can be found at the start and end of life.

I would argue that my mother's body's curious contortion was not similar to a foetal position; it *was* a foetal position. My mother was located in a bed in a care home on the Wirral in the summer of 2017 and simultaneously an embryo waiting to be born in the spring of 1924. She was experiencing both ends of her *linga śarīra*. But if my Cheating the Ferryman hypothesis is correct, then the Vedantist 'long body' is, in fact, not a line but a circle, an ouroboros. As the famous motto embroidered on the Chair of State at Holyrood Palace in Edinburgh announces, '*Ma fin est mon commencement*' (my beginning is my end), words echoed by Anglo-American poet T.S. Eliot in his enigmatic poem *East Coker*:

> *In my beginning is my end. In succession*
> *Houses rise and fall, crumble, are extended,*
> *Are removed, destroyed, restored, or in their place*
> *Is an open field, or a factory, or a by-pass.*

Or even more succinctly stated by Irish playwright Samuel Beckett in his similarly enigmatic work *Waiting for Godot*:

> *They give birth astride of a grave, the light gleams an instant,*
> *then it's night once more.*

We all have a subliminal knowledge that this is the actual way of life; it is not linear, it is circular, and therefore we exist forever.

Future Memory from Near-Death Experiences

If my hypothesis is correct, people should encounter their future and past in a Panoramic Life Review. About one-third of NDE experiencers have reported 'visions of future personal events', some of which have been subsequently verified to have actually occurred (Ring & Valarino, 1998, p. 151). For example, a 38-year-old woman had seen 'an enormous TV screen' in front of her that had displayed her life events from age 13 months to 38 years 'all at the same instant' (Ring & Valarino, 2006, p. 150). And once she had decided to return to her body, 'there was a second TV screen, which was just as big as the first. It showed [her] glimpses of what was to come'. And, according to Kenneth Ring, who was familiar with her situation, those events 'did indeed take place, just as she was shown' (Ring & Valarino, 2006, p. 151). From examples such as these, we can see that a type of precognition occurs during some NDEs. However, there also needs to be more careful verification to determine whether verifiable events are accurately predicted.

Panoramic Life Reviews are experienced when the brain's abilities are diminished, yet the subjective perceptions encountered at this time suggest the complete opposite; that the brain is functioning more effectively. The nature of time itself also seems to change. For example:

> Time did not make any sense. Time did not seem to apply.
> It seemed irrelevant. It was unattached to anything, the

way I was. Time is only relevant when it is relative to
the normal orderly sequential aspects of life. So I was there
for a moment or for eternity. I cannot say but it felt like a
very long time to me.[8]

In February 1892, Albert Heim, a professor of geology, presented a paper to
the Uto section of the Swiss Alpine Club. In this, he discussed his research
into time dilation and past-life reviews experienced by mountaineers
during climbing accidents. The paper was subsequently published
in the Yearbook of the Swiss Alpine Club later that year (Heim, 1992,
pp. 327–37). This work languished in comparative obscurity until it was
translated from German to English by Russell Noyes and Roy Kletti
in 1972 (Noyes & Kletti, 1972). In the paper, Heim described his own
experience of falling from a rock face and then went on to describe several
similar cases that he had collected over the previous 25 years. He was
particularly interested in the regularly reported sensation that while falling
time slows down, it stops altogether in some cases. This intrigued him
because this mirrored his own perceptions during his accident when he
stated that 'time became greatly expanded' (Noyes & Kletti, 1972, p. 47).

Subsequent research has shown that the sensation of subjective time
dilation during NDEs is quite common (Wittmann, Neumaier, Evrard,
Weibel & Schmied-Knittel, 2017). For example, in a survey by NDE
researcher Ken Ring published in 1980, 65 per cent of experiencers
stated that time stopped for them during their NDE, with 6 per cent
describing that time as 'extended' (Ring, 1980).

The question is, why should this be? We know that subjective time
perception slows down during times of stress and accidents. But what
mechanism is taking place here and, more importantly, what is this
additional time to be used for?

The vast majority of the cases collected by Albert Heim also had the
respondees describe another subjective experience that accompanied the
time-dilation effect; they also perceived life reviews. For example, Heim
told how during his own fall, he saw himself:

> . . . as a seven-year-old boy going to school, then in the
> fourth-grade classroom with my beloved teacher Weisz. I
> acted out my life as though I were on a stage upon which
> I looked down from the highest gallery of the theatre.
>
> Heim, 1992

This effect is the most interesting of all the perceptions reported during NDEs. A comparatively recent (2014) analysis discovered that around 14 per cent of NDE accounts include some form of life review (Long, 2014). It is particularly enlightening that past-life reviews tend to occur when individuals know they are about to die. However, and almost as a contradiction, the death threat has to be unexpected. This is supported by empirical research. In a report describing interviews with over 200 individuals who had been close to death, Noyes and his assistant authors reported that 44 per cent of respondents who believed they were about to die from a life-threatening situation recalled past-life reviews.

In contrast, only 12 per cent of those who did not think they were about to die had the experience. So, it seems that a significant factor is believing that you are about to die (Noyes, Hoenk, Kuperman & Slyman, 1977).

Several cases describing a Panoramic Life Review have been intriguing. During the terrorist attacks in London on 7 July 2005, a young Australian, Gill Hicks, was injured by one of the bombs on a London underground train as it drew out of Kings Cross Station. When she had recovered from her injuries, she described how she had experienced a vivid life review:

> . . . my life was flashing before my eyes, flickering through
> every scene, every happy and sad moment, everything I
> have ever done, said, experienced.[9]

In 2007 a hiker called Paul Simms fell down a thousand-foot sheer granite face in Yosemite. As he was falling, he was hit in the face by a tree branch and then passed a climber negotiating the cliff face. He describes how it was at that point he realized that he was going to die:

> . . . and that's when my whole life flashed before my eyes. It seemed to go chronologically but super-sped up.[10]

He experienced in vivid detail his life, with certain sections brought out in distinct clarity, including rewatching the whole of the film *Arthur 2: On The Rocks*. Then:

> . . . in the next .00075 seconds of free fall, I saw the rest of my life flash before my eyes. Everything up to and including the moment when I thought, 'Hey, if I turn around and retrace my steps right now it'll all be downhill from here, and I can – oops! What the—'[10]

He had reviewed the whole of his life right up to the point where he slipped off the ledge and then experienced the fall again up until the actual microsecond he was experiencing at that moment. In effect, he experienced a past-life review to the moment of his potential death and then experienced a second review in an even smaller piece of time. This incident is of great significance regarding my Cheating the Ferryman hypothesis, which proposes multiple lives during a near-death experience. Simms survived to tell the tale because he didn't directly hit the ground but landed on a group of fellow hikers, killing one and seriously injuring a few others.

If my model is correct, then people should be able to encounter their future as well as their past in a Panoramic Life Review. It is therefore not surprising to discover that an experience of a life review can not only reach backwards in time but forward as well. About one-third of experiencers have reported 'visions of personal future events,' some of which have been subsequently verified to have actually occurred.

In his 1988 book, *The Light Beyond*, NDE researcher Raymond Moody describes a very peculiar incident that took place a few months before his ground-breaking first book, *Life After Life*, was published. On 31 October 1975, his wife Louise had taken his children out trick-or-treating in their local neighbourhood. The little group knocked on a front door and were greeted by a pleasant man and woman. As a way of making general conversation, the couple asked the children their names. Moody's son proudly announced that he was 'Raymond Avery Moody, the third'. On hearing this, the woman looked quite startled. Turning to Louise, the woman announced, 'I must speak with your husband'. Later on, Raymond visited the woman and was surprised to discover that a few years earlier, in 1971, she had experienced heart failure and a collapsed lung during surgery and had been clinically dead for a period of time before being revived. She explained to Moody that while in this state, she encountered a being who took her through a classic panoramic life review. After reviewing her past life, the entity then described her events that were yet to occur. Towards the end of the experience, the being showed her a photograph of a man. It said that the man's name was Raymond Moody, adding, 'when the time is right, you will tell him about this experience'.

And there she was, four years later doing exactly what the being predicted she would do (Moody, *The Light Beyond: Explorations into the Near-Death Experience*, 1988, pp. 22–23).

Sometimes the life review only involves the future. For example, at the age of 16, an apprentice builder called Tony Kofi fell from a building he was working on. He didn't see his past, but his future:

> In my mind's eye I saw many, many things: children that I hadn't even had yet, friends that I had never seen but are now my friends. The thing that really stuck in my mind was playing an instrument.[11]

He survived the fall but, on leaving the hospital, felt that he had been shown an alternative future, which he was keen to make happen this time. He decided he wanted to be a professional musician. His problem was that he did not recognize the instrument he saw himself playing in his future flash-forward. One day he saw an image in a magazine of a saxophone. He immediately realized that this was the instrument he saw in his review. He used his accident compensation to buy a saxophone, and he is now one of the most successful jazz musicians in the UK.

This ability to perceive the future during extreme stress cannot be explained using the present scientific paradigm. The explanation will be simply that these people are hallucinating. But two questions have to be answered if this is to be a valid explanation. The first is how it is that those who experience these things implicitly believe that they saw their own futures. Remember that they are the best placed (indeed only), qualified witnesses to the events and have no doubts. Secondly, modern science has no understanding of precisely what 'hallucinations' are. It is just a label of convenience by which any experiences that don't fit in with the present paradigm can be dismissed, locked away and forgotten.

An even more intriguing question is who, or what, are these mysterious beings that accompany the near-death experiencers through their experience? It is reported regularly that they sensed a presence close to them during their NDE. This presence seems to be an essential aspect of the whole near-death experience.

This 'Being of Light', as this entity has become known, seems to be waiting at the 'other side' to guide the disincarnate soul, take it through the panoramic life review, and decide what happens next. There have been countless reported cases over the years, so many that it is clear that this is a standard element of the NDE. For example, a case that was described to British Near-Death researchers Peter and Elizabeth Fenwick. The individual in question was involved in a motorcycle accident when he was 17. After the accident, he experienced a classic out-of-the-body sensation and became aware of a 'person in white clothing'. He found himself standing in front of two doors, and he knew that he had to decide which one to go through. It is fairly reasonable to suppose that this was a mental fabrication of his own, but the reason for making the choice is obvious. He made his decision and found himself back in his injured body, lying in the road. However, from then on, he regularly experienced overpowering feelings of déjà vu, which, in turn, gave him an uncanny ability to 'anticipate' major future events in his life. He believed that these precognitions had been facilitated by something else he experienced during his NDE. He explained to the Fenwicks that he saw a 'speeded-up video of his future life' (Fenwick & Fenwick, 1995, p. 122).

The Fenwicks argue that this is of great significance in understanding the true nature of the phenomenon:

> People who are given these glimpses of the future often find that they subsequently experience various psychic phenomena such as feelings of déjà vu, almost as though they have been shown a speeded-up video of their future life, and later recognize and remember odd frames from it.
>
> Fenwick & Fenwick, 1995, pp. 120–21

Who, or what is the Being of Light? How does it know so well the life of the near-death experiencer?

To some researchers, this entity represents a projection from the subconscious of the dying person (Twemlow, Gabbard & Coyne, 1982; Sedahely, 1987). This is evidenced by the seemingly culturally biased nature of its manifestation. To believers in the afterlife, it is what it seems to be: a relative, an angel, or even God. However, this entity is the single most intriguing element of the phenomenon because it may be proof of another long-held belief that all human beings consist of not one but two mutually independent consciousnesses.

Another influential researcher in the field of near-death experience is Phyllis (P.M.H.) Atwater. Over many years she has brought together an astonishing collection of first-hand descriptions of altered states of consciousness during the NDE state. Unusually for writers in this field, Atwater also argues that NDE-like perceptions of time-flow can be experienced during the everyday waking state (Atwater, 2013). She cites many examples of individuals who have reported a number of temporal anomalies such as the freezing of time-and-space relationships, expansion of space along with oneself and a sensation that future events are being overlaid upon the present. These take place suddenly, only to be followed by a resumption of normal time flow. Atwater is fascinated by such experiences because, in July 1978, she found herself falling out of time and seeing her own future.

At that time, Atwater was almost fully recovered from the life-threatening miscarriage that had facilitated several near-death experiences the previous year. She had just returned to Idaho from a vacation with relations in Chicago and had, on a whim, decided to put her house on the market. She was in her office at the First National Bank in downtown Boise when something very strange happened. She felt a surge of heat racing through her body, and she noted that everything around her 'froze in place'. She then saw her desk fade from view, replaced by a field of brilliant sparkling lights that fell from the ceiling. She found herself in a place that she subsequently was to call 'The Void'. She recognized it straight away. It was the place she had visited during the second of the three NDEs she had experienced the year before.

I feel it is crucial to quote her in full as she describes this experience in her book *Future Memory*:

> Now that my house had sold, I rented an unfurnished room from a fellow analyst and slept on the floor in a sleeping bag until the time came for me to leave the state. For three weeks, I attended a party a night, saying goodbye to everyone I knew. Only what I stuffed into my small Ford Pinto went with me, as everything else I owned was either sold, given away, or stored. Four times during my trip I rested, and for four days in each place – Southern California, New Mexico, Indiana, Kentucky – before

I reached northern Virginia and a temporary stay in Reston with a cousin and his family whom I hardly knew. Eventually I found a job in Washington, D.C., and an apartment in Falls Church.

This scenario I both watched and lived simultaneously and in great detail, as if each physical motion was being performed in actuality, each thought, feeling, taste, touch, and smell thoroughly experienced.

Atwater, 2013, p. 33

Things then became very strange because, within the future dream, she experienced another advancement that progressed her further into her own future. In the dream version of spring 1979, a dream within a dream had her experience the following:

After leaving Idaho, though, I journeyed first to Escondido, California, where I attended the Death and Dying Seminar conducted by Elisabeth Kubler-Ross on August 22. I fulfilled all my childhood dreams and wishes when I meandered across the United States, including a chance to watch the sun set silver on the Pacific, then later rise golden over the Atlantic. I explored the Carson Sinks of Nevada, meditated with the Bristlecone Pines in the Patriarch Grove near Big Pine, California, enjoyed Sea World and called upon long-time friends Diane Pike and Arleen Lorrance of 'The Love Project' in San Diego, conversed with the grandfather cacti of the Arizona deserts, touched my first cotton plant in Yuma, walked across London Bridge at Lake Havasu, rode a mule train to the bottom of the Grand Canyon, ate fry bread in Albuquerque, discovered a special bear claw at Old Town, saw a miracle staircase in Santa Fe, prayed in the Air Force Academy Chapel near Colorado Springs, found a marble grave like none other in northern Kansas, hopped aboard a steamboat on the Mississippi, traced tales of Tom Sawyer and Huckleberry Finn in and around Hannibal, followed in the footsteps of Abraham Lincoln, and much, much more. Everything I had ever vowed to do since childhood I did, as well as things unknown to me; yet each scene, each place, each stranger or friend, was important and reflected some aspect of my life. A sacred journey it truly was, for at each turn of every bend and in the depths of everyone's eyes, I met parts of my own soul looking back at me.

Atwater, 2013, p. 34

She then found herself coming back to this reality, back seated at her desk at the bank. The experience of nine months of her life had taken place in around ten minutes of normal time. Then, to her utter surprise, she was, in a very literal sense, as the film title states, 'back to the future' when she found herself reliving the future memories in yet another reverie.

But this second future review had one subtle difference. In this new variation on the year, her future self decides to go for a walk in the countryside in South Virginia:

A sudden turn put me face-to-face with my right and perfect partner. He was taller than I, younger, with dark curly hair and bronze skin, a conservative fellow, refined, well traveled and well educated, a lover of grand opera, unique in his devotion to the spiritual path and the reality of God. He recognized me instantly, but it took me three days to realize who he was. We married soon after, for once our hands joined so too did our hearts. A streamer of time years hence revealed twins at our side, a boy and a girl, and nearly continuous writing, public speaking, and travel.

Atwater, 2013, p. 35

On coming round from this second, revised, future memory, she immediately started to make arrangements for her trip to South Virginia. To her surprise, some of the future-memory events came to pass exactly as she perceived them in the vision, whereas others didn't. However, one crucial factor which did happen was that she met the man on the walk and they did, indeed, marry.

This suggests to me that Atwater was given a vision of a number of alternative futures, all encoded within the information field, in a similar way to the alternate outcomes suggested by Hawking and Hertog in their Top-Down hypothesis. Atwater's 'attention' collapsed the wave function of a number of alternate futures, both within the two dream sequences and in actuality.

It is not just during a near-death experience that a panoramic life review can be experienced. A number of cases have been reported during hypnotism whereby a person has reported living a large section of their past life while in a trance state. This is not surprising as taking a person back to a period in their past is regularly used by police when investigating crimes, or therapists while isolating the source of trauma – one case I found of particular relevance to my research. In my book *Is There Life After Death?: The Extraordinary Science of What Happens When We Die*, I cited a case reported by the American psychiatrist Milton H. Erickson. It has wrongly been stated by various writers, including Marilyn Ferguson in her classic book *The Aquarian Conspiracy*, that the subject in question was Aldous Huxley. This is not true. It actually involved a student in his mid-twenties who was hypnotized by Erickson. But, interestingly, Huxley did experience a very similar past-life review which may explain the confusion.

I have managed to find the original article by Milton Erickson. It is called 'A Special Inquiry with Aldous Huxley into the Nature and Character of Various States of Consciousness', which I think may be why there has been much confusion. Although Huxley is mentioned in the title, he was not the young man in question: Erickson reports that the incident occurred in 1950 when Huxley himself would have been 56.

The original academic paper that described the Huxley-related incident was initially published in the *American Journal of Clinical Hypnosis*. It is here that Huxley describes his own very similar experience. While in a 'deep trance state', Huxley says that he found himself in a deep, wide ravine. In the vision, Erickson was perceived to be, by Huxley, sitting on the edge looking down. Huxley could hear Erickson's questions but found them intrusive. Huxley said he could see a nude infant lying in the sand in front of him. Huxley could also sense what the child was experiencing. He then saw the child growing before his eyes, creeping, sitting, standing, toddling, playing. He watched the child grow up. He followed in distorted time all the child's experiences at all times, sensing its physical and subjective mental experiences. He shared the child's joy and sadness. Finally, he realized that he had watched the child mature to a young man of 23. He went closer to see what the young man was looking at. On doing so, he realized that the young man was himself. He saw that this young Huxley was looking at another Huxley, obviously in his early fifties, just across the vestibule in which they both were standing; and that he, aged 52, was looking at himself, Aldous, aged 23. Then Huxley, aged 23 and Huxley, aged 52, apparently realized simultaneously that they were looking at each other.

The same thought arose in each mind, 'Is that my idea of what I will be like (was like) at 52 (23)?' Each tried to understand which the 'actual reality' was and which was the 'mere subjective experience outwardly projected in hallucinatory form'. Indeed it became more complicated because both Huxleys knew everything up until the age of 23, but the memories from 23 to 52 had been blotted out so that only Huxley aged 52 should remember them. They both knew each other's thoughts and tried to speak to the person above (Erickson) but realized that they could speak only as one. On trying to do this, Huxley lost the trance state and had post-hypnotic amnesia. However, three times Erickson was able to lift the amnesia of the memory, but it was then forgotten again (Erickson, 'A Special Inquiry with Aldous Huxley into the Nature and Character of Various States of Consciousness', 1965). Huxley had planned to publish a book on these experiences, but unfortunately all his notes were destroyed in a bushfire that destroyed his house.

It is then that Erickson says that this was not his first encounter with regression. He explained that he had had a subject who went into a trance state while in Erickson's laboratory. He requested that Erickson wake him up after two hours. This is the subject that Ferguson wrongly identifies as Huxley. Erickson describes it thus:

> He gave an account of finding himself on an unfamiliar hillside and, on looking round, he saw a small boy whom he immediately 'knew' was six years old. Curious about this conviction about a strange little boy he walked over to the child only to discover that the child was himself. He immediately recognized the hillside and set about trying to discover how he could be himself at 26 years of age looking at himself at age six years. He soon learned that he could not only see, hear, and feel his child-self, but that he knew his innermost thoughts and feelings. At the moment of realizing this, he felt the child's feeling of hunger and his wish for 'brown cookies'. This brought a flood of memories to his 26-year-old self, but he noticed that the boy's thoughts were still centring on cookies and that the boy remained totally unaware of him. He was an invisible man somehow regressed in time so that he could see and sense completely his childhood self. My subject reported that he 'lived' with that boy for years, watched his successes and his failures, knew all of his innermost life, wondered about the next day's events with the child and, like the child, found to his amazement that even though he was 26 years old, a total amnesia existed for all the events subsequent to the child's immediate age at the moment, that he could not foresee the future any more than could the child. He went to school with the child, vacationed with him, always watching the continuing physical growth and development. As each new day arrived, he found that he had a wealth of

associations about the actual happenings of the past up to the immediate moment of life of his child-self.

He went through grade school, high school and then through a long process of deciding whether or not to go to college and what course of study to follow. He suffered the same agonies of indecision that his then-self did. He then felt his other self's elation and relief when the decision was finally reached and his own feelings of elation and relief were identical to that of his other self.

My subject explained that the experience was literally a moment by moment reliving of his life with only the same awareness he had then and that the highly limited, restricted awareness of himself at 26 was that of being an invisible man watching his own growth and development from childhood on, with no more knowledge of the child's future than the child possessed at any particular age'.[12]

Erickson, 1980

According to Erickson's paper, this was not a unique incident. What varies is how the experience is achieved rather than the nature of the incident itself. One girl, who had younger twin sisters, found herself being one of two identical twins of herself. For example, another subject created a robot that he endowed with life, only to discover that it was his own life.

These examples all suggest to me that some of us can, under certain circumstances, sense the presence of our own Daemon. Indeed, I would further suggest that in some cases, such as the Huxley example, we can access the viewpoint of our own 'Higher Self'. This is because we are, in fact, both the Daemon and the Eidolon. Indeed, the coming together of the two to create what I call the 'Daemon-Eidolon Dyad' is, in my opinion, the ultimate aim of existence. As I shall discuss later, I suggest that we are living in a virtual environment similar to a computer game and that the Daemon is the game-player and the Eidolon is the in-game 'avatar'. Because the Daemon has lived many iterations of its game-of-life it, in effect, knows what is likely to happen in the future. One of the most extraordinary examples of a Daemon encounter reported to me took place one cool autumn evening in 1999.

Bill Murtha's Life Review

On that fateful evening, a young man called Bill Murtha decided to take a bicycle ride along the sea wall near his home in Dawlish on the south coast of England. The tide was exceptionally high that evening, and the weather was stormy. Suddenly a large wave came over and knocked him off his bike. He pulled himself up off the ground, but as he did so, a second wave crashed in and swept him off the wall into the sea.

After a few seconds, Bill managed to swim up to the surface. He was a semi-professional sportsman and had always been a strong swimmer, so initially he was not too concerned. However, one look at the high sea wall made him realize that he was in trouble. It would be impossible for him to scale it. But there was something even more concerning. The tide was going out, and he was being drawn out to sea.

He started to shout for help but to no avail. He knew that he could keep himself afloat, but doing so was draining his energy. As the cold bit into him, he realized that another far more immediate danger was taking place: hypothermia. As he felt the intense cold make its way up his body, he realized that his body was shutting down; he was dying.

What then took place was strange in the extreme. He felt himself disassociating from his body and floating upwards. And then his perceptual world changed completely.

He found himself running across a road in East London. It was a hot summer's day, and he was paying no attention to anything or anyone. He was back as a child. For a second, he felt confused, but then he heard the squeal of brakes. He looked up to see the front of a car moving towards him at speed. He had no chance of getting out of the way. He looked above the bonnet and saw the face of a young woman gazing at him in horror. He heard a sickening thud, and all went black.

In a radio interview he did with me on BBC Merseyside in January 2011, Bill described what happened next:

> I then found myself looking down at my hands, and I have nail varnish on, and I am driving a car. I then look up to see a child suddenly run in front of the vehicle. I hit the child and, in panic, park the car and walk back to look at the injured boy. As I walk along, I see that my tights are all ripped. I walk towards him, and all I could feel was remorse and fear.

His consciousness had switched from being himself as a young boy to that of the woman who drove the car that injured him many years before. Not only had he gone back in time, but he also perceived the incident from the viewpoint of another human being.

Everything faded again, and he found himself in the hallway of his house in Dawlish. It took him a moment to realize that his point of consciousness was hovering near the ceiling. There was a knock on the door. He watched his wife and daughters walk down the hall and open the front door. Standing there was a police officer. He listened intently as the police officer explained that a body had been washed up on the beach at Dawlish, and they had reason to believe that the dead person was a Mr William Murtha.

Yet again, the scene faded, and he was back in the water, waiting to die. It was then that a voice manifested in his head. It told him that he had been shown a possible future, one of many potential outcomes. The voice also told him that he needed to get his life into order.

He then heard other voices shouting to him from the shoreline. He had drifted away from the sea wall, and he was subsequently able to grab a lifebuoy that was thrown to him. Fortunately, Bill Murtha had been spotted that evening by somebody looking through a telescope. He was pulled out of the water with broken ribs and a severe case of hypothermia. But he survived.

The Concorde Precognition

Another incident involved a university lecturer friend of mine who regularly experiences precognitive dreams. They are so accurate that he keeps records of them and subsequently discusses them with friends and associates. In one such dream, he found himself in a hotel room. He knew it was in France, possibly Paris. In the dream, he walked towards the window and found he was overlooking an airport runway. As he looked out, he saw a plane cross his field of vision. It was one of the supersonic airliners known as Concorde. He was horrified to see that flames were shooting out of the plane's rear. An even greater horror overcame him when the plane crashed. He described to me how in the dream, he then sensed the distress of those on board. He felt their souls pass through him and, as they did so, he heard their thoughts. Of significance was that the voices were speaking in German, a language my friend spoke fluently. He then awoke. He was so disturbed that he sent a fax message to British Airways, one of only two carriers that flew Concorde, warning them that a Concorde would crash with a significant loss of life. Not surprisingly, he received no response. At that time, the small Concorde fleet had a 100 per cent safety record with no crashes or incidents having taken place.

A few months later, on 25 July 2000, an Air France Concorde, Flight 4590, a charter from Charles de Gaulle Airport to John F. Kennedy Airport in New York, ran over debris on the runway during take-off. This sent the heated debris into the fuel tank, causing it to rupture with sparks ignited by the fuel. It crashed into a local hotel, killing all 109 people on board and four on the ground. This is precisely what my associate saw in his dream. But what is extraordinary is that the flight had been chartered by a German cruise company, Deilmann, and the passengers, mostly German, were on their way to join a cruise ship in New York.

Unfortunately, the details surrounding precognition are rarely shared with others before the event. However, all that is needed is one irrefutable case as evidence. As the great American psychologist William James stated in a lecture he gave in 1890:

> If you wish to upset the law that all crows are black, you mustn't seek to show that no crows are; it is enough if you prove one single crow to be white.
>
> Fontana, 2005, p. 121

My 'white crow' is somebody called Graham Nicholls and an event that took place in 1999.

Graham Nicholls

If we exist in a simulation of our life and – like in a computer game – we have the opportunity to experience that life over and over again, then there must be evidence for this. If we have experienced this life before, we may recall events and circumstances experienced in a previous life. These perceptions will be interpreted as precognitions of the future whereas, in actual fact, they are memories of the past. Over recent years I have been made aware of a large number of cases whereby a person experiences an element of their own future. One such case – and one that I think presents powerful proof of 'future memory' – was experienced by author Graham Nicholls in 1999. On 25 April that year, he was presenting to a discussion group when he suddenly found himself being pushed to the ground:

> In the next moment I realized I was no longer in the space but was now in a powerful out-of-body experience. I found myself sliding down the side of a ridge in a heavily forested landscape. Roots and rich jade green leaves twisted and turned around me; there was something almost primordial about this place like I was in some distant time, some unknown part of prehistory. I came to a halt as I reached what appeared to be a clearing at the foot of the ridge.
>
> Nicholls, 2011, p. 42

He then found himself blacking out for a few seconds. When he again became conscious the forested landscape had changed to a city centre, a city centre he immediately recognized. He was in the centre of his home city, London, in the area known as Soho. He was standing on the corner of Moor Street and Old Compton Street. He felt as if he was looking down a tunnel onto the streets. Then something even more extraordinary happened:

> Suddenly there was an explosion. I saw people running; I watched one man in particular as he ran towards the site of the explosion on the opposite side of the road and maybe just over a hundred metres from where I was standing. The explosion and the emotional impact of the event suggested to me that this was a future event. I'm not really sure why I knew that; it was like I was picking it up from some part of my unconscious mind. I felt the experience was far too strong to be a meaningless hallucination. In fact it was probably the strongest experience I'd ever had. If a future event could be witnessed in this way, then this was it.
>
> Nicholls, 2011, p. 43

He then slowly recovered his consciousness, and after a few moments, he sat the group in a circle and recounted to them in detail what he had seen.

Five days later, on 30 April 1999, Graham was supposed to be meeting friends for a meal in a restaurant in Old Compton Street. The vision he had seen had quite disturbed him, and he decided to cancel. That evening he switched on the news to discover that a nail bomb had exploded in a pub called the Admiral Duncan in Old Compton Street. This killed three people and injured around seventy, many of whom had life-changing injuries. Had Graham actually gone out that night, he would, at best, have witnessed the event — or worse, been directly impacted. Something created the 'future memory', a memory that disturbed him so much that he decided not to visit Old Compton Street that evening.

Every member of the group subsequently signed affidavits stating that Graham told them in detail that a terrorist attack was about to occur soon in a specific location in London. This would involve a pub being destroyed by a bomb. The probability of such a specific statement coming true with total accuracy within a few days of being announced is vanishingly small. The only alternative explanation for this prediction is that Graham and all of his group are lying. If so, we have to ask what would motivate such a conspiracy? Furthermore, even many years later, the group continue to claim that the events happened as described. We are obliged to ask, using a popular legal term, '*cui bono*'?

So what do all these cases suggest with regard to the phenomenal world? It seems that we can perceive the future, relive the past and glimpse another reality that hides behind this one, a greater reality known as the Pleroma. But what is the true nature of these two realities? Could the Gnostics, the Vedantists, the philosophers and the mystics all be correct? Is this world we live in, the Kenoma, a mind-created illusion and we are trapped with Maya?

Could it be a mind-facilitated simulation?

PART 5

The Instantiation Argument

Introduction

To address the question of whether reality could be a mind-facilitated simulation, it is important to define our terms first. In his groundbreaking book *Alien Information Theory: Psychedelic Drug Technologies and the Cosmic Game* (Gallimore, 2019), discussed earlier, neurobiologist Andrew Gallimore makes the valid point that the word 'simulation', suggestive of a copy of something existing elsewhere, is incorrect in this particular case. He proposes that the correct description should be an *instantiation* of a reality rather than a *simulation* of one (Gallimore, 2019, p. 193).

Instantiation is a term used in computer programming. It is the process by which an abstract object is turned into something real. In this way, virtual worlds can be created out of data, and when viewed through a virtual-reality headset, they become three-dimensional and seemingly real.

In this section, I will present evidence from cosmology and from information theory suggesting that what we believe to be 'reality' may be created out of binary code and at its purest level is simply information, information that is processed by the human mind to create the illusion of an eternal reality. Let us now consider the evidence for such a seemingly outrageous statement.

The Paradox of the Big Bang

To appreciate just how strange this universe is, we need to go back in time to that moment 13.8 billion years ago. Before that time, there was nothing. No space and no time. It is vital that we understand what is meant by this statement. Try to imagine nothing. I guarantee that you will immediately think of space, a kind of receptacle that contains things. The main difference between normal space and what you envisage is that there is nothing within the receptacle. The enclosed space is empty. But 'before' 13.8 billion years ago, there was literally nothing, no receptacle or enclosed space within the receptacle. There could not be, simply because space itself did not exist. More importantly, to exist at all, space needs time to exist within, and that didn't exist either.

It seems that from literally nowhere, a Big Bang erupted. We need to ponder on this 'fact' for a second. The website www.physicsoftheuniverse.com makes the following statement:

> . . . all the matter, energy and space in the universe was once squeezed into an infinitesimally small volume, which erupted in a cataclysmic 'explosion' which has become known as the Big Bang.

I am intrigued as to what an 'infinitesimally small volume' means. Where was this 'infinitesimally small volume' located? Remember that before the Big Bang, space did not exist. Space was brought into existence by the Big Bang. So, if this infinitesimally small volume was not in space, where could it be? Indeed, even asking the question of where the infinitesimally small volume was *before* the Big Bang also makes no sense. The Big Bang created time, so how could there be a 'before'?

The website then goes on to state:

> Thus, space, time, energy and matter all came into being at an infinitely dense, infinitely hot gravitational singularity, and began expanding everywhere at once.

Okay, let's break this down. Everything that now exists, the whole universe together with its energy fields, dark matter, anti-matter and dark energy all just spontaneously and for no reason erupted from nowhere into an 'infinitely dense, infinitely hot gravitational singularity'. Let's focus on two things. Firstly, the word 'infinitely'. This is defined in Webster's Dictionary as being 'limitless or endless in space, extent, or size'. So we are expected to believe in something being infinitely dense and infinitely hot. So how hot is 'infinitely hot', and how dense is 'infinitely dense'? Clearly, something got lost 'infinitely' quickly as we know that the present universe is not infinitely dense. According to my research, the current density of the universe is 5×10^{-30} g/cm, which is a tiny number but, also by definition with regard to infinities, infinitely smaller than the density of the initial state of the universe immediately after the Big Bang. So, where did that infinite density go? We have a similar issue with heat. According to the scientists, the temperature of the singularity was also infinite. But at the point of the Big Bang, the temperature was 1000 trillion degrees Celsius. This is a peculiarly rounded figure and suggests that it was infinitely smaller than the temperature of the singularity. So, the singularity managed to lose an infinite amount of heat and an infinite amount of density. Where did it all go?

Now, remember that time didn't exist before the Big Bang, so how it found 'time' to come about is beyond comprehension. If there was no sequential flow of time, then nothing can, by definition, happen. But we are supposed to accept it just did.

Let's assume, for argument's sake, that time just spontaneously came into existence first. If this were the case, then space would have the time it needed to erupt. The problem here is that time may be available, but, as I have already stated, space itself expanded into nothing. So why didn't it just cease to exist? But we are told that by some magical process, it continued to expand. After the duration of a hundredth of a billionth of a trillionth of a trillionth (10^{-34}) of a second, it really got going. Up until that point, its rate of expansion had been comparatively slow. By 10^{-34} of a second, the universe was smaller than an atom in area but, once it had got its act together it found the energy to expand many times faster than the speed of light, doubling in size at least 90 times so that almost instantaneously it was the size of a golf ball. This period in the history of the universe is called, not surprisingly, *inflation*.

That the universe came into existence literally from nothing suggests that it was 'switched on' by something outside of it. So the Big Bang was neither big nor a bang. There was no sound, just the sudden and seemingly totally random appearance of matter. It is also essential to understand that this matter was not previously appearing in any location because space and time also did not exist before. Indeed, even using the expression 'before' makes no sense with regard to the Big Bang. Absolutely nothing spontaneously and seemingly for no reason became 'something'. With the simultaneous creation of space and time, matter had something to expand into. Indeed, it existed within an expanding space-time bubble. The bubble itself expanded rapidly. By rapidly, I mean really rapidly. The present expansion of space has been calculated as 67.4 km (41.9 miles) per second per megaparsec. As an aside, in September 2019, a team at the Max Planck Institute in Germany increased this expansion rate to 82.4 km (51.2 miles) per second per megaparsec. But even with this new increase, the expansion of space in the first few milliseconds of the Big Bang was much greater than this. How much greater? Well, I suspect that most of you reading this will believe that the fastest speed anything can travel is restricted by Einstein's theory which states that nothing can travel faster than the speed of light. Not true; the infant universe's expansion was much faster than the speed of light. Why? Well, there are two reasons. The first one is that space (or, more accurately, space-time) has no physical existence. Space, by definition, is nothing or, again, more accurately, no-thing. So a literal answer is that 'no-thing' can travel faster than the speed of light. Indeed, we generally consider travelling to be moving from one location in space to another. But it is space itself which is doing the travelling. So through, or more accurately, into what was space expanding? – because it certainly wasn't space. Confused? You should be. If it was creating space as it expanded, then it was, in a very real way, creating itself.

So, in less than 10^{-34} seconds the universe expanded out at 25 times the speed of light and then slowed down somewhat. It is now an ever-expanding sphere of space.

The concept of inflation was first suggested by a young post-doctoral student, Alan Guth, in 1980. But there are two significant issues with it. Cosmologists have been able to measure the temperature of space for 10 billion light-years in one direction and 10 billion light-years in the other, and the temperature of 2.73 kelvin is found in all directions. For the furthest reaches of either direction to have been in close enough proximity to equalize their respective temperatures in an expanding universe requires a universe that came into existence 20 billion years ago. With a universe only 13.8 billion years old, this is simply impossible.

To appreciate this expansion, let us imagine that the Big Bang took place five minutes ago. It would have expanded (but not into anything, as there is/was nothing to expand into) out from the original location of the Big Bang (which, again, is not quite right because, before the Big Bang, there was no location for it to start from). Now, imagine you are standing at that inception location. How far can you see in either direction? In order to 'see' anything, we need to have photons hitting our eyes. As photons travel at the speed of light, the furthest you could see would be around 56 million miles. So, in five minutes after the Big Bang, you could see 56 million miles in all directions. This would be a sphere of space with a radius of 56 million miles and a diameter of 180 million km (112 million miles). In effect, the width of the universe after five minutes would be 180 million km. The furthest you can see in all directions is known as the 'visible universe'. But here lies a huge problem. As time progresses, more of the universe becomes part of our own personal 'visible universe'. An hour after the Big Bang, information carried by photons will be available to us for a distance of 1078 million km (670 million miles) in any direction and a diameter of 2,157 million km (1,340 million miles). But even now, after 13.8 billion years, our visible universe is still revealing new stars and galaxies. This suggests that stars and galaxies exist outside of our 'light cone' (the technical term for the area that we can 'see'). But how did they get there? If the speed of light is the absolute limit, how can new objects be revealed? This suggests that the universe has expanded faster than the speed of light.

Final proof of the Big Bang was two discoveries from the 1960s. Firstly, it was shown that the early universe did not look how the universe does now and, secondly, in 1964, something known as the cosmic microwave background was discovered. This is the hot afterglow of the Big Bang fireball. This measured that the temperature of space is 2.73 degrees above absolute zero (expressed as 2.73 kelvin because the Kelvin temperature scale starts at absolute zero, −273.14°C). Using data from its Planck telescope, the European Space Agency has calculated how long it would take for this temperature level to have been reached by gradual cooling from the inferno of the Big Bang. From this, it has been concluded that the actual age of universe is 13.813 billion years old.

But as we have already discovered, the curious thing is that this temperature of the universe is the same in all directions. Why should this be? Science tells us that in the first seconds of the Big Bang, the universe was incredibly hot and has been cooling down ever since. But surely, as it expanded, it would cool down at different rates, particularly as the parts further away from the original source would become cooler. But it seems that the temperature is smooth in all directions. How can photons from opposite ends of the universe have the same energy levels?

We also know that modern science has an explanation for both these questions. Alan Guth's concept of inflation can be plugged in as a 'just-so story' to accommodate why the universe seems to be bigger than it should be if the speed of light had always been the maximum speed possible. As a reminder, to explain this mismatch, it seems that in less than 10^{-34} seconds, the baby universe expanded at 25 times the speed of light.

It is important here to realize that space itself was expanding at 25 times the speed of light in that new space was welling up from somewhere and pushing the already created space outwards at this colossal speed. Because space is literally nothing, it has no intrinsic mass and is not restrained by Einstein's rules. The baby universe increased its size by more than 10^{25} in less than 10^{-32} seconds. This huge expansion over a short period of time accounts for the existence of galaxies and stars outside of the light cone. In this short period, space expanded faster than light could traverse it, which explains how there still remain objects that have been pushed out so far that we have still not received the light they emit.

Guth's Inflationary Model also explains how the photons creating the background microwave temperature all have the same energy level (2.73 kelvin). Supporters of the model argue that before the period of rapid expansion, all the photons would have been crammed together in a vanishingly small area of space-time. It was then that they managed to share the same initial temperature level, and, ever since, they have been losing energy at precisely the same rate, wherever they are located in the visible universe.

The issue here is how do particles billions of light-years apart share the same information about themselves? Could the answer be the mysterious state known as entanglement?

Also known as 'superposition', entanglement is when two subatomic particles initially share the same quantum state and are sent off in different directions in space. If something is done to one particle, the other 'knows' instantaneously and reacts to it. This is irrespective of the distance between the two particles; they can be the other side of a room from each other or the other side of the universe. But, rather like Alan Guth's inflation speed of the early expanding universe, this information transfer takes place far faster than light speed.

It is essential to realize that this expansion of space has continued, albeit at a much slower rate than during Guth's inflationary period. As we have already discussed, in 2017 the European Space Agency calculated from the cosmic microwave background that the universe is 13.813 billion years old. The observable universe is a sphere that is 93 billion light-years in diameter. This sphere is expanding outwards at a rate of either 41.9 km (45.4 miles) per second per megaparsec or 73 km (45.4 miles) per second per megaparsec. A parsec (a parallax of one arc-second) is a unit of measurement equivalent to 3.26 light-years, so a megaparsec is 3.26 million light-years. This is like a balloon being inflated.

It is not the case, as you would naturally assume, that galaxies are pushing out from the edges of the universe, but that new 'space' is being created in the same way that new air is introduced into an expanding balloon. For example, this means that a galaxy a megaparsec away from Earth should be moving away at 67.4 km (41.9 miles) per second, while a galaxy two megaparsecs away should be moving away from us at a speed of 134.8 km (83.8 miles) per second.

Let us consider this in more detail. Space is, by definition, nothing. And yet, it seems that more 'nothing' is spontaneously appearing across the universe continually. This 'nothing' is spilling into this universe from . . . nowhere. It just magically appears. If this newly created 'nothing' is appearing everywhere, it means it is appearing at every point of space, including inside your brain. Of course, this gets even stranger when you apply Einstein's concept of space-time. Space and time are aspects of the same thing. So, if space is spontaneously being created at every location point in the universe, so is time. And what about gravity? Where does this fit in?

The Curvature of Space

You will regularly hear the statement that 'space is flat'. What does this mean? Some have confused this and suggested that if science states that space is flat, so is the earth as it is located in space. But this is not what is meant by this term. It is simply that on a flat surface, parallel lines will never come together. However far they stretch off into the distance, they will never get closer to each other and never diverge. It is important to realize that space stretches in all directions around us, and parallel lines setting off in any direction, up, down, sideways, will likewise never diverge or get closer. A flat universe can exist in a three-dimensional space. This is known as Euclidian geometry, named after the Greek philosopher and founder of the science of geometry, Euclid. For nearly

2,000 years, no one thought that any other geometry was possible. But then, in the mid-19th century, mathematicians such as the German Bernhard Riemann demonstrated the theoretical possibility of spaces whose dimensions are curved. In these geometries, lines that are parallel do intersect or diverge.

Within a flat universe, gravity is an issue. We all know how Isaac Newton supposedly saw an apple fall and, from this, formulated his laws of gravity. Newton was able to create a mathematical formula that could accurately calculate the strength of the gravitational force.

Newton realized that it was all to do with mass. More massive objects 'attracted' less massive objects. His apple was 'attracted' to the much larger earth just as the earth is 'attracted' to the much larger sun.

But there was a problem, a huge problem. Although Newton could create mathematical models that could be applied to small objects here on the earth and apply the same formulae to the stars and planets, he had no idea how gravity actually worked. What caused the attraction and, more importantly, how was the attractive force propagated through the vacuum of space? Also, there was the issue of whether gravity worked instantaneously throughout space or took time for its effects to reach out. For example, what would happen to the earth's rotation around the sun if the sun suddenly disappeared? Would the gravitational field stop instantly, or would it take time for the absence of the sun to affect the earth?

You may be surprised to discover that it was only in December 2012 that it was finally proven that gravity does, indeed, travel at the speed of light. What is even more surprising is that it was as late as October 2017 before it was discovered that the speed of gravitational waves was also equal to the speed of light (Cornish & Blas, 2017).

It was Albert Einstein who finally solved the mystery of how gravity works. In his General Theory of Relativity, he argued that gravitation is not a force but an effect of space-time curvature by matter. Any object with mass curves the space-time around it; the greater the mass, the greater the curvature. In this way, an object of less mass is 'attracted' to an object of greater mass because the space surrounding the larger mass is warped, which pulls the smaller object towards the larger.

If you check out any book that illustrates how the mass of objects curves space around it, you will probably be presented with a picture of a chequerboard pattern superimposed over a flat universe going off into the distance. The image will then show how an object like a star warps the space around it in a similar way to how a heavy object, when placed upon a sprung mattress, causes a depression around it. But the point has to be made that this analogy makes no sense. What is the 'depression' which causes the curvature pressing down into? It cannot be space because it is space itself that is being curved. But what does space 'curve' into? More space? Going back to our spring mattress analogy, the surface of the mattress is depressed into the space within the mattress itself. So what is this other 'space' that our regular space 'curves' into? This implies that there is another dimension that has to be created in order to accommodate this model. This really makes no sense in a physical universe.

But what, exactly, is 'space'?

Quantization of Space and Time

Imagine that we had the world's most powerful microscope. So powerful that you could magnify anything to infinite resolution. Let's imagine zooming at a part of your brain. We start with the grey matter and then zoom into the cells themselves, the neurons. From there, we magnify even more until we see the molecules that make up the neuron. We then focus in on the atoms and the space between them. Focusing on this seemingly empty space, we continue zooming in. The question is, how far can we zoom in? At present, the smallest size that can be viewed using an electron microscope is about one ten-millionth of a millimetre or 1 angstrom (a unit of length 10^{-10} metre named after the Swedish scientist Anders Jonas Ångström). But if we zoom in further, we find that space becomes very strange. We leave the theoretical strings from which modern science thinks elemental particles originate far behind as we dive deeper and deeper into smaller and smaller areas of space. Eventually, we will reach a resolution that cannot be magnified any more. This is known as the Planck length. This incredibly small distance is about 10^{-20} times the diameter of a proton.

But is space and time quantized? A sound wave of music is sampled on a music CD at 44,000 times a second. In doing so, time is chopped up into little chunks of 1/44000th of a second. But we hear the result as a continuous melody. Similarly, a digital photograph comprises thousands of single pixels, yet we see a seemingly continuous image. Could the quantum of space be the Planck length? Well, actually, no, because the Planck length is the distance between two points. This does not enclose an area of space. For the Planck length to be an area, it needs to be a Planck square – that is, a square: four Planck lengths. Is this the 'pixel' equivalent with regard to our reality? It has been further suggested that the smallest quantum of time is the time it takes to travel the Planck length at the speed of light: 5×10^{-44} seconds. This is called, not surprisingly, 'Planck time'. Are these quantized bits of time Julian Barbour's 'nows' discussed earlier?

We need, at this point, to add some form of perspective. There are more atoms in a glass of water than there are glasses of water needed to fill all the seas and oceans of the earth. So, atoms are tiny. But the nucleus of each atom is even smaller. We could cram a thousand billion atomic nuclei into the area of a single atom. According to quantum physicist Jim Al-Khalili, a single atomic nucleus can accommodate as many Planck lengths as there are cubic metres in our galaxy.

Furthermore, regarding Planck time, there are considerably more quanta of time in a single second (10^{-43}) than there have been seconds since the birth of the universe (10^{-18}).[13] Our best optical microscopes can probe down to the wavelength of light (around 10^{-7} metres). Electron microscopes can get down to 10^{-10} metres, and particle colliders can look inside the proton at distances of about 10^{-20} metres. Even the last level is 15 orders of magnitude away from viewing reality at the Planck length. Okay, what does this mean? Well, imagine that the smallest ruler you had was 1,000,000,000,000,000 (10^{15}) metres long, so this was, in effect, the smallest thing you could use to measure anything by. 10^{15} metres is around 100 times bigger than the width of the solar system. So an awful lot can be going on in that 15 orders of magnitude of size between what we know about and the Planck length.

And what is in that 15 orders of magnitude? Yet more space? But space is far stranger than we can ever imagine. Using the terms *vacuum* and *space*, it is natural to assume that space is absolutely empty of anything. After all, is that not what space is? Well, not really. Modern science has made another incredible discovery that most people are totally unaware of. Space is not a vacuum; it is a 'plenum'.

The word *plenum* is the neuter form of the word *plenus*, which literally means 'full'. This has its origins in Greek with the word *plérés*, which also means 'full'. Do you recall our earlier discussion about the ancient Greek belief in two realities, the Kenoma and the Pleroma? The Kenoma is this facsimile universe created by the Demiurge, based upon a real universe that exists outside of time and space. This was known as the Pleroma. Why? Well, because the ancient Greeks and their later Gnostic equivalents considered that the Pleroma was a place 'that fills' the emptiness. Quite literally, the Greek word *pleroma* means 'that which fills'.

Why did the Gnostics create such a concept? Could it be that they were aware in some way that hidden within the vacuum of space can be found the building blocks of the phenomenal world, a possibility that our science has only very recently begun to explore? Could it be that the duality of reality suggested by the Kenoma and Pleroma is more than just ancient speculation?

The Mystery of Zero-Point Energy[14]

You will likely have used a vacuum cleaner in the last few days or kept a drink hot or cold by using a vacuum flask. Like most elements of the modern world, we take these things for granted. However, the concept of a vacuum was, for centuries, considered to be an impossibility. The idea that there can exist space containing absolutely nothing was totally counter-intuitive. If a space contains nothing, then what constitutes the space itself? This question fascinated the early Greek philosophers. Aristotle and his followers believed there to be an absolute truth. For them, the statement 'nature abhors a vacuum' was beyond question.

But to understand this, it is necessary to define what we mean by a 'vacuum'. Imagine a completely empty universe. This universe contains no physical objects, just space. Can we reasonably say that this 'space' exists at all? For example, can such a place have distance in that distance is defined by physical objects? To state that my face is a metre away from my computer screen makes sense only if there is a physical computer screen and a physical face. If both disappear, the statement becomes meaningless. Distance needs objects to define it. Imagine now that there is just one object in space. Have we any idea in what direction it is moving? Indeed how can we tell if it is moving at all? The only way we can define the movement of one object is to define it against the position of another object. In this case, we can determine *relative* motion between two objects, but we can never objectively know which of the objects is moving. Speed similarly cannot be defined except in relative terms.

So space is simply the backdrop in which physical objects exist. Take away the physical objects, and you have a vacuum. However, existing within this vacuum can be found 'forces' that act in 'force fields'. For example, if the vacuum of space had two magnets in it, then one magnet's positive pole would attract the negative pole of the other and vice versa.

Conversely, the two positive poles would repel each other, as would the two negative poles. But how does this force work? Between the negative and positive poles is a total vacuum. The two poles are not in physical contact, and there is no medium between them, only empty space. Indeed this mystery is of profound significance because another 'force', known as gravity, seems to affect stars and planets millions of miles apart and galaxies millions of light-years apart. How does gravity cross such vast distances, and even odder, how does it have an immediate effect whatever the distance? Clearly, these 'force fields' are very strange indeed.

Modern science now knows of four different fundamental 'forces'. These are the electromagnetic force (the force that attracts or repels the poles of a magnet); gravity, the force that attracts objects to each other (but note that gravity only attracts and never repels); and the weak and strong nuclear forces that have been found within the atom itself.

It is fascinating to note that humanity had no idea of gravity for centuries, even though it is a force that sustains all life. This force was everywhere. It allowed the birds to fly free in the sky and turned the sails of a windmill in the same way that a fast-running stream of the substance called water turned a mill-wheel. Indeed it was an ongoing practical problem linked to milling and the movement of water that was to facilitate a huge breakthrough in man's understanding of his environment. In the mid-1640s, the pump-makers employed by the Grand Duke of Tuscany found that the maximum height to which water could be raised by using a suction pump was 10 metres (32.8 ft). This was a real problem because the Duke's valuable mineral mines were regularly filled with water, and it was crucial that this water be removed as quickly as possible. The Duke demanded a solution and approached the then professor of mathematics at the University of Pisa to consider how the 10-metre barrier could be overcome. The professor, Evangelista Torricelli, was intrigued and set about finding a solution. He became convinced that the weight of the air pushing down on the pools of water in the mines was the problem.

Following up on a suggestion by Galileo, Torricelli had his assistant, Vincenzo Viviani, fill a long tube of glass with mercury. Viviani then placed his finger over the tube's opening and inverted it over a bowl containing some more mercury. Torricelli observed that the mercury did not all flow down the tube and into the dish as might have been expected but that a small space above the mercury within the tube did appear. He realized that this space was absolutely empty of anything;

it was a vacuum. This discovery intrigued many thinkers. Finally, in 1654, the burgomaster of Magdeburg in Germany, Otto von Guericke, spectacularly proved the power of a vacuum when he made a globe from two copper hemispheres, removed the air from inside and had two teams of eight draft horses attempt to pull the two hemispheres apart.

Further experiments were done at this time, and it was found that sound was not transmitted through a vacuum. This was understandable because there was no medium for the sound waves to be transmitted in. However, it caused universal puzzlement when it was also discovered that light could be transmitted through a vacuum.

From this, it was concluded that normal vacuums, such as the ones created by Torricelli and Guericke, were not true vacuums because they still contained heat in the form of thermal radiation. It is now known that the only condition in which a complete vacuum can ever exist is if a regular vacuum is created at absolute zero, the temperature at which all thermal energy also disappears. Heat is understood to be a physical effect of electromagnetic energy. So when, at the coldest temperature possible, heat disappears, its source, electromagnetic energy, logically does so too.

Even modern experimental science cannot reach absolute zero, now calculated to be $-273.15°C$. This point has brought about a new temperature measurement known as 'kelvin' or 'K'. Absolute zero is the starting point of this scale, 0 K. As we have already discovered, due to the existence of cosmic microwave radiation, the average temperature of the vacuum of space is 2.73 K. This is because even space itself is not a pure vacuum. As we have already discovered, it contains cosmic microwave background radiation – the 'afterglow' of the Big Bang.

However, under certain artificial laboratory conditions, temperatures approaching absolute zero have been reached. These techniques are known as laser cooling or, more popularly, Doppler cooling. At this temperature, some extraordinary effects have been observed. Matter begins to act in ways unknown at higher temperatures. These include superconductivity, superfluidity, the mysterious Bose-Einstein condensates and, of extreme relevance to this discussion, the Casimir Effect, discovered in 1948 by Hendrik B.G. Casimir of the Philips Research Laboratories in the Netherlands.

Casimir placed two electrically conducting parallel plates a small distance apart in an enclosed container. The container was then turned into a vacuum. If the plates were initially charged, elementary electrostatics laws predict that a force would exist between them. However, and this is what surprised Casimir and his associates, even when the plates carried no charge, a force was still measured surrounding them. In 1958 a Dutch physicist, M.J. Sparnaay, discovered that this mysterious energy source would continue to be detected even at just above absolute zero.

Experiments using Doppler cooling have brought helium to within microdegrees of absolute zero. Even at this temperature, the helium remains in liquid form (Gasparini, 2012). Theoretically, there should be absolutely no natural energy existing in this state. Again, this is evidence that a form of energy exists just above absolute zero, a place where none should be found. It seems that quantum physics has an answer to this mystery.

In classical physics a pendulum that is not moving is said to have zero energy. It is at rest, so it has zero kinetic energy, and it is at its lowest point, so it has zero potential energy, and that's all the energy there is. However, in quantum mechanics, there is a principle known as the Heisenberg uncertainty principle, and this states that a system's momentum and position cannot both simultaneously be zero. Since potential energy is the energy of position, and kinetic energy is the energy of motion (velocity or momentum), Heisenberg's principle states that a quantum swing must have some energy even at a temperature of absolute zero. This is called Zero-Point Energy.

Since the discovery of Sparnaay, evidence for this energy has also been found in other phenomena, most notably something known as the Lamb shift, in which slight frequency fluctuations have been measured in light being emitted by an excited atom.

The idea that all empty space is full of energy was first suggested by British researcher Dr Peter Higgs back in 1964. Higgs proposed this as a solution to one of the greatest mysteries of particle physics: why some subatomic particles have a relatively huge amount of mass whereas others have a barely measurable amount and, indeed, some have none at all. Higgs suggested that there may be an as-of-yet undiscovered energy field that fills all space and that it is this field that brings about the mass of objects. On 4 July 2012, it was announced that the existence of the Higgs boson had been experimentally confirmed. This is an astounding discovery that has enormous implications for my Cheating the Ferryman hypothesis.

If the Higgs boson exists, then so does the Higgs field. A 'boson' is simply the carrier of information about a field. For example, the photon is the boson for the electromagnetic field. It is now believed that the Higgs field is everywhere. So as particles fly through the 'vacuum', they are slowed down by the surrounding Higgs field. Imagine that the Higgs field is like an ocean. The larger the fish, such as a whale shark, the more the fish will be slowed down as it swims through the water. This is simply because its body area ensures that it interacts with far more water molecules. A smaller fish, such as a sardine, can slide through the water because the level of 'water-drag' is much less. So it is within the 'Higgs ocean'. The level of drag on each fundamental particle is what scientists call 'rest mass'. It is this that creates the solidity of the objects we perceive around us. It is a direct reaction with a vast, invisible field of energy that fills everything. This force is external to objects in that it comes about from the interaction of particles with the external environment in which they move.

What is fascinating about this energy is that it exists within a vacuum. To do this, it must conform to the accepted basic ideas that modern science has about vacuum conditions. To be a true vacuum, the vacuum must define no unique places or directions. It must have no location in either space or time, and it should look the same in all directions. In other words, to be an element of the 'quantum vacuum' as this place has become known, the mysterious energy must be everywhere in every direction. This means that the 'vacuum' is not a vacuum at all but the absolute opposite: a plenum, an area of space that is full. This energy is now known as Zero-Point Energy (ZPE) and has the potential to be the most significant discovery humanity has ever made. For example, it is believed that it is the 'quantum vacuum' that subatomic particles appear from and disappear into in nanoseconds, the very subatomic particles from which the supposedly solid and physical 'material' universe is built.

Could it be that there is a direct link between dark energy, information and the Zero-Point Field? Could dark energy actually be Zero-Point Energy?

If this is the case, then there is a vast amount of Zero-Point Energy within the universe. Indeed John Archibald Wheeler calculated that a cubic centimetre of 'vacuum' contains so much raw energy that if this was condensed into matter, there would be more matter than is known to exist in the observable universe.[15] What is also intriguing about ZPE is that according to a new theoretical concept known as 'quantum holography', it may be a medium in which huge amounts of information can be stored. Not only that, but quantum holography also provides a model by which all self-organizing systems, such as life itself, use the information stored within the Zero-Point Field to evolve.

Could it be that the universe itself is created from holographic principles? This is far from a new idea. Earlier, we discussed the four Vedas of Hinduism. Of these, the most intriguing for me is the Atharva Veda, the Veda of 'magical formulae'. Somewhat contradictorily, it is also the most practical because it sets out procedures for the living of everyday life. But one section that is far away from the mundane and the everyday contains a description of something known as Indra's Net.

The Atharva Veda tells of the powerful god Indra who owns an infinitely large net of cords. On each cord is a jewel, and each jewel is a reflection of all the other jewels. If you could inspect one of the jewels, you would quickly discover that all the others were reflected in its surface. While each jewel is unique, they all reflect the magnificence of the whole.

The Mahāyāna Buddhists adapted this concept in their own *Avatamsaka Sutra*, written in the 2nd century:

> In the heaven of Indra there is said to be a network of pearls, so arranged that if you look at one you see all the others reflected in it, and if you move into any part of it, you set off the sound of bells that ring through every part of the network, through every part of reality.

In the same way, each person, each object in the world, is not merely itself but involves every other person and object and, in fact, on one level is every other person and object.

What is of enormous significance for our developing argument is the idea of Indra's Net and how it reflects modern science, specifically the science of holographics.

The Model: Holograms

Many of us carry round in our purses or wallets clues to the fact that the universe may be far stranger than we can ever imagine. Do you have a credit card or charge card? Take a close look at it. When you tilt a credit-card hologram, you see an image of something like a bird moving 'inside' the card. This is just one of the many applications of the amazing and comparatively recent science of holography.

The word *holography* (and an image created using holography known as a *hologram*) is taken from the Greek words *holos*, which, not unsurprisingly, means 'whole', and *graphos*, which means 'to write'. The word *gramma* means 'a thing written', so holography is the process of creating holograms.

To understand how a hologram works, we firstly need to understand what a laser is.

The word *laser* is shorthand for the descriptor 'light amplification by stimulated emission of radiation'. This is, in effect, an intense beam of light of a single colour. It is very different to everyday light. As we have already discovered, light is the part of the electromagnetic spectrum to which our visual system is sensitive. The human brain is programmed to present to consciousness specific visual colours directly related to particular wavelengths. The actual section of the electromagnetic spectrum to which our eyes are sensitive ranges roughly from 400 nanometres (violet) to 700 nanometres (red). Within this range, we find the specific colours. Violet light has the shortest wavelength, which means it has the highest frequency and energy. Red has the longest wavelength, the shortest frequency and the lowest energy. Specifically, the complete list is: violet, 380–450 nm (688–789 THz frequency); blue, 450–495 nm; green, 495–570 nm; yellow, 570–590 nm; orange, 590–620 nm; and red, 620–750 nm (400–484 THz frequency).

A laser generates a beam of very intense light. This has three elements that differentiate this from ordinary white light generated by, for example, a light bulb. Firstly, a laser is monochromatic; it is light of one single wavelength. Ordinary white light is polychromatic; it is made up of all wavelengths of visible electromagnetic energy. As we have already discussed, this is electromagnetic energy with a wavelength of between 400 to 700 nanometres. Each colour of the visible spectrum is contained within this range. When combined, all the colours merge, and this is perceived as pure white light by our eyes and brain. Of course, to stress again, these colours are simply how our brain interprets each wavelength. They have no independent existence outside of our perception of them. Secondly, laser light is directional. This means that the beam has a very low divergence.

Ordinary white light coming from a conventional source – again, think of a light bulb – spreads out in all directions. The further it spreads, the more it loses its intensity. Laser light does not do this. It maintains a thin beam that loses very little intensity over a considerable distance. The third difference is that laser light is coherent. All the waves of light in a laser are in phase with each other. This simply means that the peaks and troughs of their individual waves all match perfectly.

To create a laser, you will need something known as a lasing material. The perfect example is the precious stone known as a ruby. A single ruby is placed in a chamber between a pair of mirrors. Light is flashed into the chamber and runs back and forth between the mirrors. Within the ruby, each photon of light entering it pushes up the energy of any atom that absorbs it. A second photon then hits the electron and – rather than being absorbed – triggers the release of the first photon. The ruby acts as a light amplifier (LA) in which every photon that enters the ruby facilitates the emission of two photons, hence the LA section of the 'laser' acronym. The two emitted photons are in phase, which, as we have discovered, means that they are emitted in a tight beam. Very quickly, as billions of atoms are emitting in-phase coherent light, a powerful beam is created. This runs backwards and forwards between the mirrors, building up energy all the time. However, the second mirror is only partially silvered, which allows some of the photons out to produce the laser beam.

To further create a holographic image, we take this laser light and split it into two beams, one of which is reflected off the object to be recorded. This beam arrives at a photographic plate where it interferes with the first beam. To the naked eye, the pattern on the photographic plate is seen as simply meaningless swirls and patterns. An amazing effect occurs when this plate is illuminated with laser light; the swirls become a three-dimensional image of the original object. This image can be viewed from any angle. The photographic plate contains a hidden or enfolded order. This is well known. What is less well known is that if a holographic film is cut into pieces and again illuminated with laser light, each piece does not, as one would expect, hold a part of the whole image, but has a miniature copy of the entire original image. This is slightly fuzzy but nevertheless can be identified as such. The form and structure of the entire object is encoded within each region of the photographic record. The technical term for this is *mereological*. So a hologram is mereological – as is, possibly, the universe itself.

And it was this process that fascinated physicist David Bohm. Bohm believed that holograms could be used to explain his belief that our perception of separate things is an illusion and that there exists an underlying order of wholeness. He likened this to a flowing stream. He asked us to visualize the surface of this stream. We see an ever-changing pattern of vortices, ripples, waves and splashes. These seem real, but in actual fact, they have no independence from their underlying cause, the continual flowing of the water. They have no autonomy of their own. They cannot exist without this underlying motion. And so, he argued, it is with what we believe to be perceived reality, including human consciousness itself. He wrote:

> In the implicate order the totality of existence is enfolded within each region of space (and time). So, whatever part, element, or aspect we may abstract in thought, this still enfolds the whole and is therefore intrinsically related to the totality from which it has been abstracted. Thus, wholeness permeates all that is being discussed, from the very outset.
>
> Bohm, 1980

From this, Bohm suggested a model whereby the whole universe can be thought of as a kind of giant, flowing hologram, or holomovement, in which a total order is contained, in some implicit sense, in each region of space and time. The explicate order is a projection from higher dimensional levels of reality. The apparent stability and solidity of the objects and entities composing it are generated and sustained by an ongoing process of enfoldment and unfoldment. Subatomic particles are constantly dissolving into the implicate order and then recrystallizing.

This underlying structure can be found in the vast area of magnitude that we cannot measure with any of our instruments, effectively the space between the smallest thing we can see and the smallest part of space that exists, the Planck area. As we have already discovered, this is the Planck length, which is a two-dimensional line roughly equal to 1.6×10^{-35} m or 0.000 000 000 000 000 000 000 000 000 000 000 016 metres. This is about 10^{-20} times the size of a proton. To put it another way, suppose that you measured the diameter of an atom in Planck lengths, and that you counted off one Planck length per second. To measure the atomic diameter in Planck lengths would take you 10 million times the universe's current age.

On this scale, the entire geometry of space-time, as predicted by general relativity, breaks down. The main reason for this breakdown is that the Planck scale, which we discussed earlier, is smaller than the quantum wavelength of the universe as a whole.

Of possibly great importance here is linking Bohm's model of holography and the implications of John Cramer's Transactional Interpretation of Quantum Physics, discussed earlier. You will recall that Cramer argued that there are two forms of electromagnetic energy that manifest as 'retarded' and 'advanced' waves. Retarded waves travel forwards in time, and advanced waves travel backwards in time. I have suggested from this that when they encounter each other, advanced and retarded waves create an interference pattern which is identical to one that creates a holographic image. In doing so, they create the seemingly three-dimensional universe that we perceive all around us. We shall return to the implications of this later.

You will also recall earlier that I discussed Daniel Dennett's concept of the Cartesian theatre and how I adapted this to reflect a much broader expanse of human experience, something I call the 'Bohmian IMAX'. I hope you will now appreciate why I chose this particular term. According to David Bohm, human consciousness and the universe it perceives are linked in a much broader (and deeper) uber-reality whereby everything is consciousness, and by the act of observation, we draw out of the Implicate Order the Explicate Order which is, in effect, Kant's 'phenomenal world'.

Towards the end of his life, and in his last published work, Bohm was to write the following:

> Consciousness is much more of the implicate order than is
> matter . . . Yet at a deeper level [matter and consciousness]
> are actually inseparable and interwoven, just as in the
> computer game the player and the screen are united by
> participation in common loops. In this view, mind and
> matter are two aspects of one whole and no more separable
> than are form and content.
>
> Bohm & Peat, 1987

This comment has proven to be amazingly prescient. There is growing
suspicion that the physical universe is, in fact, a huge hologram and that
everything is, in a very real sense, a single unity, a single unity that may
be a form of all-pervading consciousness. But what evidence do we have
for such a belief? Well, quite a lot, actually, and all of it has to do with a
subject closely related to holographic imagery; information.

Dark Matter and Information

A few years ago, something extraordinary was discovered with regard
to the rotation of galaxies. They rotate with such speed that they should
have ripped themselves apart many years ago. But they have not. All
observable galaxies retain their shape, as do globular clusters.

Why this is so can be tested for yourself. Tie a weight to the end of
a piece of string of, say, three metres. Holding onto the other end, start
to spin round. The weight will soon lift off the ground and will rotate
around you. The speed you have to rotate to keep the weight in the air is
not great. Now pull the string in to, say, one metre, and continue to spin.
You will have to spin a great deal faster to keep the weight in the air.
This is similar to how gravitation works in the solar system. The planets
further out revolve around the sun much slower in relative terms than
those nearer in. This law relates to all orbiting systems. The balance
between gravitational pull and centrifugal forces means that the further
something is away from whatever is holding it in orbit, the slower it will

move. The stars, star clusters and nebulae that make up a galaxy all revolve around a central core. So all galaxies are rotating in the same way that planets revolve around a star.

But here lies a problem. Experimental science states that the further away from the gravitational force, the slower an object should go. But, in 1933, Swiss astronomer Fritz Zwicky noticed something odd about the Coma cluster of galaxies. According to his calculations, the stars on the edge of the galaxies were moving far too fast in relation to the galaxy's mass. Zwicky calculated that the actual mass of the Coma galaxies needed to be 400 times greater than what had been measured. As with much of modern science, when an anomaly is observed – something that doesn't fit in with what the scientific paradigm demands – scientism takes over. Scientism is an approach to scientific analysis whereby prior held beliefs on the nature of reality are more important than observed, empirical information. As Zwicky's observations contradicted the rules of faith, they were simply ignored. That was, until 1970, when Carnegie Institute American astronomer Vera Rubin, after many years of detailed observations, concluded that the rotational curve of the Andromeda galaxy was the total opposite of what should be expected. As with Zwicky's Coma galaxies, the star velocities on the edge of the galaxy made no sense. This time all the stars, irrespective of their distance from the central source of gravitational attraction, revolved at the same speed. These stars, according to the rules of centrifugal force, should be regularly flung into deep space. Andromeda should have been falling apart. It wasn't. But our cosy idea of a nice materialist-reductionist universe was!

However, it took until the early 1980s before astronomers gave up trying to fudge the unpalatable fact that a large percentage of the universe was missing. They continued to debate the actual implications of Rubin's discovery but were less keen to share this information with the public.

The missing mass was termed 'dark matter', not because it is dark but simply because we cannot detect its presence directly; we can only detect it by its effect on the matter around it. It is totally invisible. It has been calculated to bring about its impact, there must be six times as much dark matter as matter. In simple terms, this means that 26.8 per cent of the universe is 'missing'.

In 1997 astronomers noted that throughout its history, the universe has expanded at different rates. It expanded rapidly immediately after the Big Bang and then slowed down for around seven billion years, and then expansion started speeding up again. This suggested the existence of another mysterious and invisible form of energy. Not surprisingly, this became known as dark energy. When the amount of dark matter and dark energy are calculated into the mass of the universe, it is found that ordinary, 'baryonic'[16] matter contributes 4.9 per cent of the total mass of the universe.

Various theories have been proposed to explain the true nature of dark matter and dark energy, but none have explained what these mysterious forms of matter and energy consist of. I would like to propose that dark matter is made of something we are all very aware of – information. This may sound crazy, but I am not alone in this idea. Dr Melvyn Vopson of the University of Portsmouth has proposed a model he calls the mass-energy-information equivalence theory. In simple terms, Vopson argues that information has mass and is the basic building block of the universe. To understand this, we have to go back to the 1940s and the work of revolutionary thinker Claude Shannon.

Shannon was a mathematical engineer working at the Bell Laboratories in New Jersey. In 1940 he was tasked with making telephone switching boards more efficient. He then made an association between how switching circuits worked and a relatively obscure form of mathematics called Boolean algebra.

In 1854 English primary school teacher George Boole published a book entitled *The Laws of Thought*. In this extraordinary book, Boole showed that all algebraic manipulations could be done using two numbers: zero and one. A digit that is either zero or one is technically known as a binary digit, or 'bit' for short. Shannon applied this model to information transfer and, in 1948, he summarized his findings in an academic paper. This single paper revolutionized our understanding of information theory and changed telecommunications forever. In this, Shannon wished to define precisely what information is. He observed that when acquiring information, we learn something we didn't know before. We are, therefore, less uncertain about that something.

For example, we know there can be two outcomes, heads or tails, when tossing a coin. When analyzed in terms of certainty and uncertainty, we can make the following observations: toss the coin but do not look at the outcome – uncertainty 100 per cent (1). Look at the coin and discover that it came up heads – uncertainty 0 per cent (0). As there are only two outcomes (heads or tails), this is a binary choice, 1s and 0s. This is an example of George Boole's concept of a 'bit'. By observing the result of the coin toss, you have gained one bit of information.

By quantifying information as bits, Shannon showed that information was identical to entropy. Disorder is directly related to the number of outcomes of an action, which relates to the number of things involved. For example, a single molecule cannot be considered disordered, but the more molecules added to the assemblage, the greater opportunity for disorder.

There may be far more entropy and information to be had than simply what is immediately apparent. For example, our coin example involves a non-described coin type. But what if an expert in coinage was viewing it? When she looks at the coin and sees, say, heads, she can elicit far more information. She may be able to identify a specific type of coin, the year it was produced, what country, and many other factors that she did not know before she looked. In this way, entropy is in the eye of the beholder. This brings the universe back to the 'observer' status that has already been discovered in quantum mechanics.

But what we are discussing here is how information is described, and this is by using mathematics and language. But words are not accurate descriptors, whereas numbers are. Objects can be measured using number systems. These can involve measures of distance and weight. These number systems can be manipulated in various ways using geometry, arithmetic and algebra. In itself, this is quite a curious thing. Is mathematics a creation of the human mind, or is it something intrinsic to the universe? Do mathematical equations exist independent of the human mind in that we 'discover' them, or are they a creation of human intelligence, a structure that we have imposed on a chaotic cosmos?

From mathematics, we can create physics, the direct study of physical objects and the space in which they exist. Once we have the physical sciences to open up our understanding of the universe around us, we create something else, information. The model is a simple progression of mathematics – physics – information.

In recent years several scientists have argued that this progression is incorrect and that the primary entity from which reality is built is information itself.

And yet again, it is the great John Archibald Wheeler – the physicist whose work we have already discussed regarding the role of the observer in collapsing the wave function (Wheeler J.A., 'Information, physics, quantum: The search for links', 1989) – who first suggested, with Rolf Landauer, the German-American physicist and pioneer thinker in the field of information technology, that information was prime (Landauer, 'Computation and Physics: Wheeler's meaning circuit?', 1986). A few years later, in 1998, Wheeler created the powerfully descriptive slogan 'it from bit', a concept that we are now going to review in some detail (Wheeler & Ford, 'It From Bit' in *Geons, Black Holes, and Quantum Foam: A Life in Physics*, 1998).

According to Einstein's Theory of Relativity, observers moving at different speeds will disagree about both their personal measurement of time and distance. But one thing we can all seemingly agree on is the speed of light. Light will always be perceived as travelling away from us at 299,338 km (186,000 miles) per second from whatever position we are. By joining space and time in a new reality called space-time, Einstein created an external structure by which all duration and location can be objectively measured. However, Wheeler argued that his delayed-choice experiment, discussed above, suggested that space-time itself is not fundamental and that there is another level of objectivity from which space-time is created. For Wheeler, everything that is 'it' is created from information, 'bits'. He very succinctly defined this as being 'it from bit'. In a work published in 1990, he described this quite precisely:

> It from bit. Otherwise put, every it – every particle, every field of force, even the space-time continuum itself – derives its function, its meaning, its very existence entirely – even if in some contexts indirectly – from the apparatus-elicited answers to yes-or-no questions, binary choices, bits. It from bit symbolizes the idea that every item of the physical world has at bottom – a very deep bottom, in most instances – an immaterial source and explanation; that which we call reality arises in the last analysis from the posing of yes-no questions and the registering of equipment-evoked responses; in short, that all things physical are information-theoretic in origin and that this is a participatory universe.
>
> Wheeler, 1990, p. 5

In effect, Wheeler suggested that everything, from space-time to subatomic particles, is created out of binary choices. And it is from Wheeler, Shannon and specifically Landauer that Vopson takes his starting point for his own mind-blowing proposition that information itself has mass and energy.

Earlier, in 1961, Landauer had argued that even the destruction of one bit of information would generate a tiny amount of heat. This became known as the Landauer Principle. This effectively links thermodynamics and information in that the irreversibility of the deletion is the same as the irreversibility of entropy. Vopson takes this further, arguing that, once created, information has 'finite and quantifiable mass'. His mass-energy-information equivalence theory calculates that the mass of one bit of information at room temperature of 26.85°C is 3.19×10^{-38} kg.

Not only that, but he also suggested in a paper published in September 2019 that the mass of a data storage device such as a disc drive or an SD card would increase by a small amount. For example, for a 1Tb device, the mass change from empty of data to full of data would be 2.5×10^{-25} kg (Vopson, 2019). But it is the conclusion that Vopson draws that is simply mind-blowing. Read this very carefully:

> Assuming that all the missing dark matter is in fact information mass, the initial estimates (to be reported in a different article) indicate that 10^{93} bits would be sufficient to explain all the missing dark matter in the visible Universe. Remarkably, this number is reasonably close to another estimate of the Universe information bit content of $\sim 10^{87}$ given by Gough in 2008 via a different approach. In fact, one could argue that information is a distinct form of matter, or the 5th state, along with the other four observable solid, liquid, gas, and plasma states of matter. It is expected that this work will stimulate further theoretical and experimental research, bringing the scientific community one-step closer to understanding the abstract nature of matter, energy and information in the Universe.
>
> Vopson, 2019, p. 4

Here Vopson suggests that dark matter is, in fact, information, and that it is also the fifth state of matter. But can this be extrapolated to dark energy? We know from Einstein that matter and energy are related, so the same relationship must be found between dark matter and dark energy. And what are the implications for the Holographic Principle whereby 'information' is smeared on the event horizon of a black hole? This is discussed on p.207.

Sadly, at the moment, the ultra-accurate mass measurement needed to quantify this minute weight difference is not available. Our technology simply cannot measure differences so small. But there is no reason to believe that such a machine cannot be created in the future.

What is even more exciting here is how Vopson describes how many bits of data are needed to describe all the missing dark matter (10^{93}). This is reminiscent of how many Planck squares containing one bit of data are required to describe the visual universe using the Holographic Universe model. But there is much more, and this comes from research into the other great 'dark' area of modern cosmology, black holes.

Black Holes and Information

Recently some startling discoveries have been made with regard to the fine-structuring of the observed universe. These discoveries are the first to show that the perceptual cosmos may, indeed, be created out of digital information and that it is, in effect, a huge hologram.

In physics, there is something known as entropy. In effect, any system moves from a state of order to a state of disorder in a gradual but inexorable process. This only ever goes in one direction. It has never been observed that something in a state of disorder gradually changes to order. For example, an egg in its initial state is in a state of total order. Its shell is intact, and the yoke and white are perfectly separated. If that egg is dropped onto the floor, it smashes. The shell is shattered, and the yolk and white are mixed up. This process can never be reversed. We interpret this uni-directional process as a series of changes through time. Indeed, it is correct to state that this process is time or at least a visible and measurable aspect of time itself. And time, like entropy, only ever goes in one direction. As a system becomes more disordered, its state of entropy is said to be increasing.

States of entropy are described by information. An ordered, stable, low entropy system needs less information to describe it than a disordered, high entropy system. This shows a link between information and entropy; more entropy needs more information to describe it. As such, information is integrally linked with physical objects, according to Einstein, created out of energy. For example, a nuclear bomb's power comes from the release of a huge amount of energy from a tiny amount of matter. From this, a direct link can be made between energy and the information that describes that energy.

The Law of the Conservation of energy is an axiom of modern physics. In simple terms, it states that the total energy of any isolated system remains constant; it can be neither created nor destroyed. Of course, in our everyday world, energy does seem to disappear. For example, your coffee gets colder, showing the power of entropy again. The heat energy is not lost; it is converted and spread over a wider area. Another issue is that the heat is lost because however much you try, your study is not an isolated system. But the universe is. The universe cannot lose energy or the information that describes that energy. But it seems to.

It all comes down to black holes. But what exactly is a black hole? In simple terms, it is a star that has collapsed upon itself and becomes so massive that nothing can escape from its gravitational field, not even light. Let me explain this. The mass of an object causes gravity. The more massive the object, the greater the gravitational force it contains. You and I are held on the surface of the earth because the earth is much more massive than we are. However, at specific speeds – known as 'escape velocities' – an object can escape the gravitational force of a much more massive object. To overcome the earth's gravitational force, an object needs to travel away from the surface at a speed of 40,266 km (25,020 miles) per hour. As the moon is much less massive (and is captured by the earth's gravitational field, hence why it is in orbit around us), its escape velocity is only 8,568 km (5,324 miles) per hour. However, black holes are so massive that the escape velocity is greater than the speed of light. This is why it is a black hole. It gives off no electromagnetic energy (light) and therefore is totally black. However, as nothing can travel faster than the speed of light, nothing can escape a black hole once it has been sucked inside. But this is where things get weird. According to modern science, when anything is sucked in, it is destroyed; it ceases to be. This violates the law of the conservation of energy. The universe is an enclosed system, yet energy and accompanying information are totally destroyed, not converted into anything else.

So, let us imagine throwing a mobile phone into a black hole. All the information in that phone, digital and physical, is destroyed. But this contradicts the First Law of Thermodynamics – that energy (information) is always conserved. It may be changed, but it cannot be lost in an enclosed system (such as the universe). But it is lost if it is thrown into a black hole. A solution to this issue has recently been proposed. This suggests that as an object is sucked in, a copy of all the information describing the object is smeared out along the surface of the black hole. This means that all the information describing everything inside a black hole is on the surface of that black hole. Any surface is a two-dimensional surface, including the surface of a sphere. A sphere also has an inner surface that faces inwards. Of course, a black hole is, in effect, a vast sphere, and so is the expanding universe. And just like any sphere, the universe has an inner edge.

Could it be that the edge of the universe may function in the same way as the surface of a black hole? That it contains a two-dimensional area within its inner surface that encodes all the information about everything inside the sphere? This inner surface is technically known as the Cosmological Horizon.

Assuming the universe is isotropic (meaning it has a physical property which has the same value when measured in different directions), then it is a spherical region centred on the observer (and this in itself tells us something about the role of the observer). Its diameter is 8.8×10^{23} km, and it consists of 4.9 per cent ordinary (baryonic) matter, 26.8 per cent dark matter and 68.3 per cent dark energy. Could all the information needed to describe all the matter in the universe be similarly smeared along the inside edge of the Cosmological Horizon?

In 2013 research was published in *Nature News* by Yoshifumi Hyakutake and colleagues from Ibaraki University. This discussed a calculation involving the gravity-related string theory of Juan Maldacena of Princeton, who, in 1997, suggested that gravity arises from infinitesimally thin vibrating strings which exist in nine dimensions of space plus a tenth of time.[17] Maldacena argued that the universe actually consists of two separate areas; the ten-dimensional universe of strings and a simpler, flatter cosmos where there is no gravity. The former exists as a hologram. The Japanese team have shown that there is a precise mathematical link between the two realities.

In one paper, Hyakutake computes the internal energy of a black hole, the position of its event horizon (the boundary between the black hole and the rest of the universe), its entropy and other properties based on the predictions of string theory as well as the effects of so-called virtual particles that continuously pop into and out of existence (Hyakutake, 2013). In the other, he and his collaborators calculate the internal energy of the corresponding lower-dimensional cosmos with no gravity – the two computer calculations match (Hanada, Hyakutake, Ishiki & Nishimura, 2013).

In response to these extraordinary findings, one of the founding fathers of the Holographic Theory, Leonard Susskind of Stanford University, commented:

> They have numerically confirmed, perhaps for the first time, something we were fairly sure had to be true, but was still a conjecture – namely that the thermodynamics of certain black holes can be reproduced from a lower-dimensional universe.
>
> Cowen, 2013

In other words, another universe exists in a 'lower dimension' of reality, and it is this universe that facilitates the creation of this one. So what do we mean when we use the term 'dimensions' in this regard?

I suspect that the 'lower-dimensional universe' is made of pure information. That information is encoded in the Zero-Point Field, and the perceptual universe is a programme using this information to create itself. The questions then have to be, what is the nature of this programme and, more importantly, who has written the code?

The Universe as Information

In 1965, Gordon E. Moore, the co-founder of Intel, made an astounding prediction. He stated that the number of transistors that could be placed on an integrated circuit would double every year. Later, in 1975, he revised this to a doubling every two years. This has recently been revised to every three years. One can only imagine what processing power will be available to software designers in, say, 300 years.

What will our descendants do with all this processing power? If today's technology is anything to go by, they will attempt to create, among other things, computer-simulated virtual realities. For example, on 16 September 2020, Oculus announced a virtual-reality headset known as the Oculus Quest 2. This challenged the marketplace of similar headsets such as the PlayStation VR Headset and the HTC Vive Pro, which needed to be attached to a powerful laptop or PC. The Quest 2 carried its own processor and could be worn anywhere. When activated, the headset plunges the 'observer' into a totally believable three-dimensional environment indistinguishable from everyday reality. Such is the effect of the simulation that software designers have deliberately made the virtual-reality environment less real because there have been concerns that photo-realistic environments could be psychologically damaging. But in the final analysis, these are game-related environments that are, by their very nature, unreal.

But recent developments in technology have allowed researchers to create accurate renditions of actual reality. It is all to do with applying something known as quantum chromodynamics, a process that describes the workings of one of the four fundamental forces of nature; the strong nuclear force. This is the force that binds the basic building blocks of matter, quarks and gluons together to form protons and neutrons. We are now in the position to be able to programme computers to simulate how this force develops. Using the world's most powerful supercomputers, scientists have simulated a tiny corner of the cosmos a few square femtometres in area. A femtometre is 10^{-15} of a metre. This may sound like a ridiculously small amount of space (a quadrillionth of a metre or 0.000000000001 mm). This small area of space is, to all intents and purposes, indistinguishable from the real thing (Beane, Davoudi & Savage, 2012). The only restriction in creating more extensive areas of simulated reality is the available computing power.

It is only a matter of time before the region of a few micrometres will be reached. This is large enough to simulate a human cell. If this is the case, then it is not beyond comprehension that we may, in the far future, have sufficient computing power to simulate a whole universe. With this in mind, could it be possible that a hugely advanced civilization has already simulated a universe – and that we exist within it?

The point at which humanity reaches this ability to simulate reality has been called the Omega Point or the Singularity. The former was suggested by French priest-scientist Pierre Teilhard de Chardin and the latter by futurologist Ray Kurzweil.

Kurzweil is the inventor of, among other things, the flatbed scanner and the Kurzweil keyboard. As a convinced futurologist, he believes that computing power is developing so quickly that we will be able to digitize somebody's life and upload it into an on-screen 'avatar' within a few decades. In his best-selling book *The Singularity is Near,* he suggests that in time human consciousness will become digitized and as such will cease to be embodied within what we generally call 'reality' (Kurzweil, 2006). Our awareness will exist in a 'virtual reality' created from information located inside a vast computer. But there is more to this than simply the idea that humanity will somehow relocate into a virtual world. Kurzweil argues that humanity has been evolved explicitly for the cosmos to bring itself to 'self-awareness'. We are on the road to 'cosmic awareness'.

The idea that our reality may be an instantiation, to use Andrew Gallimore's terminology, was first suggested by Oxford University philosopher Nick Bostrom in 2003. In an article published in the *Philosophical Quarterly* (Bostrom, 2003) he suggested that it was almost certain that we were all living in computer-generated simulations of our lives. In simple terms, his argument goes as follows. We know from the famous Moore's Law that computer processing power doubles every two or three years. There is no reason to believe that this will not continue for some time to come, the only restrictions being how small we can make printed circuit boards. Indeed, a new area of research called quantum computing suggests that processing power may be almost limitless for future generations. If humanity survives and moves into a 'post-human' phase – in other words, that we evolve in such a way that our technology and ourselves will become melded in some way – then this infinite processing power will be readily available. So what will our post-human ancestors do with this processing power? Bostrom suggests that it is inevitable that they will create ancestor simulations and populate them with the people who lived in history.

If today's technology is anything to go by, it is reasonably clear that Bostrom was right in his assumption that future scientists will attempt to create ever-more realistic computer-simulated virtual realities.

Of course, a virtual-reality programme needs a perceiver to bring it into existence. For example, I have recently acquired an Oculus Quest 2 virtual-reality headset. Yesterday I downloaded a virtual-reality version of one of my all-time favourite computer games, Myst. In its original version from the early 1990s, it consisted of a series of images of a mysterious island that the game-player explored and, in doing so, was tasked to solve a series of puzzles. It was immensely enjoyable but very static. You viewed the island on your computer screen, and by pointing and clicking on a particular location, the image would change, and you would be viewing that location from a new vantage point. In 2020 the game was completely redesigned for a virtual-reality environment. In this new version of Myst, you find yourself, after donning your Quest headset, surrounded by the island. You can wander around, and in every direction you look, it feels as if you are there. It feels totally real. But the stereo images rendered on the internal screens are not a continual image. They are made up of millions of pixels. What initially presents itself as a three-dimensional reality is a two-dimensional projection made up of pixels, and each pixel is a single point of light that is individuated and surrounded by others. The illusion of an island location disappears as we look closer and realize that it is, in fact, just individual pixels. Without a game-player whose visual and auditory systems interpret the results of these binary instructions, and whose brain then creates and presents to the conscious 'observer' the illusion of an island with all its buildings, artefacts and geography disappears.

In other words, the instantiation needs consciousness to 'collapse its wave function' in precisely the same way that particles need consciousness to collapse theirs. Is this simply an extraordinary coincidence, or is this evidence that the Kenoma is a facsimile of the Pleroma?

If this is the case, then there should be observable and quantifiable effects to prove that time and space and all the things they contain are subjective experiences that have no independent reality. We have already discussed one clue to this, the Unruh effect. I would now like to introduce to you another, the simply mind-blowing concept known as Momentum Space.

Evidence: Momentum Space

As we have already discussed, the four dimensions of 'space-time' (height, width, breadth and time) had long been considered the absolute and unchanging scaffolding of the universe. Then Einstein changed all this by showing that nothing in space is consistent, and the length of an object or the timing of events are different for every observer. This is literally what he meant when he applied the word 'relativity' to his theory. Everything is *relative* to the viewpoint of the observer. This is a crucial point to appreciate, particularly when linked to the fact that quantum physics tells us there is a direct relationship between the behaviour and possibly even existence of subatomic particles.

Einstein argued that space and time were aspects of the same underlying something he called 'space-time'. This does not mean that they are related somehow, but they are actually the same thing. Space can become time, and time can become space. However, for Einstein, this relative perspective related only to space and time, but not space-time itself. When unified, there is an ultimate objective reality that is consistent for all observers and independent of them.

But it seems that our understanding of space-time is only half the picture, quite literally, as it appears that there may be four more dimensions to add to the four we already know of.

Look around you now. You will see this book (or an on-screen equivalent), and beyond that, you will see objects, maybe a table or a chair, a cup of coffee and four walls. But what you do not see is space and time. Instead, what you do see is energy and momentum existing within the container we call space-time. Everything you see around you, again including this book, is 'seen' by your brain when photons of electromagnetic energy bouncing off objects hit your retina. By detecting the photons' energy and momentum, your brain reconstructs a facsimile of the world around you, in effect, the space and time that makes up your experiential world. Indeed, every scientific measurement we make regarding the physical world uses the same process. For example, when we look through a telescope at a distant quasar, we measure energy and momentum, not space and time.

In 1938 German physicist Max Born noticed that several fundamental equations used in quantum mechanics could also be applied equally effectively to momentum space. This was significant because one of the most important problems of modern physics has been that when equations used in quantum mechanics are applied to relativity, they come up with impossible results such as infinities. For science to have a consistent understanding of the universe, the maths must work in the same way for quantum mechanics and general relativity. General relativity deals with space-time and quantum mechanics deals with momentum and energy. This idea, which has become known as the 'Born reciprocity', offered a considerable advance in our understanding of the universe and maybe even provided a long-sought-after theory of quantum gravity. Sadly, at that time, the mathematics to prove such a model were not available and, of greater significance, there was no idea what form of entity could curve momentum space.

However, recent advances in mathematics have led Lee Smolin and Laurent Freidel of the Perimeter Institute for Theoretical Physics in Waterloo, Canada, Jerzy Kowalski-Glikman of the University of Wroclaw, Poland and Giovanni Amelino-Camelia of Sapienza University in Rome to present a new application of Born's reciprocity which they term 'phase space'. This is an eight-dimensional world that merges into our familiar four dimensions of space-time – the other four dimensions that make up phase space to collectively create momentum space.

From this observation, Smolin and his associates argue that we do not live in space-time; we live in momentum space. Momentum space has a similar structure to space-time (time on one axis and the three dimensions of space on the other), but it has energy replacing time on one axis and momentum, with its three coordinates, populating the other. Smolin and his team then applied the maths to the curvature of momentum space and came to some extraordinary conclusions. They discovered that space-time itself is also effectively different for each observer. Of even greater significance was that the team found that over time and distance, the difference increases. This is of great significance because how can we ever say that there is an objective 'reality' outside our perceptions if a different version of space-time exists for each perceiving consciousness?

An article in *New Scientist* published in August 2011 showed just how reality will differ for two observers within momentum space. For example, if you are 10 billion light-years away from a supernova, your measurement of its location will be different to where a local observer knows the supernova is. This is calculated at being around 300,000 km (186,411 miles). And both you and the local observer are right. In a very real sense in your personal universe, the supernova is in one place, whereas in the local observer's universe, it is in a completely different location. You and the local observer are existing in different universes. And remember, this happens with regard to *every* event. Scientists now call this phenomenon 'relative locality'.

As the author of the article, Amanda Gefter, rightly observes:

> Relative locality would deal a huge blow to our picture of
> reality. If space-time is no longer an invariant backdrop
> of the universe on which all observers can agree, in what
> sense can it be considered the true fabric of reality?
>
> Gefter, 2011, p.36

Relating to our earlier discussions regarding the Unruh Effect, I stated
that if an observer is just above the event horizon of a black hole and is
released and, in doing so, accelerates in one direction or another, they
will perceive no radiation. But if that same observer, or another observer,
is held stationary, they will perceive an infinite amount of radiation. So,
which set of information is correct? No radiation or infinite radiation?
When taken into account with regard to our discoveries regarding
Momentum Space, we must quickly conclude that we all exist within our
own 'relative' sensory universe whereby space, time and location are all
intensely personal concepts. In this, I am reminded of the concept of the
phaneron as proposed by American philosopher Charles Sanders Peirce
(1839–1914). In his collected papers he describes this as being:

> . . . the collective total of all that is in any way or in any
> sense present to the mind, quite regardless of whether it
> corresponds to any real thing or not.
>
> Peirce, 1931, p. 284

In my opinion, this is a powerfully effective description of what modern
cosmology and quantum physics are telling us about the true nature of
the matter-mind interface. What is the contents of the mind at any point
in time is, in effect, reality as far as that consciousness is concerned.

Indeed, if we apply this to the Cheating the Ferryman hypothesis, we
move into some very challenging areas of speculation. We have already
discussed evidence that each consciousness 'collapses' its own wave
function and, in doing so, creates its own refined version of reality. But
there is also an argument that each consciousness *contributes* to a broader

reality created by all observers conscious at that moment in time. In the past, I have termed this 'consensual reality', but in my last book, *The Hidden Universe: An Investigation into Non-Human Intelligences,* I changed this to the far more descriptive 'egregorial reality' (Peake, 2019).

We have now discovered evidence of the relationship between the observer and the instantiation, but what about the components of the instantiation, the quite literal 'bits' from which it is created. Have we any proof that we can sometimes spot the joins, as it were? Possibly yes, and it is all to do with the speed of light.

Maximum Speed

Time is flexible. When we travel at great speeds, time slows down. Time also speeds up the greater the gravity field (or curvature of space). Why should this be?

This can be explained by using virtual-reality (VR) game analogy. Every computer user knows that when the server is busy, the frame-rate drops off. Time suddenly slows down within the game environment. We need to explore this in more detail to see if this may be more than just an analogy, possibly even a clue to what is actually happening.

Within a VR environment, distance is measured in pixels and time in cycles. These are similar to the frames in a film with regard to time and the spaces between the image dots in relation to its space. When we watch a film, what we are really looking at is a series of still images. When originally recorded, the film camera took snapshots of a scene at a rate of 24 still images (frames) every second. Each image is therefore slightly different to the one before as objects in the scene change position. These are located in sequence on a cine film. When passed in front of a light source with a focusing mechanism at a rate of 24 images per second and projected onto a screen, the light image gives the illusion of pure movement in space and time. What is moving in physical space is the cine film, not the two-dimensional objects projected onto the screen. The illusion of motion perceived when observing a film running at 24 frames a second seems continuous only because our eyes refresh 30 times a second.

And the same may be the case for the universe itself. As we have discovered, the smallest possible amount of time is known as Planck time, which is 10^{-43} of a second. This is effectively the 'refresh rate' of the universe. Planck time is the time needed for a light photon to travel the Planck length. In turn, the Planck length is the smallest piece of space that is possible. In digital terms, Planck time can be defined as an equivalent to cycles and each Planck length to a pixel. From a quantum point of view, the value of the speed of light is simply one. Does this explain the mystery of why the universe has a seemingly arbitrary speed limit?

Our universe seems to have a restriction to it that makes no sense. Nothing can travel faster than the speed of light. Why is this? The equations work, but they give no explanation as to why they work. But if we assume that this universe is a digital universe similar to a vast computer programme, then the restriction is simply the refresh rate of the programme. This would suggest that the speed of light is always one pixel per cycle within our universe, which is the Planck length divided by Planck time. For us, from our perceptual position, 299,337 km (186,000 miles) per second are simply values we apply.

When you play a computer virtual-reality game, a photon, in the guise of a screen pixel, can move from point to point only as fast as the screen refresh rate allows. In a virtual reality, the screen cycle rate defines a maximum pixel transfer speed across a screen.

Now imagine that each unit of Planck time is similar to the individual frames of a cine film. There is a gap between each unit of 'quanta' of time as there is a black line between each film frame. Similarly, each unit of Planck length (or, more accurately, Planck 'space') is quantized and in isolation from its neighbouring Planck units.

That space and time are not continuous but come in unique and self-contained 'bits' may sound bizarre, but this is simply a reflection of the fact that matter and energy are 'quantized'. As Einstein proved, both matter and energy are aspects of the same thing, as are space and time.

Indeed, space-time is now a scientific term that is universally accepted. So, if matter-energy is quantized, why not space-time? Indeed, this may be evidenced by an ongoing issue with field theory. In order to work, it needs continuity, not individuation, but mathematically such a model suggests infinities when a mathematical trick known as 'renormalization' is applied.

As we discussed earlier, a Planck length is the linear distance between two points. To be an area of space, it needs to be a Planck square, with each side being a Planck length. From this, it becomes clear that the smallest area of three-dimensional space will be a Planck cube.

And Planck squares play a crucial role in one of the most exciting discoveries in recent years; that the universe may be a two-dimensional holographic projection.

Earlier, we discussed the mystery of why the cosmic microwave background is very close to 2.73 degrees above absolute zero in all directions that it has been measured. This cannot be explained if the universe has simply expanded at up to light speed. We have also discussed how Alan Guth proposed something known as *inflation*, in which space expanded at many times the speed of light straight after the Big Bang. This period of rapid expansion allowed the universe to reach a uniform temperature very quickly so that at the end of the inflationary period, all parts of the universe had the same temperature, cooling down, in the same way, to reach the 2.73 K observed today. Any tiny fluctuations around this temperature are known as low multipole moments, and it was data on these supplied by the Planck satellite in 2017 which suggested something quite extraordinary.

A group of scientists based in Canada, the UK and Italy, analyzed the multipole data against what would be expected if the standard cosmological model was correct or if the holographic model discussed extensively in this book was a better fit with regard to the experiment's results. Of crucial significance regarding my CTF model, the data received fitted better with what would be expected if the holographic model was correct (Afshordi, Coriano, Delle Rose, Gould & Skenderis, 2017).

So why is the holographic model of great importance with regard to my Cheating the Ferryman hypothesis? In simple terms, it proposes that anything you can know about a particular volume of space can be learned by looking at the surface enclosing the volume. You will recall this is precisely what a hologram does when it contains a three-dimensional image within a sheet of glass or plastic. The holographic model argues that this is exactly what the universe does. It stores all the information needed to create a seemingly three-dimensional universe on a two-dimensional surface.

In 1981 the Israeli cosmologist Jacob Bekenstein published an article in the journal *Physical Review* (Bekenstein, 'Universal upper bound on the entropy-to-energy ratio for bounded system', 1981). In this, he proved that the amount of information you can squeeze into a specific region of space is proportional to the area of the surface surrounding that space. Many years later, in August 2003, Bekenstein expanded this idea in a much-discussed article that appeared in *Scientific American* (Bekenstein, 'Information in the Holographic Universe: Theoretical results about black holes suggest that the universe could be like a gigantic hologram', 2003). In effect, this means that the amount of information that can be stored depends upon the area, not the volume. The information is encoded on the boundary rather than within its bulk.

Of course, there is one massive issue regarding both the holographic and instantiation models, and that is the nature of self-referential consciousness. If consciousness is central to the collapse of the wave function and to the perceptual creation of the universe, what creates consciousness? A simple answer is that it is the brain, and the brain is created out of information and data in the same way that everything else is. But, as Australian philosopher David Chalmers pointed out in a paper published in 1995, modern science has no idea how self-referential consciousness can be created out of brain processes (Chalmers, 1995). He called this the 'hard problem'. Within the present paradigm of science, no answer can ever be found to this question. However, while Kurzweil's model also flounders on the rocks of Chalmer's 'hard problem', as we shall discover later, the theories of Jesuit palaeontologist Pierre Teilhard de Chardin do not. And this is because de Chardin argued that consciousness is prime, and it is consciousness that creates reality.

The Omega Point

After he had co-authored *The Anthropic Cosmological Principle* with John D. Barrow, Frank Tipler bravely took the findings of his book to its logical conclusion, presenting an argument that not only had the universe been designed, but it also had hard-wired within it an ultimate purpose. This purpose was to bring about what he called the 'Omega Point'. Tipler had borrowed this term from the writings of the great French Jesuit palaeontologist Pierre Teilhard de Chardin.

In his studies into palaeontology, de Chardin had noted that the evolution of consciousness seemed to run counter to the Second Law of Thermodynamics. Unlike physical systems which are characterized by entropy (chaos increasing with time), evolution imposes increased order on biological systems as they respond more effectively to environmental conditions.

In his book *The Phenomenon of Man*, he suggested that energy exists in two forms, 'tangential' and 'radial'. The former is the energy that scientific instruments can measure. The latter is a form of psychic energy. Tangential energy is governed by the Second Law of Thermodynamics, whereas radial energy is not. In the early 1950s, de Chardin began to believe that his tangential energy could be related to 'information' and that information in itself countered the Second Law.

For de Chardin, information processing, when taking place within the electrical circuits of a computer, were similar to how the brain generates thought. Both are seemingly non-physical effects created by a physical process.

From this model, de Chardin suggested that just as non-conscious life had spread across the planet to create a vast, interrelated biosphere, consciousness had similarly spread to cover the earth in a non-physical form which he termed the *noosphere* (from the Greek *noos* meaning 'mind' and *sphaira* meaning 'sphere'). Therefore, the biosphere is created by tangential energy and ruled by the Second Law of Thermodynamics, whereas the noosphere is created by radial energy. This was powerfully prescient in that we now know that information has created its own niche regarding the World Wide Web and the creation of virtual realities that are rapidly becoming indistinguishable from what we believe to be 'real' reality.

In an earlier book *Cosmogenesis*, published in 1922, de Chardin argued that evolution does not end with humanity but has a teleological imperative by which inanimate matter evolves over billions of years to a state of divine consciousness. Over time, matter comes together to create life which, in turn, brings about consciousness. In its initial state, life adds another level to the universe by collectively manifesting a *biosphere*, a sphere of life. As it acquires consciousness and then self-consciousness, another level is added, the *noosphere*, as described by de Chardin and his associate, Ukrainian biochemist Vladimir Vernadsky. In effect, both the biosphere and the noosphere are additional layers similar to layers of sediment in geology.

In time, humanity will evolve and, in doing so, will escape the 'heat death' inevitability inherent in the Second Law of Thermodynamics. We will do this by reaching what de Chardin calls the 'Omega Point'. This is where consciousness incorporates itself into a single unity, which will be what we know as God. De Chardin saw this to be linked in some way to information as data, and that the Omega Point existed both inside linear time and outside of it.

In *The Phenomenon of Man*, de Chardin proposes that the evolution of consciousness through time is analogous to taking a series of sections through a cone, starting at the base and working to the top. Each section is a circle that decreases in size from the one before. Eventually, it reaches a point state, a *singularity*. It is at this point that the universe itself becomes 'self-aware'. In doing so, he gave the universe, and everything in it, a purpose.

Could the link between my Cheating the Ferryman hypothesis and the philosophy of the eternal return and the theological concept of Maya be exactly what I am trying to impart in this book: information? I would now like to pull all the threads together and review what has been termed the Science of Immortality.

PART 6

Models of Immortality

Michael Mensky's Quantum Concept of Consciousness

In a fascinating new theory, Russian physicist Michael Mensky has proposed a radically new interpretation of Everett's Many-Worlds Interpretation. Mensky, based at the Lebedev Physics Institute in Moscow, calls his model Quantum Concept of Consciousness (QCC) or the Extended Everett Concept. He believes that this model offers a scientific basis for, among other things, the Jungian collective unconscious.

Mensky focuses on the observer's consciousness when a 'measurement' occurs. The mystery is how the observer unconsciously chooses one actual reality from all the other potential realities available to them. Why does this outcome occur rather than the trillions of others? Mensky has an interesting solution to this problem.

He argues that all alternatives are realized and that the observer's consciousness splits between all the alternatives. However, the observer, in some way, chooses to witness just one of the outcomes. Mensky argues that this happens because the observer is, in some way, 'entangled' with the actual outcome of the experiment. This cleverly side-steps the issue of how consciousness collapses the wave function by having the observing consciousness and the wave function of the system being intrinsically linked. The implications of this model are quite profound; it suggests that the observed world is simply a projection of the quantum world that comes into existence when that world is 'selected' by the consciousness of the observer. In effect, this means that each perceptual universe – what I call the *phaneron* after the writings of Charles Sanders Peirce, which we discussed earlier – is unique to each observing consciousness. Even more intriguing is that the observer's interests and biases also affect the nature of the universe brought into existence. We not only create our own reality, but we can influence how that reality is presented to us. In an extraordinary statement, Mensky writes:

> If, for instance, a close relative dies in one of these realities and remains alive in another, the conscious subject is highly motivated to select the latter alternative. If he believes in this case that he is able to affect the selection, it is not inconceivable that he will actually increase the probability to some extent that he will witness precisely the latter alternative.[18]

This is very much in keeping with my own 'egregore' model which I presented in my last book, *The Hidden Universe*. In this, I argue that the actual experiential phaneron of each person is influenced by them. In this way, they witness events that reinforce their belief system. For example, one person sees a ghost, and another does not. This is because the two people are existing in subtly different (but probably overlapping) Everett Universes.

But what about all the other universes that exist in parallel with the one perceived? Mensky argues that all these universes are 'observed' by his version of Carl Gustav Jung's 'collective unconscious'. He terms this the 'super-consciousness'. This super-consciousness has access to information that exists in both the past and future. He believes that any singular consciousness experiencing a singular Everett Universe can, under certain circumstances, access the knowledge banks of the super-conscious, a process he calls 'super-intuition'. The emotional response to such acquisition he calls 'cognitive euphoria'. This is when spontaneous creativity breaks through. Those of you who are aware of my 'Daemon-Eidolon Dyad' and 'Huxleyian Spectrum' will see immediate parallels here.

Interestingly enough, Mensky makes particular reference to anticipatory scientific discoveries, which he argues in a 2014 paper involve the scientist accessing information from the super-conscious mind (Mensky, 2014). I agree with this, but for me, it is more the access to the knowledge of the Daemon, the part of the Dyad that has access to all other lives and all the information gleaned in those lives. This can then be viewed within the structure of Mensky's QCC and my own CTF model. By attending to the possible existence of specific scientific outcomes, the scientist brings into existence the very particles they are looking for.

I would argue that science has already discovered powerful evidence that we, both collectively and individually, create our own versions of reality. We have already encountered the Unruh effect, Momentum Space, the Collapse of the Wave Function and a number of other scientific discoveries pointing us to this conclusion. But for my model to work, there must be evidence that the act of observation *actually* collapses the wave function rather than the collapse being inferred by the science. This may now be the case. Recently David Chalmers, who we encountered earlier regarding his 'hard problem' of consciousness, has been working with Kelvin McQueen of Chapman University, California. Together, they have come up with a mathematically grounded account of how consciousness can bring about the collapse.

In an as-yet unpublished paper, Chalmers and McQueen apply integrated information theory (IIT) to the question of the wave function collapse.[19] In effect, this states that any system that integrates information is conscious. In a recent article in *New Scientist*, science writer Anil Ananthaswamy quoted McQueen as saying:

> In this way of thinking, consciousness creates classical reality, but it doesn't create quantum reality. It's converting quantum reality into classical reality.
>
> Ananthaswamy, 2021

Read this very carefully. McQueen suggests that our perceptual reality, Peirce's 'phaneron', is mind-created, but the quantum world is independent of the observer. And yet, as we have already discovered, particles remain waves of probability without an 'act of measurement'.

Scientists who follow the Copenhagen Interpretation happily accept that the wave function collapse is real; that a statistical probability wave changes form to being a point particle. The question is, what makes this happen? It happens at the point the wave is 'observed'. The question is, what do we mean by observed? Can the measuring device be an 'observer', or does the change only occur when a consciousness observes the wave? Furthermore, does that consciousness need to be self-referential?

Assuming that consciousness brings about the collapse, then the massive question is how consciousness brings about the collapse of the wave function. What does it do to make a wave become a particle? Does consciousness and the wave function move into a state of superposition?

Chalmers and McQueen, with regard to the question of consciousness and the wave function collapse, make the following observation:

> The key idea here is that consciousness is a superposition-resistant property and that its physical correlates therefore resist superposition too. That is, it is difficult or impossible for a subject to be in a superposition of two different states of consciousness, and this results in the collapse of physical processes that interact with consciousness.
>
> Chalmers & McQueen, 2020

Effectively, for consciousness to be in a superposition state would involve the observer being in two states of awareness. Let's take a totally materialist-reductionist stance on this. The physical brain state – that is, the configuration of the neurons and the neurotransmitters, will be identical in that they are the same thing. This should be identified using brain scanners. As far as I am aware, no experiment has taken place to determine this. But surely, if we are continually collapsing the wave function of the reality around us, then the neurological effects of this should be continually evident during MRI and fMRI scans. But this is not the case. If, however, we take a dualist stance on this (that consciousness is not created by brain states but is facilitated by them), then there should be no physical evidence for neurological superposition.

I believe that science is looking in the wrong place concerning this ongoing mystery. The answer may lie in something far more interesting, the idea that consciousness is immortal and the perceiver brings into existence the perceived, but only within the phaneron of that perceiver. And this position led to a very intriguing application of quantum mechanics and immortality, something popularly known as the 'quantum suicide' experiment.

Max Tegmark's Quantum Suicide

One morning in 1985, a student was riding his bike through the streets of Copenhagen on his way to school. As he approached a cross street where he always turned left, he considered whether there was any point in looking right because there was never any traffic in that part of the city at that time in the morning. For some reason, he felt it was of great importance that he did look. As he did so, he saw a speeding 40-ton truck bearing down on him. He slammed on his breaks just in time. Had he not done so, he would have been killed instantly.

The young student was Max Tegmark, whose theories we have discussed earlier, now one of the world's leading theoretical physicists. In a recent book, he observes that his decision to look or not look right all came down to:

> . . . whether a single calcium atom would enter a particular synaptic junction in my prefrontal cortex, causing a particular neuron to fire an electrical signal that would trigger a whole cascade of activity by other neurons in my brain.
>
> Tegmark, 2014, p. 4

In 1997 Tegmark took the implications of his life-or-death decision to its logical conclusion by applying the implications of Schrödinger's cat, the Copenhagen Interpretation and the Many-Worlds to imply that death may be something that only ever happens to other people.

He proposed a thought experiment similar to Schrödinger's cat. He asked us to imagine that a machine gun is attached to a device that measures the z-spin of a subatomic particle. All subatomic particles have this, and it can be either 'up' or 'down'. However, the direction of spin is entirely random and cannot be predicted for any single particle. If the device 'senses' a particle with a 'down' spin, it instructs the machine gun to load a single live bullet into the stock. If the particle spin is detected as 'up', the gunstock remains empty with the weapon just making an audible click.

An experimenter stands in front of the gun and asks her assistant to pull the trigger to test the weapon. The assistant nervously follows the instruction and presses the trigger. The device detects that the particle's spin is 'up' and does not load a bullet into the stock. The gun makes an audible click, and the experimenter remains alive.

The experimenter suggests that they now go through a further nine repeats of the experiment. She stands in front of the gun, and on each occasion, the stock remains empty. After the tenth repeat, she tells her assistant that it is time to end the test and go home for the evening. The experimenter feels satisfied that the Many-Worlds Interpretation has been proven correct and invites her relieved assistant out for a quick celebratory drink.

Now let us go back to the start of the experiment and experience it from the viewpoint of the assistant. He follows the instructions given by his boss. He presses the trigger three times, and on each occasion, the gun clicks. However, on the fourth attempt, the subatomic particle has a 'down' spin, a bullet falls into the stock, and the trigger engages. A bullet flies out of the barrel and crashes through the skull of the experimenter, killing her instantly. In a blind panic, he phones the police and is arrested for murder.

So what has happened here? Is the experimenter alive or dead? Did they go for a drink, or did the assistant face a murder charge? Tegmark argues that in the same way that Schrödinger's cat is both alive and dead in different universes, so is the experimenter. In her universe, she did not die, but she did in the universe of her assistant. The crucial point here is that the only reality that the experimenter can possibly perceive is the one in which she survives.

Although this is a thought experiment, it has a direct relationship with this book's subject matter. Empirical science arguably shows that personal immortality is not only possible but probable. Not only this, but modern science also provides a location where all these alternate lives can be lived; it is called Hilbert Space. This is the mathematical construct that contains all the possible solutions of the variables in the Schrödinger equation. In effect, it is a space containing all the wave functions that have not 'collapsed' in this one. Although this is a mathematical rather than physical location, academics such as Tegmark argue that mathematical information creates the seeming physical universe that surrounds us. This is not as strange as it seems. If you don a virtual-reality headset, you are immediately thrown into a seemingly real, three-dimensional world, yet this 'reality' is created from digital information processed using mathematical equations. And, as we have already discovered, there is a robust case to argue that reality is, in its purest sense, created out of digital information.

Interestingly, co-travellers along this road of quantum immortality with Tegmark and myself are theologians, specifically John Hick and Eric Steinhart.

John Hick and Eric Steinhart

Earlier, in our review of a number of religious and philosophical beliefs, we used our central thesis, the Aldous Huxley model of the perennial philosophy, the idea that all religions teach the same thing at their purest level. This was also the central belief of the American-based British philosopher of religion John Harwood Hick (1922–2012).

Hick was a fundamentalist Christian who, after reading the works of Immanuel Kant, revised his position and began to take a much broader and inclusive approach to religious beliefs. He became a great advocate of religious pluralism and was the first chairman of All Faiths for One Race (AFFOR). From this, it is fair to conclude that he was open to the Aldous Huxley concept of the perennial philosophy. Indeed, such was his unorthodoxy that on two occasions, he was the subject of heresy proceedings in the early 1960s.

Hick's interest in Eastern religions and his seeking a unified, underlying belief system is evidenced in his books *More Than One Way?* and *God and the Universe of Faiths*. But it was in his 1976 book *Death and Eternal Life* that his ideas on plurality with regard to life after death took a very interesting direction.

In this book, and in keeping with his own inclusivity, Hick reviews the various models of the afterlife found in the world's major religions and takes a grounded empirical approach to the evidence for such models. This involves a philosophical evaluation of the Eastern concepts of reincarnation and the Western concept of bodily resurrection. He finds both models unsatisfactory with regard to modern science. For example, according to most Christian theologies, the human personality survives the body's death and continues to exist in a spiritual form for an indeterminate amount of time. Then, there will be a physical resurrection of the body at some stage, and the person will be reconstituted.

He discusses in detail the concept of the *eschaton*. This is the final outcome of God's plan for the universe. Hick points out, according to Christian theology, that between each soul's death and the eschaton will be a considerable amount of time. The question is, what happens to each individual soul between the death of its body and the time of the eschaton. Hick terms this period to be the *paraeschaton*.

To replace the classical post-mortem bodily resurrection model, Hick created his 'replica' theory. He asked his readers to imagine a person disappearing in a London street, and at the same moment, an absolute replica of that person appearing in New York. On examination, it is discovered that the New York person is absolutely identical to the person who disappeared in London right down to the molecular level. The only difference is what Hick terms 'continuous occupancy in space' (Hick, 1994, p. 280). Hick then asks us to imagine that the person in London died instead of disappearing, and the replica appears in New York. The difference here is that there is a corpse in London and a live version of that corpse in New York.

Hick then asks us to imagine that the replica appears not in New York but on a different planet or even a different space-time dimension. To all intents and purposes, the replica would be the dead person, but still alive. I am reminded here of the wonderful *Riverworld* series of science-fiction novels written by Philip José Farmer. In these, Farmer has every human being who has ever lived resurrected on a planet that has a river winding from pole to pole. In the novels, each being has an immortal associate known as a *wathan* which is uncannily similar to my concept of the Daemon. I cannot help but wonder if Farmer's first book, *To Your Scattered Bodies Go*, which was published in 1971, may have influenced Hick's 'replica' hypothesis.

Hick argues that the state immediately after death is 'subjective and dream-like'. Again I note parallels here, this time with the Bardo state of Tibetan Buddhism, which we discussed extensively earlier. In this transitory world, the 'replica' may experience personal memories of their past life and scenarios created out of their expectations as to what the afterlife may consist of. Although Hick fails to make a link here, I would argue that the classic near-death experience whereby dead relatives, friends or religious figures are encountered all take place in this version of the Catholic concept of Limbo. Furthermore, I would add that as this place is timeless, then many reruns of the replica's life could also be accommodated.

The final outcome of Hick's model is the achievement of the eschaton in which all humanity will meld into a singular consciousness and move into what he terms 'transcendental reality'. This converges with the Buddhist and Hindi models whereby the soul is merged into the singularity of Brahman or the One.

Interestingly, in his article 'Reincarnation and the Meaning of Life', Hick refers to a model not dissimilar to my Cheating the Ferryman hypothesis. He does this as part of a broader discussion on the meaning of Nietzsche's take on the 'eternal recurrence', which, to clarify, Hick has great problems with because it involves living the same life repeatedly. In contrast, he argues that having the opportunity to live one's life again, or a period of one's life again, with the knowledge of what you did during that period, is a far more liberating idea.

In this regard, Hick cites the Scottish philosopher David Hume who asks the same challenging question but, as Hick observes, 'without the poetic extravagance of eternal recurrence'. He uses a section from Hume's 1779 *Dialogues Concerning Natural Religion* where the character Demea says:

> Ask yourself, ask any of your acquaintance, whether they would live over again the last ten or twenty years of their life. No! but the next twenty, they say, will be better.[20]

To which Hick himself replies:

> For however satisfying our life as a whole may have been during the last ten or twenty years, we can all think of innumerable points at which it could have been better, so that, if we are comparing the way it has been with the way it might have been with these improvements, we would say No to the actual in comparison with the improved version. But we must eliminate this comparison in our thought experiment. I have to try to look back on my life as a whole during the last ten or twenty years and ask whether I would wish to live it again just as it has been, not changed or improved in any way, and without knowing that it had

all happened before. It would be exactly as though one was living it for the first time, the alternative being not having existed at all.[20]

This is precisely what I suggest takes place in Cheating the Ferryman. As I described previously, Russian philosopher Peter Ouspensky, in his 1915 novel *The Strange Life of Ivan Osokin*, has his central character, the eponymous Osokin, relive a period of his life with the prior knowledge of all the mistakes he made last time. Ouspensky has Osokin make exactly the same mistakes, suggesting that we are doomed to an eternal recurrence because even with prior knowledge, we will still make the same decisions.

Hick was a hugely influential thinker within certain theological circles, and his work stimulated a number of younger philosophers, one of these being Eric Steinhart, whose Revision Theory of Resurrection mirrors even more closely my Cheating the Ferryman hypothesis.

Steinhart, professor of philosophy at the William Paterson University in New Jersey, argues that most resurrection theories violate all natural laws, making them physically impossible. He then sets himself the task of creating a theory that does not violate these laws. In this regard, he states that:

> We are not aware of any resurrection theory that is fully consistent with natural Laws.
>
> Steinhart, 2008

In his paper, Professor Steinhart acknowledges that Hick's replication theory is the only life-after-death theory he is aware of that does not violate all natural laws. I do find this extraordinary in that there is absolutely no science of any description used by Hick to support his theory. Indeed, Steinhart subsequently uses the lack of supporting science to diverge from Hick's theory to begin his exposition of his own model. He writes:

On Hick's theory, the replica is not made by a natural combination of atoms. It is not conceived by the sexual union of a human father and mother. It does not gestate in any womb and is not born from any woman. It is not part of any biological process of evolution. The replica appears on the resurrection earth by a kind of spontaneous generation. It does not have any apparent antecedent cause. It appears as if by magic. Its appearance is miraculous. But that is not naturalistic. We want a theory in which the appearance of the resurrection body is natural and lawful. We will have to modify Hick's theory.

Steinhart, 2008, p. 71

Steinhart subsequently discusses another resurrection theory, that of P. Forrest, who suggests that a future civilization could take a copy of a human zygote, a fertilized egg cell, and a new version of the person is grown from this. This then could be reborn on a paradise version of the earth. He then suggests that this paradise earth will have an identical history to that of the original earth. He recognizes that as the regenerated version will repeat the initial life from conception to death and repeat this on an endless repeat of that life, this will be similar to Nietzsche's eternal return of the same. Steinhart considers that this will avoid Hick's spontaneous generation problem. However, as a believing Christian, he has great reservations regarding the eternal return of the same because:

… it entails neither the physiological improvement of the resurrection body nor the moral improvement of resurrection society.

Steinhart, 2008, p. 73

He argues that his own revision theory of resurrection (RTR) overcomes this problem by rejecting exact repetition in favour of ongoing improvement life after life. His 'proof' for this does not come from any form of science but simply that if God wishes to make it this way, he can:

> An earthly body has an earthly biography. Given your earthly biography, God can work out how it can be improved. Given a set of earthly biographies, God can surely work out how they can all be improved together.
>
> Steinhart, 2008, p. 73

He continues with the theological theme in his 2014 book. In this Steinhart makes this interesting statement:

> [Revision Theory] is linked to the old Buddhist doctrines of impermanence and no-self. The doctrine of impermanence resembles the digitalist theory of exdurance.
>
> Steinhart, 2014, p. 165

But he fails to point out that RTR is also not like reincarnation because, in reincarnation, the person is reborn as somebody else, or possibly even an animal or insect. In this respect, RTR is remarkably similar to CTF. However, he again falls back onto a theistic explanation by arguing that each life is better than the previous one, not through a form of evolution as suggested in CTF, but through the intervention and 'scripting' by a 'god':

> Your current life is a revised version of your previous life, which was lived out in some previous ecosystem, in some previous universe, running on some previous god. Once your previous life was over, that previous god figured out the ways to improve it. One of these ways is the script for your current life. Your current life follows this script, which was defined in its entirety, from your conception to

your death, before our universe began. This script includes
your present body-program (your present soul) as well as
its inputs. It defines a life that is better than your last life.

Steinhart, 2014, pp. 169–170

My CTF hypothesis does not need a Calvinistic-like god that
predetermines how our lives develop, just a Daemon to be aware of the
issues encountered last time. Furthermore, it successfully overcomes
all of Steinhart's reservations regarding his own theory. My evidence
presented in support of CTF is from science rather than theology
or, as Steinhart is keen to point out, 'scriptural evidence for multiple
resurrection' (Steinhart, 2008, p. 75). Later in the article, however, he
does cite – as I do with regard to CTF – supporting evidence from
the Cosmic Anthropic Principle of Barrow and Tipler and the various
multiple-universes theories. Still, I believe that he fails to make any
causal link between the science and his theory other than similarity.

I find Steinhart's RTR fascinating and I believe that it is of the utmost
importance that science and spirituality work together to answer the
ultimate questions of existence.

Epilogue

At the start of this book, I described the various scenarios that may face us when we die. We have now spent a great deal of time reviewing why I believe that my revised Cheating the Ferryman (CTF) hypothesis offers a rational, logical alternative that uses science to create a model that invalidates no religious beliefs and, in many ways, supports them. Let us now review what this model proposes and present it as a fourth alternative.

CTF suggests that your consciousness enters a timeless location at the point of death, and you are 'reborn' in a new version of your previous life. You are reborn as *you*, not as somebody else. You are born of the same parents (or possibly any scenario whereby your exact DNA profile is reproduced).

Of course, your birth location and scenario will depend upon a myriad of life decisions made by your parents, your grandparents and, indeed, all your ancestors. Each outcome of every decision is made by a consciousness that can 'collapse a wave function' and therefore creates a reality out of the information field that exists within the macroverse. Your 'rebirth' will involve you downloading an initial information field based very closely on your previous life. This allows for logical and sequential progression whereby the last life's issues can be resolved or unfulfilled scenarios followed through. These alternate realities are created from information, not physical objects (although their amalgamations are perceived as being physical objects).

This is like loading a third-person role-playing computer game. The game's scenario is rendered from digital information that appears as a location and landscape on your PC screen (more accurately, a virtual-reality world as rendered by an Oculus Rift or similar device).

Epilogue

Once you start this new life, all outcomes of all your decisions can be 'collapsed', but once 'collapsed', the scenario becomes physical and cannot be changed. Decision by decision your new life as you enfolds (to use a David Bohm reference) out of the Implicate Order and into the Explicate Order.

This sounds like reincarnation (which it is, in the literal sense of the word), but you are *you*, not somebody else. The major difference is that there is part of you in this second life which carries the memories of what you did last time. This is the immortal you, your Daemon. This is the real you that exists in orthogonal time, in the fifth dimension outside of time and space. But you, the sentient being inside this virtual-reality game, is unaware of these memories. You are an Eidolon, a being that lives just one life and then 'dies' at the end of that life.

You die. Your Daemon does not. The Daemon accesses the information of your previous lives via your DNA which, in turn, can access data from the Zero-Point Field (Bohm's Implicate Order). How open your Doors of Perception are will depend on how effective your Daemon will be in communicating with you. If it can, it will use its knowledge of your previous incarnations (games) to guide you through this one.

But the Daemon can guide you only as long as it has experienced the decision-outcomes taken in previous lives. When a completely new scenario is encountered, its only advice can be general because it, like the Eidolon, is encountering this set of circumstances for the first time. And here is the big difference between ITLAD and reincarnation. Here, there is development; here, there is a carry-through of life experiences. Here is the opportunity to learn from one's mistakes. Indeed, here is a scenario to right the wrongs and explore other avenues not taken. Over many lives (because at the end of each one, a new one is encountered), 'all roads can be taken', especially with an effective and engaged Daemon.

So what is the point of all this? Well, just as Phil Connors did in the film *Groundhog Day*, every Daemon has the opportunity to guide its numerous Eidolons to live 'the perfect life' and, in doing so, move on to the day *after* Groundhog Day.

This is precisely the logic that supports the classic interpretation of reincarnation as espoused by Buddhism and Hinduism (and the traditions of Sufism, Gnosticism and many other esoteric systems). We need to live many lives in order to reach the Buddha state. When we eventually become an 'avatar', we can move on to the next stage.

It must be stressed that *all* these 'groundhog lives' take place in the final nanoseconds of life as we experience it within linear time. By the time we reach the actual point of clinical death, we will have lived countless lives in orthogonal time, a form of time that exists at right angles to the flow perceived within this Gallimorian Instantiation.

Human beings, or indeed any process of self-reflecting consciousness existing in the material universe, have existed for hundreds of thousands of years on this planet and possibly millions of years on other planets. Each epoch of time has been seemingly different, with different technologies, cultures and philosophies. However, these 'different' cultures are different only when viewed from each of our own phanerons. The history that we experience is simply the history of this particular version of the Bohmian IMAX, the one that has evolved in time to bring about that specific observer.

In my previous books, I have regularly discussed that time is the most critical dimension. But as I stated above, we each have our own observer-universe. So for others, time will have evolved differently, meaning subtle differences in the cultural and scientific environments. Each shared phaneron will be collectively created by all the observers whose aggregated observations (created from their own psychological histories) bring about a shared cultural and technological society.

But what if this has been happening throughout 'time' and that earlier culture will, through the multiple ITLADian-based lives of their observer-collective, have also evolved into societies with 21st-century technology, culture and social environment? For example, a 9th-century, Dark Ages culture will remain like that in our world view. However, within their own subjective time perceptions (and having multiple life-iterations that will change each member of that society's beliefs, cultural sophistication and scientific knowledge), they will 'evolve' a society very similar to our own. Indeed, what year it actually is is simply a social norm accepted by all within that society. What really matters is how 'advanced' that society is.

Let's return to Cheating the Ferryman. Each consciousness, at the point of death, goes back and relives its life. This life is in the same time and culture as the previous life. But this time, the Daemon guides the Eidolon using knowledge gained from the previous life (or lives, as multiple lives are experienced, and with each life, more knowledge is achieved and an individuated evolution takes place). But − and this is a crucial point − this is happening to every other sentient intelligence that the original Eidolon interfaces within each life-iteration. Millions of Daemon-guided singular consciousnesses, embodied as Eidolons, are collectively evolving as an Uber-Eidolon, which is the collective known as society. As this society evolves, it will develop new technologies and medical advances within its own historical time period. This is again important. My example 9th-century, Dark Ages European society will, over multiple runs through its collective Bohmian IMAXs, evolve scientifically and culturally, and each individuated Eidolonic consciousness within that BIMAX will be 'reborn' into progressively more sophisticated cultural environments. Scientific and medical advances will be made by those who learn from their multiple lives and iteratively apply this knowledge. Each individual contributes to a collective change. And BIMAX after BIMAX, this will evolve a technological civilization similar and, in some cases, identical, to our own 21st-century world. This means that discoveries will be made which will eradicate diseases and illnesses, people will survive accidents that in earlier BIMAXs would have killed them. This, in turn, will allow these Eidolons to live a full life and, in turn, for them to contribute to society as a whole. So what was, and still is to us looking back on our history, a backward and technologically ignorant 9th-century society evolves into a society identical to our own. But it is so important to realize that this is still located in the past with regard to linear time.

But if time is orthogonal and not linear, these 'earlier' societies exist concurrent to our own. Indeed, how would we know if our society is not one of these earlier ones? Or, more interestingly, that there has only ever been one actual society, and we are in it? After all, if time is subjective, then why should this not be the case?

So all human beings, since time immemorial, may be actually still alive and experiencing life now. We are all evolving together. In effect, this is a variation on Pandeism in which we are all really one consciousness experiencing itself subjectively.

For me, this fourth way, Cheating the Ferryman, proposes a model of human immortality that makes logical sense. It gives consciousness a reason for being rather than simply a pointless exercise in a nihilism that achieves nothing. We are here to learn and grow towards perfection. But, most importantly, CTF is supported by the science, with which the other three alternatives are in conflict.

As we have discovered, there is overwhelming evidence that reality is not what it seems. What we believe to be a physical universe may actually be created out of digital information. Furthermore, this reality seems to work on holographic principles. Human consciousness is a receiver of information from the Zero-Point Field, projected externally to create the illusion of time and space.

But what, exactly, is consciousness? You will recall that David Chalmers has argued that how the brain creates referential self-awareness is the greatest problem for modern science, a mystery that we are no nearer solving now than we were a hundred years ago. Of course, we have had somewhat hubristic book titles such as Daniel Dennett's early 1990s book *Consciousness Explained* (Dennett, 1991) and, more recently, Terrence Deacon's similarly self-congratulatory titled book *Incomplete Nature: How Mind Emerged from Matter* (Deacon, 2013). Both of these are excellent books but, in my opinion, despite the plaudits they have received, they are far from convincing.

I would like to suggest that consciousness is the medium whereby information becomes physical in the sense that it becomes sensual. This

Epilogue

is analogous to how a computer screen, with the aid of a microprocessor, turns digital data into a three-dimensional image when we play a virtual-reality game.

But there is a feedback mechanism going on here. Consciousness needs the sensory apparatus such as eyes and ears to interface with the data. But eyes and ears, and all our other sense-processors are, in a very real sense, physical. Does consciousness collapse the wave function of the atoms and molecules that make up our eyes, ears and other sense facilitators? Indeed, do we also bring into existence the very brain that processes the data?

As cited earlier, cognitive scientist Dr Donald D. Hoffman argues a very similar case to my own with regard to the idea that our perceptual universe is a simulation or, as I call it, an instantiation. He puts together an argument as to how we all seem to share the same experience. He states:

> As members of one species, we share an interface (which varies a bit from person to person). Whatever reality might be, when we interact with it we all construct similar icons, because we all have similar needs, and similar methods for acquiring fitness payoffs.
>
> Hoffman, 2019, pp. 80–81

In his book *The Case Against Reality*, Hoffman presents his Interface Theory of Perception (ITP). In this, he argues that how our perceptions present the phenomenal world to our consciousness is analogous to the relationship between a desktop interface and a computer. In effect, consciousness causes brain activity and, in doing so, creates all objects and properties of the physical world.

Those of you who know your cinema will recall the famous line from the 1999 film *The Matrix* where a child explains to the central character, Neo, that what he sees as a spoon is not a spoon at all:

Do not try to bend the spoon, that's impossible. Instead, only try to realize the truth . . . that there is no spoon. Then you'll see that it is not the spoon that bends, it is only yourself.

But for Hoffman, if Neo looked away, then for him the spoon would cease to exist. The spoon is simply a data structure that is created when Neo interfaced with it. What exists is digital information processed by Neo's visual processing system and brain. Replacing a spoon with a cube, Hoffman writes:

> . . . we each construct our own cube, but in much the same way as everybody else. The cube I see is distinct from the cube you see. I may see cube A at the same time you see cube B. There is no need to posit a real cube that everyone sees, and that exists when no one observes.
>
> Hoffman, 2019, p. 81

This is such an important point. And please remember this is being made by one of the world's leading cognitive scientists, not a 'new age' guru!

However, Hoffman does not explain the source of the information whereby consciousness projects outwardly into the environment what we perceive. As I have argued in this book, I believe that the source of information is holographic in nature and may be found within the non-physical mystery that is Zero-Point Field (ZPF). Author Ervin Laszlo calls this the Akashic Field. In his introduction to my book *The Out-of-Body Experience: The History and Science of Astral Travel*, he explains this far better than I ever could. I, therefore, make no apology for quoting him in full:

> The ZPF is but one of the many physical manifestations of the deep-structure of the universe. At the bottom of it all is very likely the field of fields that includes the ZPF with its

zero-point energy, but includes far more than that. It also includes all universal and quantum fields, and the as yet little understood holographic field that I believe conveys the nonlocal connection underlying micro- as well as macro-level entanglement. But all that I earlier claimed for the ZPF is valid for this super-grand-unified field. It is the in-itself unobservable matrix that grounds the observable universe. We cannot define it as a separate reality because every definition we could offer would be in terms of things – fields, forces, relations, or entities – that are not only produced by this field, but are actually in that field. Or, more radically, are that field.

It is not as though there was the manifest world, and a fundamental field that grounds that world. World and field are one. This one-world is nonlocal: all of its elements are subtly but effectively linked. Microtubules, Bose-Einstein condensates, holograms, the implicate order, the ZPF, and the super-grand-unified Akashic Field are as many hypotheses for understanding its nature and its dynamics, and the possibilities for understanding it.

Laszlo, 2011

Could it be that consciousness and the universe are simply manifestations of a deeper reality, a reality that is actually unitary in nature? Are we all a singular consciousness experiencing itself subjectively as the great comedian Bill Hicks once suggested?

Today a young man on acid realized that all matter is merely energy condensed to a slow vibration, that we are all one consciousness experiencing itself subjectively. There is no such thing as death, life is only a dream and we are the imagination of ourselves.

Hicks, 2004, p. 26

If we are a single consciousness experiencing itself subjectively, then what is the nature of that consciousness? Is this just another variation on Brahman discussed in the section on theology, or is it more? I suspect that we have levels of awareness. This starts with the Eidolon, the consciousness that exists within the simulation and experiences just one life. It is the equivalent of any in-game avatar generated for a singular game-play session within a video game. It exists for one game which ends at its 'death' within the game-play. This is a single life. The Eidolon is born, experiences a life and then ceases to exist. When a new game is started, a new Eidolon is created with no memories of the last game (life).

But experiencing every game-play is the game-player who exists outside of the game. This is the Daemon. It remembers all previous games (lives) and uses this knowledge to assist each new Eidolon to advance successfully through the game. How effective it will be on doing this will depend upon various factors. For a full discussion on how this may work, check out my books *The Daemon: A Guide to Your Extraordinary Secret Self* (2008) and *Opening the Doors of Perception: The Key to Cosmic Awareness* (2016). We, therefore, have two forms of memory: Eidolonic Memory (EM), which is the recollections of experiences encountered within one run of the game; while Daemonic Memory (DM), on the other hand, is the memories of all the previous games experienced by the Daemon. EM is precisely what the famous Swiss psychiatrist Carl Gustav Jung (1875–1961) called the 'personal unconscious'. DM has an awareness of the events of which each individual EM is cognisant. What is of great importance here is to realize that there will be a point in the game when DM will have no prior knowledge. Although it can guide the Eidolon using its previous experience, its precognitive abilities will have ceased. I have argued in the past that this is why déjà vu experiences are perceived less and less as we age (Adachi, et al., 2003).

But I now believe that there may be another two levels above this 'Daemon-Eidolon Dyad'. These I call the *Uber-Daemon* and the *GoDaemon*. The Uber-Daemon is, in effect, the consciousness that created the game itself. It has full access to all the information contained within the Zero-Point (Akashic) Field that involves humanity. This is identical to Jung's second level of awareness, the 'collective unconscious'. Jung defined this as:

> The collective unconscious as the ancestral heritage of possibilities of representation, is not individual but common to all men, and perhaps even to all animals, and is the true basis of the individual psyche.
>
> Jung, 1998

I would like to argue that the Jungian collective unconscious is the source of two of the experiences that are regularly cited as evidence of survival after death, and are seemingly contradictory to my Cheating the Ferryman hypothesis. The first is past-life memories that are either spontaneously recalled or evoked through hypnotic regression. In these, individuals describe in detail elements of another life experienced in the past. These facts are subsequently checked and found to be true. I would like to suggest that what is taking place here is the person is tapping into the collective unconscious of the human species and has randomly attuned into a specific lifetime. This is a memory of a past life, but not *their* life. This information may be carried through in our DNA or simply be facilitated by attuning into a broader area of Laszlo's Akashic Field. The second area that the collective unconscious could explain is clairvoyance and psychic mediums. These individuals attune into the collective unconscious and pick up information created by the expectations of their clients. Furthermore, one could add as an additional explanation that such experiences could be related directly to my 'egregore' model extensively discussed above.

And now we turn to the GoDaemon. By this, I mean the collective consciousness of everything in the multiverse. This is what the Hindus mean when they discuss Brahman, Quabbalists when they describe the Ain Sof and the Shaivists' concept of Citi. In effect, this is pure Advaita, non-dualism, a model of understanding whereby everything is created out of pure consciousness that is information. This is the core belief of Aldous Huxley's perennial philosophy discussed in Part 3 of this book.

And so we reach the end of our journey. With the assistance of scores of philosophers, scientists, experiencers and writers, I have presented evidence that my Cheating the Ferryman hypothesis is more than simple speculation. But as with all my books, in the final analysis it is you, dear reader, who will decide if I have succeeded in this aim. But if, at a deeper level, we are all a singular consciousness, then I am just an aspect of yourself that has been manifested in your phaneron in order to help you understand exactly what you are; part of something far greater; a shard of the Pleroma working its way home through multiple lives.

Listen to your Daemon and enjoy your many journeys through your many lives.

ENDNOTES

1   For a more extensive discussion on my analysis of Kabbalah in relation to my theories, please check out my book *The Out-of-Body Experience: The History and Science of Astral Travel*, pp. 20–23

2   https://blanqui.kingston.ac.uk/texts/eternity-by-the-stars-1872/

3   https://blanqui.kingston.ac.uk/texts/eternity-by-the-stars-1872/

4   https://www.nature.com/articles/s41567-019-0663-9?proof=t&fbclid=IwAR19OMQU3_Ug5dsaSlZ4jS8Hxibld95VGBCvyH4wXjGXiUCdmebUzu69FmE

5   From Stephen Hawking's lecture 'The Beginning of Time', 1996: https://www.hawking.org.uk/in-words/lectures/the-beginning-of-time

6   *New Scientist*, 16 March 2002, p. 26

7   'Einstein is Found Hiding on Birthday: Busy with Gift Microscope', wireless to the *New York Times*, 15 March 1929, page 3, column 3, New York (ProQuest)

8   https://near-death.com/grace-hatmaker/

9   https://neurosciencenews.com/life-event-review-18617/

10   https://www.newyorker.com/magazine/2007/08/20/my-near-death-experience

11   http://www.bbc.co.uk/nottingham/content/articles/2005/08/03/tony_kofi_interview_feature.shtml

12   http://www.oocities.org/franzbardon/erickson.html

13   Al-Khalili, Jim, *Quantum: A Guide for the Perplexed*, Phoenix, London, 2012, p. 197

14   This section is taken, in part, from my book *The Infinite Mindfield: The Quest to Find the Gateway to Higher Consciousness*, Watkins, 2013. This presents a more in-depth discussion of the neurological aspects of Cheating the Ferryman and altered states of consciousness.

15   Wheeler, J.A., & Misner, C., *Geometrodynamics*, Academic Press, 1962

16   That is, matter made up of protons and neutrons, the constituent particles of the atom's nucleus

17   Maldacena, J.M. 1998. *Advances in Theoretical and Mathematical Physics*, 2, pp. 231–252

18   Mensky, 'Concept of consciousness in the context of quantum mechanics,' Jan 2005, *Uspekhi Fizicheski Nauk*, 175(4):413, p. 405.

19   Forthcoming in S. Gao (ed.) *Consciousness and Quantum Mechanics*, Oxford University Press

20   http://www.johnhick.org.uk/jsite/index.php/articles-by-john-hick/11-reincarnation-and-the-meaning-of-life

BIBLIOGRAPHY

Adachi, N., Adachi, T., Kimura, M., Akanuma, N., Takekawa, Y., & Kato, M. (2003, April). 'Demographic and psychological features of déjà vu experiences in a nonclinical Japanese population'. *J. Nerv Ment Dis*, pp. 242–247.

Afshordi, N., Coriano, C., Delle Rose, L., Gould, E., & Skenderis, C. (2017, January 27). 'From Planck Data to Planck Era: Observational Tests of Holographic Cosmology.' *Physical Review Letters. 118, 041301.*

Ananthaswamy, A. (2021, July 10). 'Does consciousness make reality'? *New Scientist Special Issue –Consciousness*, p. 43.

Anderson, S., Holliday, I. E., Singh, K. D., & Harding, G. F. (1996). 'Localization and functional analysis of human cortical area V5 using magneto-encephalography'. *Proceedings of the Royal Society: Biological Sciences. 263 (1369),* 423–431.

Atwater, P. (2013). *Future Memory.* Charlottesville: Hampton Roads.

Barbour, J. (2000). *The End of Time.* London: Phoenix.

Beane, S. R., Davoudi, Z., & Savage, M. J. (2012). 'Constraints on the Universe as a Numerical Simulation'. *arXiv:1210.1867v2.*

Bekenstein, J. D. (1981). 'Universal upper bound on the entropy-to-energy ratio for bounded system'. *Physical Review* , pp. 287–298.

Bekenstein, J. D. (2003, August 14). 'Information in the Holographic Universe: Theoretical results about black holes suggest that the universe could be like a gigantic hologram'. *Scientific American.*

Berkeley, G. (2005). *A Treatise Concerning the Principles of Human Knowledge.* Cosimo Classics.

Binkofski, F., & Block, R. A. (1992). 'Accelerated Time Experience after Left Frontal Cortex Lesion'. *Neurocase Vol 2*, pp. 485–493.

Bohm, D., (1980). *Wholeness and the Implicate Order.* London: Routledge and Kegan Paul.

Bohm, D., & Peat, F. D. (1987). *Science, Order, and Creativity.* New York: Bantam.

Borjigin, J., Lee, U., Pal, D., Huff, S., Klarr, D., Slobada, J., … Mashour, G. A. (2013).

'Surge of neurophysiological coherence and connectivity in the dying brain'. *Proceedings of the National Academy of Sciences of the United States of America*, 14432–14437.

Bostrom, N. (2003). 'Are You Living In a Computer Simulation'. *Philosophical Quarterly. Vol 53, No. 211*, pp. 243–255.

Chalmers, D. (1995). 'Facing up to the Problem of Consciousness'. *Journal of Consciousness Studies vol 2, no 3*, 243–255.

Chalmers, D. J., & McQueen, K. J. (2020, July 3). 'Consciousness and the Collapse of the Wave Function'. *http://www.consc.net/papers/collapse.pdf*, p. 14.

Chateaubriand, F. (1850). *Memoires d'Outre-Tombe* .

Chew, Geoffrey F., Gell-Mann, Murray, and Rosenfeld, Arthur H. (1964) 'Strongly interacting particles'. *Scientific American*, 210, pp.74–93.

Cooper, S. A., Joshi, A. C., Seenan, P. J., Hadley, D. M., Muir, K. W., Leigh, R. J., & Metcalfe, R. A. (2010). 'Akinetopsia: Acute presentation and evidence for persisting defects in motion vision'. *Journal of Neurology, Neurosurgery & Psychiatry, 83*, 229–230.

Cornish, N., & Blas, D. (2017, October 18). 'Bounding the Speed of Gravity with Gravitational Wave Observations'. *Phys. Rev. Lett. 119, 161102.*

Cowen, R. (2013, December 10). 'Simulations Back Up Theory That Universe Is A Hologram'. *Nature.*

Cox, B. (2012, February 20). 'Why Quantum Theory Is So Misunderstood'. *The Wall Street Journal.*

Cox, B., & Forshaw, J. (2011). *The Quantum Universe: Everything that Can Happen Does Happen.* London : Allen Lane.

Daniel, C. D. (1993). *Consciousness Explained.* London: Penguin.

Davies, P. (2019). *The Demon In The Machine.* London: Allen Lane.

Deacon, T. W. (2013). *Incomplete Nature: How Mind Emerged from Matter.* New York: Norton.

Eckle, P. (2008). 'Attosecond Ionization and Tunneling Delay Time Measurements in Helium'. *Science 322*, p. 1525.

Bibliography

Ellenbroek, B., & Youn, J. (2016, September). 'Rodent models in neuroscience research: is it a rat race?' *Dis Model Mech*, pp. 1079–1087.

Epictetus. (1998). *Discourses Book 1 (translated by R.D. Dobbin)*. Oxford: Clarendon Press.

Erickson, M. H. (1965). 'A Special Inquiry with Aldous Huxley into the Nature and Character of Various States of Consciousness'. *American Journal of Clinical Hypnosis, vol 8*, 17–33.

Erickson, M. H. (1980). 'A Special Inquiry with Aldous Huxley into the Nature and Character of Various States of Consciousness'. In M. H. Erickson, *The collected papers of Milton H. Erickson, volume I* (p. 83). New York: Irvington Publishers.

Faust, M. (2011). *Nietzsche: The God of Groundhog Day*. Michael Hockney.

Fenwick, P., & Fenwick, E. (1995). *The Truth in the Light*. London: Headline.

Fontana, D. (2005). *Is There An Afterlife?* Ropley: O Books.

Gallimore, A. R. (2019). *Alien Information Theory: Psychedelic Drug Technologies and the Cosmic Game*. Strange World Press.

Gardner, J. N. (Career Press). *The Intelligent Universe*. New Jersey: Franklin Lakes.

Gariaev, P. P. (1989). *Energy No 10*, pp. 46–52.

Gasparini, F. M. (2012). 'Viewpoint: Helium Puddles Near Absolute Zero'. *Physics.5. 136*.

Ge, X. X., Zhang, C., Gribizis, A., Hamodi, A. S., Sabino, A. M., & Crair, M. C. (2021, July 23). 'Retinal waves prime visual motion detection by simulating future optic flow.' *Science. Vol 373. Issue 6553*.

Gefter, A., (2011, 20 July). 'Existence: Why is There A Universe'?. *New Scientist*.

Giobran, G. (2007). *Everything Forever: Learning To See Timelessness*. Enchanted Puzzle Publishing: Seattle.

Greene, B. (2005). *The Fabric of the Cosmos*. London: Penguin.

Grof, S. (1993). *Holotropic Mind, The: The Three Levels of Human Consciousness and How They Shape Our Lives*. London: Harper Collins.

Halm, H. (1996). *The Empire of Mahdi: The rise of the Fatimids*. Leden: Brill.

Hanada, M., Hyakutake, Y., Ishiki, G., & Nishimura, J. (2013, November 21). 'Holographic description of quantum black hole on a computer'. *Science 344 (2014)* pp. 882–885.

Haraldsson, E., & Osis, K. (2012). *At the Hour of Death: A New Look at Evidence for Life After Death*. Guildford: White Crow Books.

Hawking, S. W., & Hertog, T. (2018, April 27). 'A smooth exit from eternal inflation?' *Journal of High Energy Physics. 147*.

Heim, A. (1992). *Notizen uber den Tod durch Absturz*. Zurich: Jahrbuch der Schweitzerischen Alpclub, 27.

Hicks, B. (2004). *Love All The People: Letters, Lyrics, Routines*. London: Constable and Robinson.

Hilgard, E. (1977). *Divided consciousness: Multiple controls in human thought and action*. New York: Wiley.

Hilgard, E. R. (1977). *Divided consciousness: multiple controls in human thought and action*. New York: Wiley.

Hines, T. (1988). *Pseudoscience and the Paranormal*. London: Prometheus Books.

Hoffman, D. D. (2019). *The Case Against Reality*. London: Allen Lane.

Hoyle, F. (1983). *The Intelligent Universe*. London: Michael Joseph.

Hughes, J. R. (2008, July). 'Gamma, fast, and ultrafast waves of the brain: Their relationships with epilepsy and behavior'. *Epilepsy and Behavior. Vol 13. Issue 1*, pp. 25–31.

Hyakutake, Y. (2013, November 29). 'Quantum Near Horizon Geometry of Black 0-Brane'. *https://arxiv.org/abs/1311.7526*.

Iaccarino, H. F., Singer, A. C., Martorell , A. J., Rudenko, A., Gao, F., Gillingham, T. Z., …Tsai, L. H. (2018, October). 'Gamma frequency entrainment attenuates amyloid load and modifies microglia'. *Nature*, pp. 230–235.

Inglis, B. (1990). *Coincidence: The language of destiny*. London: Hutchinson.

Itano, W. M., Bollinger, J. J., & Wineland, J. J. (1990, March). 'Quantum Zeno Effect'. *Physical Review A Volume 41, No 5*.

Jacques, V., & Roch, J.F. (2007). 'Experimental Realization of Wheeler's Delayed-Choice Gedanken Experiment'. *Science vol. 315, no. 5814*, 966–8.

Jaynes, J. (1976). *The Origin of Consciousness in the Breakdown of the Bicameral Mind*. New York: Houghton Mifflin.

Jung, C. G. (1998). 'The Structure of the Psyche'. In C. G. Jung, *The Essential Jung* (p. 88). London: Fontana Press.

Kak, S. (2006). 'Pythagorean Triples and Cryptographic Coding',. https://arxiv.org/find/all/1/all:+kak/0/1/0/all/0/1?skip=25&query_id=a7b95a2782affe4b.

Koob, A. (2009). *The Root of Thought: Unlocking Glia: The Brain Cell That Will Help Us Sharpen Our Wits, Heal Injury, and Treat Brain Disease.* New Jersey: Pearson FT Press.

Koob, A. (2009, October 27). 'The Root of Thought: What Do Glial Cells Do?.' *Scientific American.*

Kramar, M. (2021). 'Encoding memory in tube diameter hierarchy of living flow network'. *Proceedings of the National Academy of Sciences.*

Kurzweil, R. (2006). *The Singularity is Near.* London: Gerald Duckworth & Co.

Landauer, R. (1986). 'Computation and physics: Wheeler's meaning circuit?' *Foundations of Physics, 16(6)*, 551–564.

Laszlo, E. (2011). Foreword. In A. Peake, *The Out-of-Body Experience: The History and Science of Astral Travel* (p. x). London: Watkins.

Long, J. (2014, Sept-Oct). 'Near-Death Experiences: Evidence for Their Reality'. *Missouri Medicine*, pp. 372–380.

Main, R. (1997). *Jung on synchronicity and the paranormal.* London: Routledge.

Mare, W. D. (1935). *Early One Morning.*

Martineau, H. (1877). *An Autobiography.*

Max Planck Society. (2021, February 23). 'Researchers find a single-celled slime mold with no nervous system that remembers food locations'. Retrieved from Physics Org: https://phys.org/news/2021-02-single-celled-slime-mold-nervous-food.html

Maxwell, J. C. (1864). 'A dynamical theory of the electromagnetic field'. *Philosophical Transactions of the Royal Society of London 155*, 459–512.

Mensky, M. B. (2014). 'Super-Intuition And Correlations With The Future in Quantum Consciousness'. *Cosmology Vol. 18.*, pp. 263–282.

Misra, B., & Sudershan, G. (1977). 'The Zeno paradox in quantum theory'. *Journal of Mathematical Physics. 18, 756.*

Moody, R. A. (1988). *The Light Beyond: Explorations into the Near-Death Experience.* London: Macmillan.

Mullan, S., & Penfield, W. (1959).'Illusions of comparative interpretation and emotion: production by epileptic discharge and by electrical stimulation in the temporal cortex'. *AMA Archives of Neurology & Psychiatry 81*, 269–284.

Neppe, V. (1981). *A study of déjà vu experience. (PhD Thesis).* Witwatersrand: University of Witwatersrand.

Neppe, V. M. (1983). 'The incidence of deja vu'. *Parapsychological Journal of South Africa,* 94–106.

Nicholls, G. (2011). *Avenues of the Human Spirit.* Ropley: John Hunt Publishing.

Nietzsche, F. (1974). *The Gay Science: With a Prelude in Rhymes and an Appendix of Songs.* Vintage Books.

Nietzsche, F. (n.d.). *Will to Power.*

Nimtz, G. (2003). 'Verhandlungen der Deutschen Physikalischen Gessellschaft'. *Progress in Quantum Electronics 27*, p. 417.

Noyes, R., & Kletti, R. (1972). 'The experience of dying from falls'. *Omega, 3*, pp. 45–52.

Noyes, R., Hoenk, P., Kuperman, S., & Slyman, D. (1977). 'Depersonalisation in Accident Victims and Psychiatric Patients'. *J. Nerv. Ment. Dis, 164*, 401–407.

Ovsiew, F. (2014, June). 'The Zeitraffer phenomenon, akinetopsia, and the visual perception of speed of motion: a case report.' *Neurocase 20 (3)*, pp. 269–72.

Pascal, B. (n.d.). *Pensées.*

Paul, P. (1985). *Some unseen power: The diary of a ghost hunter.* London: Robert Hale.

Paulos, J. A. (1991). *Beyond Numeracy.* London: Penguin.

Peake, A. (2004). 'Cheating the Ferryman: A New Paradigm of Existence?' *Journal of Near–Death Studies 23 (2)*, 67–99.

Peake, A. (2006). *Is There Life After Death: The Extraordinary Science of What Happens When We Die.* London: Arcturus.

Peake, A. (2008). *The Daemon: A Guide to Your Extraordinary Secret Self.* London: Arcturus.

Peake, A. (2012). *The Labyrinth of Time: The Illusion of Past, Present and Future.* London: Arcturus.

Peake, A. (2016). *Opening The Doors of Perception: The Key to Cosmic Awareness.* London: Watkins.

Peake, A. (2019). *The Hidden Universe: An Investigation Into Non-Human Intelligences.* London: Watkins Publishing.

Peat, F. D. (2008). 'Divine Contenders: Wolfgang Pauli and the Symmetry of the World'. In L. Storm, *Synchronicity: Multiple Perspectives on Meaningful Coincidence* (p. 21). Pari: Pari Publishing.

Bibliography

Peirce, C. S. (1931). *The Collected Papers Vol. I*. https://www.textlog.de/4324.html.

Priestley, J. B. (2000). *An Inspector Calls and Other Plays*. London: Penguin.

Puccetti, R. (1973). 'Brain bisection and personal identity.' *British Journal for the Philosophy of Science*, 339–355.

Ramachandran, V. S., & Blakeslee, S. (1998). *Phantoms in the Brain*. London: Fourth Estate.

Reisberg, B., Franssen, E. H., & Hasam, S. L. (1999). 'Retrogenesis: Clinical, physiologic and pathologic mechanisms in brain aging, Alzheimer's and other dementing processes'. *European Archives of Psychiatry and Clinical Neuroscience. 249 (Suppl 3)*, 28–36.

Ring, K. (1980). *Life At Death: A Scientific Investigation of the Near-Death Experience*. New York: Coward, McCann and Geoghegan.

Ring, K., & Elsaesser Valarino, E. (2006). *Lessons From The Light*. Neeham: Moment Point Press.

Rosenblum, B. &. (2006). *Quantum Enigma: Physics Encounters Consciousness*. London: Duckworth.

Rudolph, K. (1984). *Gnosis: The Nature and History of Gnosticism*. Edinburgh: T. & T. Clark Limited.

Ryle, G. (1949). *The Concept of Mind*. Chicago: University of Chicago Press.

Saavedra-Aguilar, J. C., & Gómez-Jeria, J. S. (1989, June). 'A neurobiological model for near-death experiences'. *Jornal of Near-Death Studies*, pp. 205–222.

Salaman, E. (1970). *A Collection of Moments*. London: Faber.

Schopenhauer, A. (1966). *The World as Will and Representation*. Denver: Dover Publications.

Schrödinger, E. (1935). 'Die gegenwärtige Situation in der Quantenmechanik'. *Naturwissenschaftern, 23*, 823.

Sedahely, W. J. (1987). 'The near-death experience: is the presence always the higher self?' *Omega 18*, 129–134.

Sperry, R. W. (1975). 'Mental phenomena as causal determinants of brain function'. In G. G. Globus, G. Maxwell, & I. Savodnik, *Consciousness and the brain:* (p. 170). New York: Dutton.

Steinhart, E. (2008). 'The revision theory of resurrection'. *Religious Studies. 44*, 63–81.

Steinhart, E. C. (2014). *Your Digital Afterlives: Computational Theories of Life after Death*. New York: Palgrave Macmillan.

Stetson, C., Fiesta, M. P., & Eagleman, D. M. (2007, December 12). 'Does Time Really Slow Down during a Frightening Event?' *PLoS ONE 2 (12) e1295*.

Tart, C. T. (1976). *States of Consciousness*. New York: Dutton.

Tegmark, M. (2014). *Our Mathematical Universe: My Quest for the Ultimate Nature of Reality*. London: Penguin.

Tegmark, M., Hut, P., & Alford, M. (2006, October 21). 'On Math, Matter and Mind.' *Found. Physics 36*, pp. 765–794.

Tonkonogy, J. M., & Puente, A. E. (2009). *Localization of clinical syndromes in neuropsychology and neuroscience*. New York: Springer.

Twemlow, S. W., Gabbard, G. O., & Coyne, L. (1982). 'A multivariate method for the classification of prexisting near-death conditions'. *Anabiosis 2*, 132–139.

Vopson, M. M. (2019, September 6). 'The mass-energy-information equivalence principle'. *AIP Advances 9, 095206*.

Wheeler, J. A. (1989). 'Information, physics, quantum: The search for links'. *Proceedings of the Third International Symposium on the Foundations of Quantum Mechanics*, (p. 354). Tokyo.

Wheeler, J. A. (1990). *A Journey Into Gravity and Spacetime*. New York: Scientific American Library.

Wheeler, J. A., & Ford, K. (1998). *It From Bit. In Geons, Black Holes & Quantum Foam: A Life in Physics*. New York: Norton.

Wittman, M., Neumaier, L., Evrard, R., Weibel, A., & Schmied-Knittel, I. (2017). 'Subjective time distortion during near-death experiences: an analysis of reports'. *Zeitschrift fur Anomalistik*, 309–320.

Zihl, J., Von Cramon, D., & Mai, N. (1983, June 1). 'Selective Disturbance of Movement Vision After Bilateral Brain Damage'. *Brain, Volume 106, Issue 2*, pp. 313–340.

INDEX

Index

Index